SEASONS AT HIGHCLERE

Gardening, growing and cooking through the year at
THE REAL DOWNTON ABBEY

THE COUNTESS OF CARNARVON

This book is dedicated to my sisters,
some of whom cook and some of whom garden;
to Nanny, who observes each activity offering her opinion;
and to Edward and Geordie, with whom and
for whom I love to cook and garden.

For everything there is a season,
to grow, to cook and to hope for reason.

CONTENTS

INTRODUCTION

Seasons at Highclere – Gardening, Growing and Cooking Through the Year at The Real Downton Abbey shares the history and reality of living in a great landed estate, from its Anglo-Saxon origins through 800 years as a medieval bishops' palace and then into the great Victorian and Edwardian gardens of the 'real Downton Abbey'. From the enduring timelessness of the iconic cedars of Lebanon, to rooms with a view within the Castle, this book is an opportunity to share the layers of historical research about the gardens and landscape, to retell anecdotes and include recipes, from family picnics to formal dinners in the great State Dining Room.

The Highclere Estate has a uniquely long history spanning nearly 1,300 years, with very few changes of ownership. For 800 years it was owned by the Bishops of Winchester and it still stands, more or less, on the same footprint as it did then, with the old medieval walls lying within the curtilage of the current Castle and gardens.

From a bishops' palace, Highclere became an elegant Tudor family residence, which was purchased by my husband's forbears in 1679. Later, the Carnarvon family built a symmetrical, classical, stone Georgian home around the Elizabethan building. This lasted until the 3rd Earl of Carnarvon commissioned the pre-eminent Victorian architect Sir Charles Barry to design and build the current Castle which is so known and loved today. Barry was inspired by his travels in Italy, by the colours and sights he saw there, and he regarded Highclere as perhaps his most successful project, and far more enjoyable than his contemporaneous one: the Houses of Parliament.

Initially, this 'new' Highclere was also called a 'palace' before being renamed Highclere Castle. It has a cosy splendour, with between 250 and 300 rooms, and sits in 1,000 acres of Capability Brown parkland. We still look after farmland, downland and woodland comprising another 4,500 acres.

There are certain practicalities of looking after a twelfth-century monks' garden, of understanding the development of a classic eighteenth-century English garden, the sweeping changes of Capability Brown and the need and desire to allow space and peace for wildlife. After all, it is their home too.

There is no subject of more general use than the cultivation of land and improvement of the vegetable world.
Richard Bradley, *New Improvements of Planting and Gardening*, 1739

Despite the impact of modern technology, we are all affected by the changing seasons and by the memories they trigger. The bursts of colour, sounds of birdsong, frisking lambs and fresh bright light that herald spring and the warmth and drowsiness of an English summer: insects amongst the wildflower meadows, the sound of a tennis ball being hit and the thought of fresh homemade lemonade in a tall jug. Autumn has a crisp smell in the air, with the crunch of leaves underfoot and the crimson colours of distant views, whilst winter is pale, with brisk walks on ancient white-chalk downlands, eating hot stews or roasting chestnuts by the fire and sharing cosy conversations with friends and family. Our four seasons involve all the senses: sight, hearing, smell, taste and touch, and they all live in our memories.

Every autumn, at our harvest festival, we sing the Hymn of the Hampshire Countryside (overleaf) whilst a variety of patient animals, tractors and bags of wheat, oats and barley wait outside. It is not

Hymn of the Hampshire Countryside

Praise we The Lord, the great Author of Nature
Praise we the maker of upland and plain;
Praise we the Spirit through whom every creature
Gathers its life and renews it again.

Once did The Son of God - mighty the wonder -
Walk this Earth's dusty paths, tread on its loam;
Once did he look on the harvest and ponder:
Where is the labour to fetch it all home?

Lord, we would serve Thee and turn to Thy glory
All our best efforts of mind and of hand;
Lord, we would see the old heavenly story
Made flesh again in the soil of our land.

Are not the waters of Test and of Avon
Meet for thy christening as Jordan's of old?
May not our downs, with thy footprints engraven,
Like Judah's mountains thy cradle unfold?

Of in the starry night, waking or sleeping,
On the hard stones Thou reclines thy head:
Wilt no Thou not rest where our forest is heaping
Leaves for thy pillow and ling for thy bed?

Once for a gardener did Mary mistake Thee
In the first mists of the first Easter Day:
Lord, we have gardens, and fain would we make Thee
Master of all their resplendent array.

See, where his flock the young shepherd is guiding,
Hard by the track on Old Winchester Hill;
See, where 'mid Alton's shy slopes lie in hiding,
Kilns where the hops their soft odours distil.

Jesus, our Saviour, in mercy be near us:
Shepherd and Sower and Reaper art thou;
Pardon our sins - let thy charity cheer us:
Hallow the harvest we bring to thee now.

short but it does proceed at a steady beat, which gives me time to think as we move from praise for 'the maker of upland and plain' to the ancient paths in which footprints are 'engraven' to the 'leaves for thy pillow and ling (heather/moss) for thy bed'. One verse sensibly asks of the farmer and his harvest 'where is the labour to fetch it all home?', which always wrings a wry smile from my husband, Geordie. It is an endlessly repeated cycle in which the land gathers up its life to start again each year as we look up into 'the starry night, waking or sleeping'.

Rather like the majestic trees circumscribing the Castle, this home is rooted in one place. Neither can move to escape but both need to adapt in order to survive in unpredictable conditions. The weather, of course, remains a daily topic of conversation concerning the Castle, trees, garden and farm. So used are we to shops, fridges and delivery companies, it is easy to forget where and how our food arrives on our table. The gardens of today may be less productive and have become more of a retreat than they used to be, but the farm is largely as it has always been, albeit more mechanised: a balance between producing a good harvest and conserving nature.

Arriving visitors find themselves following a road around a corner, down a hill, that curves playfully through an Arcadian parkland before they discover the Castle before them, sitting resolutely in the middle. It is the setting, the sense of place, the deep knowledge of history and the lives of the preceding residents that anchor us into the ground: the generations who lived, strived and laughed here before my husband and myself. It is a visible reminder both of achievements and heritage.

We know what we are but know not what we may be.
William Shakespeare, *Hamlet*

For Geordie and I it is a privilege, a responsibility and an extraordinarily busy life at all hours alongside a community who love this building, its gardens, farmlands, woods, nature on Earth and in the sky and all the values, cultures and dreams that it stands for. To quote the French author Victor Hugo: 'If you don't build castles in the air, you won't build anything on the ground'.

FIONA — 8TH COUNTESS OF CARNARVON

SPRING

THE GOLDEN STONES AND PINNACLED TOWERS OF HIGHCLERE CASTLE SIT ASTRIDE an extraordinary landscape in southern England. Climbing up the twisting, closely constructed staircase to the very top of the Tower, I push open a small doorway and step out to gaze silently at the horizon, the open view that stretches out in every direction. Grass parklands, downlands, woods, fields, the remains of earlier farming homesteads and prehistoric boundaries snake their way through both time and distance ...

IN THE BEGINNING

GEORDIE AND I ARE THE STEWARDS not just of the beautiful, inspirational home known to millions as 'Downton Abbey' but also of the complex remains of a great diachronic landscape. This is not a static heritage captured at one architectural moment but an evolving landscape that embraces a widespread natural diversity in geography, farming, flora and fauna. The longevity of consistent ownership, with its consequent lack of radical change, means that those who wish to can walk, live or pause in this landscape today and glimpse moments of these past communities. For some 800 years, long before my husband's family came here, Highclere was a great ecclesiastical estate, its history well represented in the Bishops' Rolls in Winchester and other lay returns. Looking south from the Castle Tower, the horizon takes you back beyond even these times to the prehistoric, to Bronze Age barrows and bowls and an Iron Fort on the summit of Beacon Hill that encircles the remains of some 20 homesteads and storage pits. It was already a busy cultivated land when the Romans marched in during the first century BC.

Highclere lies between what were the large Roman towns of Winchester and Silchester, and the old roads here still mark the grids that linked the urban-inclined Roman settlers. Surmising from the coins and broken pottery that have been found here, there may have been a villa settlement at this time at the northern foot of Beacon Hill. Later, as the Roman civilisation disintegrated and the Saxons moved across the Channel, the Roman market life dissipated and their rural villas, buildings, fields and homes were either destroyed or amalgamated into Saxon farming life. Bede's *Ecclesiastical History of the English People* records that the tribe in this area was called Gewisse, though there is little real record of them.

From an early beginning in Anglo-Saxon times, the assets of the Bishops of Winchester evolved into one of the most extensive manorial holdings in England. Five charters, the first in 749AD, set out the boundaries and ownership of the lands at 'Clere', and Alfred the Great even mentioned *aet cleran* in his will.

The location was clearly prized. The geology of the lands allowed arable farming on the light soils, grazing on the downland, cows and horses on good pasture, and pigs in the *panne* with Highclere as the *caput*. By 1086 a church had been built on a site near the current Castle. It was

Bronze Age vistas on the
Highclere Estate

named for St Michael (who was associated with high places, apparitions and cemeteries) and the first recorded priest was one Aluric.

During the thirteenth and fourteenth centuries, under the Bishops of Winchester, William Edington and subsequently the famous William of Wykeham, Highclere was further transformed. Situated at a natural crossroad for travellers, Old Burghclere became the centre of the farming enterprise whilst the existing buildings were gradually transformed into a medieval palace with inner and outer courtyards, orchards, herb gardens and a deer park. The pipe rolls record the aggrandisement of the manor, the great building works and the rents from tenants that came in to help pay for it. The manor of Highclere was notable for its sport, for the deer park, warrens and the fish ponds. Agriculture was undertaken beyond the boundaries of the park palings, whilst trees to the north of the courts and house masked the village settlements. Although much of the architecture and life was either not recorded or lost, it is probable that the vernacular houses would have been constructed in either wattle or timber.

During the reformations, the lands of 'clere' passed out of ecclesiastical ownership and, after a hiatus of around 100 years, into that of the ancestors of the Carnarvon family. Into the park laid out and bounded by the Bishops of Winchester 300 years earlier they added the more formal avenues, perspectives, glades, exotic trees and follies of a gentleman's estate.

Later, the great eighteenth-century landscape architect 'Capability' Brown reworked the Elizabethan gardens and park on a grand scale, removing the vernacular dwellings to the north of the Castle to 'rationalise' the setting. Sweeping vistas were created and a more fashionable 'arrival' and 'departure' story built to suit the social standing of the Earl.

The famous diarist William Cobbett, on riding into the park, observed it as a paragon of presentation and management, the sharply contrasting topography flattered by the hand of man.

Today, walking through the gates, taking the time to stand and stare, you enter into an Arcadian world that, in spirit, might not be that different from that seen by priest Aluric 1,000 years earlier.

THE GARDEN OF EDEN

WHETHER IT IS THE *EPIC OF GILGAMESH* or other legendary myths about the origins of life, it all seems to begin in a garden. A man is created from the soil by a god, and lives in a natural setting amongst the animals. He is introduced to a woman who tempts him and he succumbs. Most of us are able to resist everything except temptation, and thus nothing much has changed.

The difference between farming and gardening is often blurred. Farming – *agriculture* – involves livestock as well as plants, and its goals are utilitarian. Gardening – *horticulture* – does not involve raising animals, and the goals might be utilitarian but can also be recreational or ornamental, often in combination.

Some time before his coronation as Holy Roman Emperor in 800, Charlemagne published *Capitulare de Villis Imperialibis*, which set out a framework within which was listed the plants that should be grown in every town. This guidance could be adapted according to local conditions – Charlemagne's empire spanned a large geographical area – but some aspects, such as the need for good drainage and guttering, were universal. The same principles apply today; shelter and good drainage are imperative but so is a deep familiarity with the land and gardens, a knowledge that is both practical and recurrent.

The equinox on 21 March marks the official start of spring and the beginning of summer daylight hours, at least in the UK. In Roman times it was called the 'day of joy' and it was celebrated amidst a week of festivities. However, nature is often at least one step ahead, and in reality, by this point 'spring' has been underway for several weeks. The earliest bulbs have already come and gone and fresh green shoots are everywhere. Crocuses light up the shadows under the trees, a woodpecker flashes through the Wood of Goodwill, toads are spawning in the lake, and Mike Withers' bees (Mike is Highclere's beekeeper) are emerging from their hives. The sap is starting to rise in the mighty oaks that ring the parkland and the skylark flies up towards the fresh sky to sing. In the words of Shakespeare: 'April ... hath put a spirit of youth in everything.'

From the sharp, green, vibrant shoots unfurling from tree branches, to the open grassland and glades which are host to golden daffodils, spring is transforming the wintry grey trunks and silent landscape into the 'blossomed peartree in the hedge, Blossoms and dewdrops – at the bent spray's edge', as Browning beautifully describes it. Everywhere, vivid shards of colour on the ground are counterbalanced by the first clouds of effervescent blossom.

From an indeterminate date known only to themselves, the mornings become a much noisier world, full of competing songbirds, but what is rather joyous is that, thanks to still mostly bare branches, you can see the tiny birds balanced high in the trees. In fact, spring time can generally become quite competitive at Highclere: John the Castle Manager is already listening out intently to make sure he is the one to hear the first cuckoo.

A watch of nightingales · A charm of goldfinches · A wisp of snipe
A murmuration of starlings · A parliament of rooks

The tempo and decibels pick up as blackbirds whistle and wrens and robins join in with remarkable variation, joined by ever more collections of birds returning from southern climes. They all seek shelter in evergreen oaks and thick tall viburnums as early spring showers eddy sharply and immense white cloud banks hurry across the skyline. Shy spotted woodpeckers give their presence away by their drumming on the trees, early queen bees emerge to look for nectar, and a bumble bee flaps its way into the stables behind the Castle before slowly, almost drunkenly, reversing out.

THE SHEEP DELL

IT IS A GOOD WALK ACROSS LARGE PARK FIELDS, 'down dell', following the edge of a path along a woodland before turning down an old track to reach the blackened, slatted barn with its matching roof at Ivory Farm. Behind it lies a more modern version, with a long, grey metal roof, supported by practical metal pillars, all of which offer a measure of shelter but also plenty of circulating fresh air.

The sound of the ewes and lambs can be heard long before you draw close and is quickly followed by the familiar earthy smell of sweet haylage, straw and the promise of tiny white bundles of legs and triangular heads. Inside the barn, on one side, are the small pens inhabited by ewe and lambs, whilst much of the central space, now framed by large straw bales, is filled with extraordinarily wide ewes waddling as they munch on haylage or sit down, exhausted, panting, on thick beds of straw. A radio plays in the background over a well-organised table laid out with everything that might be needed from sanitiser spray, gloves, various gels and a kettle, to powdered milk and red heat lamps.

The gestation time of a sheep is five months. Rams are put with groups of ewes in sequence to create some semblance of planning so that lambing can take place over a number of weeks. If possible, the single and sometimes the twin lambs can arrive outside, but the ewes carrying triplets are always brought into the barn.

Spring birth remains a miracle each year. The ewes stand up and sit down again, grunting, lurching and, typically, looking helpless. Then, with a heave, the water bag that protected the head of the unborn lamb in the womb, bursts. Hopefully, at that point, the lamb 'dives out' of the ewe, its two front feet closely followed by its nose and head. The fluids and mucus need to be cleaned from the lamb's face and shortly after it sneezes and takes a breath. Every time it is a moment of awe. Then, not much more than ten minutes later another lamb emerges. The lambs are picked up and, followed by the ewe, put safely into a single pen with water buckets and hay in the hope that the ewe bonds with her babies and will begin to clean and lick them. Unless the weather is truly appalling, the ewes and newborn lambs will be turned out into the more sheltered fields in the park the following day. Playing chase and tag over old logs and tree stumps, the lambs grow ever stronger.

However, some years we have had times of freezing spring frosts and even snow during lambing. In those times every corner of every barn comes into play to offer some temporary shelter until the cold snap is blown away by energetic gusts of April weather. Twenty-four-hour 'food and room service' of water, hay and bottle-feeding orphans is a gruelling effort. In the frozen March of 2018 Geordie and I enjoyed a lovely supper with friends in the Castle before swapping evening dress for wellington boots at 11pm to head down to the lambing barns for a couple of hours to help through the dark night, topping up the ewes' water, putting wedges of haylage into corners of pens and enough straw around their perimeters to help the lambs survive the icy temperatures. The process today remains the same as it was hundreds of years ago, and it is both exciting and exhausting depending on the time of day and the amount of hours of sleep.

Sheep were once a vital part of the economy: in the thirteenth and fourteenth centuries they contributed a third or more of England's export revenues and they have played a role in Highclere's finances since the estate's earliest days. Early eighth-century Anglo-Saxon charters defining boundaries at Highclere mention sheep 'dells' – sheltered areas that are good for grazing. The Bishops' records document that in 1208 ...

554 [sheep] remain from last year and 250 were added from the stock and 1 found. Sum 805.

At that time, the flocks were under the care of the Sheep Reeve, who was sufficiently important himself to merit assistants. Records from 1350 detail expenses of '6 gallons of tar ointment read achre, 24 hurdles wattling and shearing beyond what the customary tenants were able to do on account of their fewness' (the result of the Black Death).

Shearing was so important it was supervised and everyone turned out to help. The wool was sent to London to be exported and was the nation's most important income source during this period. If wool was an important part of Highclere's income, then fortunes were made from it in London. A newly arcaded and two-storied custom-house was built at Wool Wharf in 1382 and the Comptrollership of Wool Customs was a role that was much fought over from which enormous wealth could be accrued.

In contrast, today each fleece fetches perhaps £1, which is less than the cost of shearing. Our sheep, however, form part of the stewardship of the landscape on the chalk down-lands, keeping scrub bramble at bay and having a role in the long rotations that make up the agricultural cycles. There is no intense farming at Highclere, but rather the intention to maintain a balance to allow the relationships within nature to continue. Their grazing forms part of the complex relationships that allow grasses and other plants to thrive, while in turn providing a home and feeding conditions for birds, butterflies, moths and many insects.

AND OTHER ANIMALS

THROUGHOUT THE MEDIEVAL PERIOD, the hogs in the woods were also always noted. Beechmast and acorns offered pannage through the winter whereas today we have bags of feed, although the hogs are still happy to snuffle through their paddocks next to the woods. Spring is a good time for piglets to arrive and in a short time they are up and about, enquiring into their world and squeaking noisily when unsure or worried, which wakes up the sows.

At the opposite side of the park is a court-yard of stables in which the thoroughbred brood mares spend early spring while we wait for the foals to appear. Inevitably the foals will be born in the small hours of night, although we are now blessed with cameras to alert us to head over, armed with Thermoses of tea and coffee. The telltale signs of pacing and looking around start and stop until suddenly the mare is down, then hooves and a face appear, followed by a collection of long legs landing on the straw. The next two hours tend to be spent watching and helping as need be until the foal has started drinking and has gained the essential colostrum as the mare's contractions ease.

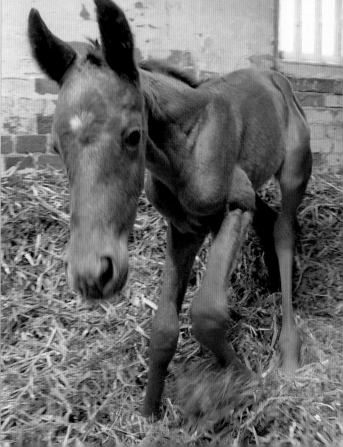

The pasture around the Castle 'has the smooth character belonging to the downs or pastures of chalky districts', which is as good for horses' bones as it is for ours. Horses have been part of Highclere since forever, recorded endlessly by number and function, but it was the 5th Earl who, in 1902, began a stud here. He passed his passion on to his son who was a good amateur jockey and also created a business out of it. The 7th Earl, Geordie's father, worked tirelessly planning his breeding and racing operations and likewise passed his interest in horseracing on to his children. Like his father, Geordie is utterly enthralled by working out the mating plans for his mares, deciding where they should be trained and then consulting with the trainers on all the upcoming meetings to find suitable races for them, though always realising this is a game of triumph and disaster 'and treat those two imposters just the same' (some wise words from Rudyard Kipling's poem 'If').

Animals are part of our imagination and dreams. In many ways the romance of spring is embodied within them – in the impossibly long legs of a foal unfurling to shakily stand shortly after birth, in the lambs curled up in the straw, the piglets emerging noisily and in some numbers, the chickens shaking out their feathers and becoming more vocal and productive as the weather warms. They offer us promise and relationships and, whilst we do not depend on them in the same way today as we once did, they add so much to our life and awareness.

TIME-LAPSE PLANTING

'What is Spring?
Growth in everything'
Gerard Manley Hopkins, 'The May Magnificat', 1918

APRIL AT HIGHCLERE OFTEN BEGINS with sharp showers, brisk breezes and the occasional flurry of snow, all of which catch out the unprotected walker. It is a month of transformation, as the muted browns and mossed greens suddenly acquire golden highlights of colour, and melodic voices in different registers echo high in the trees, complementing the time-lapse colour and scent of spring below. As if from nowhere, one day, the tiny cowslips cover the entire wildflower meadow like a sunny carpet of pale gold. Their natural habitat is the chalky soil of unmown meadows and if once plentiful, they are now quite rare. Happy cousins of the primrose and welcomed as a portent of spring, they bear a cluster of small yolk-yellow flowers above large, green crinkly leaves. Thankfully, they know no boundaries and so they cheerily colonise paths and borders.

As if brought in by nature's orchestral conductor, taller clouds of daffodils – double-heads, single-heads, whites, yellows and orange – and yellow eyes begin to open into colour by paths, borders and in glades. In the Wood of Goodwill, daffodils and narcissi are naturalised around trees, scattered along the Walnut Walk, with varieties such as 'Minnow', 'Pheasant's Eye', 'Dutch Master', 'Cheerfulness', 'Actaea', 'Ice Follies' or 'Jonquilla Ice Follies'. We began the project twelve years ago, buying a thousand mixed daffodils and laboriously planting them by hand, which took time and, in such a large area, originally made a small showing. However, it is about persistence and, to the gardeners' immense pleasure, we then found a Dutchman called Michael Lubbe who arrived bearing gifts of Edam cheese and a clever machine to run behind a small tractor. He was able to plant 5,000 bulbs in just two hours (for example, 'Standard

Value', 'Holland Sensation', 'Flower Record', 'Dutch Master' and 'Carlton'), which transformed all our lives. In fact, the first time Michael arrived, Don Dowsett, our original gardener, immediately perceived the enormous advantage and rushed off to collect and tip all the rest of the bulbs he thought he might have to plant into Michael's machine. In his haste every bulb on the estate went in, including the 'Tête-à-tête' and 'Paperwhite' bulbs that had been intended to grow in large cache-pots to bring into the Castle. There would be other years …

Long celebrated in art and literature, daffodils and narcissi are associated with a number of themes in different cultures, ranging from death to good fortune. Many varieties have scent but the fragrance of narcissi above all is intoxicating and uplifting. William Wordsworth summed up all views of daffodils with his immortal poem written around 1804:

'When all at once I saw a crowd,
A host, of golden daffodils;
Beside the lake, beneath the trees,
Fluttering and dancing in the breeze.'

In the early days, our planting was perhaps a little linear but we soon became more sophisticated and in subsequent years, Michael would arrive and drive in great sweeping curves. Later, we added Snakeshead fritillaries (*Fritillaria meleagris*), Grecian windflower (*Anemone blanda*), Glory of the snow (*Chionodoxa luciliae*), *Narcissus cyclamineus* 'Rapture' and the forest tulip (*Tulipa sylvestris*), as well as alliums to give longevity to the flowering in the woodland gardens.

As the yellow golds gather strength for a final flourish, tulips in all colours begin to take their place. Every autumn, Geordie diligently peruses bulb catalogues for both old and new favourites in order to carefully plan his campaign. Tulips go in later in the autumn than other bulbs, and deeper – at least three times the depth of the bulb. They are, however, much liked as food by small mammals, so various wire nets and other stratagems are constructed to keep the bulbs safe. Come early spring there is a certain anxiety to see if these defences have worked and that there are at least some pale leaves, the shape of hare's ears, peeking through the ground.

Once again, the tulips are planted in sequence so that they can be enjoyed over a longer season. Early, mid- and late-flowering choices are mixed with the differing shapes of lily, parrot, early doubles or Darwin tulips. If much-admired today, it is hard now to contemplate the mania around tulips that took place in Holland in the 1600s. Symbols of wealth, they were painted by the greatest artists and their perceived value led to sky-high prices followed by an inevitable crash.

It all started with a single tulip bulb brought to Holland from Turkey, called the *tulipan* (turban in English; *tulband* in Dutch), perhaps named for the shape of the turbans worn by Turkish men. By 1630 prices had risen to as much as 6,000 guilders for a single bulb (the *Semper Augustus*), the same as a beautiful house in the most fashionable district of Amsterdam. For economists, it became the first great financial bubble, followed by the South Sea Bubble of 1720 and continuing all the way to the more recent tech bubbles.

IRISES AND RAINBOWS

IN GREEK MYTHOLOGY, Iris was the goddess of the rainbow and a messenger for Zeus and Hera and many believe that the flower is named after her. She carried messages from heaven to Earth on the arc of the rainbow and was a companion to female souls on the way to heaven. To this day, Greeks plant purple irises on women's graves so that Iris will guide them to their resting place in heaven.

Each iris is a work of art, with extraordinarily beautiful, large flowers on strong, tall stems above sword-like leaves. They are best planted to sit near if not on top of the soil. When they have flowered, they can be split, leaving the healthy rhizomes undisturbed and gearing up to flower the following year. With proper care they should keep flowering for up to twenty years.

Each year we collect more species: 'Lion King', 'Golden Beauty' and 'Red Ember' from local suppliers along with the exceptional French Cayeux family breeding irises such as 'Baie des Anges' and 'High Chaparral'.

Loved by royalty since the times of the ancient Egyptians who immortalised them as symbols of life, the iris was adopted as the fleur-de-lis by the French monarchy and incorporated into the royal standard and coat of arms, then later depicted for evermore in one of the world's most famous paintings, Vincent van Gogh's *Irises*. Closer to home, the British artist Sir Cedric Morris was the only person of his generation to achieve national stature both as a painter and a plantsman. In his famous gardens at Benton End, in Suffolk, he grew about 1,000 new iris seedlings each year, displaying the collection on open days. He produced at least 90 named varieties, usually prefixed with 'Benton' and, unsurprisingly, they provided a frequent theme for his paintings.

AS SPRING PROGRESSES TOWARDS SUMMER, THOUGHTS TURN TO COCKTAILS and friends with whom to share the gardens and evening celebrations. The elder brother of the novelist Evelyn Waugh is often credited with inventing the cocktail party.

'Some years ago I remarked to my brother Evelyn that I believed I had invented the cocktail party,' Alec writes. 'His eyes widened and whitened in the way they did. "I should be careful about making that boast in print"... He may well be right, but I have, I trust, reason for maintaining that in the literary bohemian circle I did frequent in London, I gave the first cocktail party.'

Evelyn Waugh, of course, married in turn two nieces of the 5th Earl of Carnarvon, and wrote that something was 'very Highclere' when it was very good. These cocktail recipes are very Highclere and our croquet was consequently very good, too.

Spring Cocktails

The Lavender Lady

The prettiest of cocktails, and it perfectly highlights the botanicals in Highclere Castle Gin.

50ml (2fl oz) Highclere Castle Gin
25ml (1fl oz) lavender syrup
25ml (1fl oz) lemon juice
1 egg white

Combine the gin, lavender syrup and lemon juice into an ice-filled cocktail shaker and shake until cold · Strain out the ice, add the egg white and shake again (this is known in the trade as a reverse shake) · Strain into a chilled coupe glass.

BUTLER'S NOTE

You can buy lavender syrup or make your own very easily · Pick lavender flowers before they have properly opened · Add 250g (9oz) sugar to 250ml (8fl oz) cold water in a pan, making a one-to-one syrup · Bring to the boil, drop in a handful of flowers and let them steep until cool · Leave for more or less time, depending upon how strong a lavender flavour you prefer · Strain into a jug · Kept in the fridge, this syrup will last for up to a week (or pour into an ice cube tray to freeze, so it is always there when you need it).

Bramble

Created just 40 years ago, this has already become a classic – a fantastic splash of summer colour.

50ml (2fl oz) Highclere Castle Gin
25ml (1fl oz) lemon juice
12·5ml (scant ½fl oz) sugar syrup
15ml (½fl oz) *crème de mûre* (blackberry liqueur)

To garnish

Blackberries
Lemon slices

**Fill an old-fashioned glass with crushed ice ·
Add the gin, lemon juice, sugar syrup and
stir together · Pour the *crème de mûre* over ·
Spear the garnishes on a cocktail stick.**

BUTLER'S NOTE

You could substitute *crème de cassis*
(blackcurrant liqueur) for the *crème de mûre*,
or garnish with a sprig of rosemary.

The English Garden

This is such a quintessentially British cocktail
filled with summer flavours, best served in a long,
tall glass and enjoyed in a deckchair on a lawn.

50ml (2fl oz) Highclere Castle Gin
25ml (1fl oz) elderflower liqueur (St. Germain)
15ml (½fl oz) lime juice
75ml (3fl oz) apple juice

To garnish

Apple slices
Cucumber ribbon

**Shake all the ingredients in a shaker and strain
into an ice-filled glass · Garnish with slices of
apple and a cucumber ribbon.**

Hanky Panky

Created by the bartending legend Ada 'Coley' Coleman in the 1920s, who became the first female head bartender at the Savoy. The recipe is from the 1930 *Savoy Cocktail Book*. It has a beautiful colour and scent and is one to sip slowly.

50ml (2fl oz) Highclere Castle Gin
50ml (2fl oz) sweet vermouth
2 dashes Fernet-Branca
  (a bitter herb-based liqueur)

To garnish

Orange twist

Combine all the ingredients into a mixing glass with ice · Stir until well chilled · Strain into a chilled cocktail glass · Garnish.

His Lordship Cocktail

We make and sell excellent marmalade and it is an essential part of Lord Carnarvon's life!

50ml (2fl oz) Highclere Castle Gin
25ml (1fl oz) elderflower cordial
25ml (1fl oz) lemon juice
1 bar spoon orange marmalade

To garnish

Ice cube
Strip of orange zest

In a cocktail shaker, stir all the ingredients (before adding ice) until the marmalade dissolves · Add ice to the shaker and shake until cold · Double strain into a cocktail glass, leaving the ice in the shaker · Add a single ice cube if it's a hot day, and a strip of orange zest.

BUTLER'S NOTE

Double straining is when we use two strainers of different mesh size to ensure that no crushed ice passes into the glass.

AZALEA ALTA-CLERA

Biking up the hill of the main drive to the castle at the end of my morning circuit of the park with the dogs, I am always glad to see the banks of dark green rhododendrons. With more energy than I possess at this point, the dogs run off towards them and disappear into the tangle. They are quite deaf to my calls as I carry on through the black gates and then turn back to pedal through the longer grass towards the folly, Jackdaw's Castle.

Highclere Castle sits on a chalk escarpment which therefore really only encourages lime-loving shrubs and trees but the mass of rhododendrons also shelters a collection of azaleas. Once, this whole green lawn was covered with herbaceous beds filled with plants brought back from travels abroad. They were first planted by the 2nd Earl (1772-1833), an enthusiastic horticulturist, ably abetted by his younger brother, William Herbert, who was a botanist. To provide a suitable environment in which his collection could flourish, Lord Carnarvon arranged to have huge pits dug out to an area between 1–2 acres in size which were then backfilled by cartloads of humus-rich acidic soil collected from down by a lake in the north part of the park. From these, an extensive mass of beds and formal walks were created, beginning near the Library windows of the Castle.

The 2nd Earl also collected seeds, notably from America, and raised the plants here in his nurseries with Mr Carton, his gardener, with further help from a Mr Gowan. The gardens gradually became noted for the many fine achievements of these gentlemen and the new hybrids they raised. To quote a *Gardening Magazine* article from the time: 'the most striking crosses have been effected between *R. arboreum* and the hardy species ... which are really splendid'. In 1813, he raised about 1,800 seedlings by crossing the flowers of *R. ponticum* and *R. maximum*, which he gave to many friends as well as desiring that they might be distributed among the wider community of nurserymen. Various notable azalea successes were also achieved, in particular, a cross of *Azalea calendulacea* and

Azaleas coming into bloom
in front of Jackdaw's Castle

Azalea nudiflora var. *rubescens*. As a result of all these efforts, this part of the Castle garden became much admired in Victorian times and was known as the American Garden.

Our magazine information continues:

> The history of the hybrid *R. alta-clerense* is curious in the way of floricultural anecdote. To obtain it had been a great desideratum; but the specimens of *R. arboreum* at Highclere had shown no disposition to flower. The only places in England where it then (1826) flowered were Hylands (Mr. Labouchere's), and at The Grange. From the latter place an umbel was obtained and conveyed to Highclere in a tin case. By means of its pollen the flowers of *R. ponticum* and *R. maximum* were fecundated ... Those which were retained at Highclere have now attained a flowering age, and form extensive shrubberies round the house.

During the two world wars most of the gardens were grassed over but some of the azalea beds at the very back remained, although increasingly overgrown. In November 2015 I decided to spend a few hours each weekend armed with really thick gloves, a fork and long shears pulling out brambles to see what lay underneath. All the dogs happily snuffled around digging as well, if for a different purpose. Sometimes it seemed overwhelming, sometimes really satisfying, but the project has continued, helped by the gardening team. We have progressed as far as digging out the bramble roots and it is a joy to be able to see again the shape of these aged azaleas and to think on when they were planted. I fuss around them, looking for other old beds full of the right soil which you can sometimes see as indentations in the grass.

In May the grass bursts into growth – it has all the rain it needs followed by sunshine, so the lawnmowers are in overdrive but so too are the ancient azaleas. They explode forth in colours, entirely forgetting their age. Blooms of yellow, red, peach and pink, orange, white and mauve shroud the shrubs, leaving only a few leaves to be seen. Gloriously clashing and scented, they are in fact rare Ghent

azaleas introduced from North America in 1734. The *Azalea ponticum* or *R. luteum* (yellow and highly scented) dates to 1806, whilst other hybrids include 'Ignea Nova', 'Coccinea Speciosa Narcissiflora' and 'Gloria Mundi'.

One specific bed always excites interest as gloriously coloured and scented; a number have been identified, including 'Pallas', 'Gloria Mundi' and 'Sang de Gentbrugge'. Their branches are covered in lichens, so I look carefully every April hoping they will return in splendour the following month.

THE DARLING BUDS OF MAY

'Blossom by blossom the spring begins' wrote Algernon Charles Swinburne, Victorian poet and novelist. Walk down to the south east of the Castle, past the huge head and shoulders of Charlemagne, and push open the wooden gate to hear the birds sing in the cherry trees as the thousands of white- and pink-tinged blossoms seem to create a light-filled snow heaven above you. The slim, almost invisible branches move gently in the breeze, disseminating a faint light scent.

Since ancient times, the Japanese have heralded the arrival of cherry blossoms as the symbol of the ephemeral beauty of life, its fragility and transience. For all their beauty, the blossom is short-lived, but in some ways the finale of spring – in which the petals are soft scattered over the serpentine green paths of the Secret Garden – is almost more beautiful, even if it represents the passing of the flowers. The Secret Garden shelters a collection of cherry trees from the time of its original creation by Jim Russell in 1962. However, a further 21 new white and pink Sakura trees have been kindly gifted to us from the Japanese Embassy in London. Planted in groups around the gardens, they will give so much pleasure for many years to come.

In contrast, on other walks, there are now clouds of apple blossom, pink and white, quietly buzzing with the sounds of the many bees drawn to the sweet nectar. The songbirds perform longer and more complicated melodies in the morning but I owe them a thank you at evensong too. Another ten days though, and the glory will already be fading. As Shakespeare put it in his famous *Sonnet 18*:

> Rough winds do shake the darling buds of May,
> And summer's lease hath all too short a date.

The blossom of blackthorn is also long gone by now but hawthorn has taken its place with a mass of white blossom overwhelming any glimpse of the leaves or spiny, prickly branches. Hawthorn in particular has ancient associations with May Day (1 May), which in the country calendar marks the point when spring becomes summer. Hawthorn flowers traditionally adorned May Day garlands as well as the wreath of the 'Green Man'. You are not supposed to bring hawthorn into the house but you can use the haws in jellies or salads, and in folklore it was in these bushes that the faeries lived. In fact, the site of Westminster Abbey was once called Thorney Island after the sacred stand of thorn trees that grew there. It does create an almost impenetrable hedge that's useful for keeping in cattle, whilst the bark can be used to make yellow dye.

To my mind, 1 May, is above all a general rejoicing at the return of better weather, and whilst there are many medieval references to such celebrations throughout Europe, their roots are much older.

The Romans dedicated a day in early May to the goddess Flora, which is practical given that if April brings showers, May brings flowers. Irises, tulips and philadelphus, vigorously growing lawns; everywhere there is an energy and light that Paul, Highclere's Head Gardener, and his team are working to keep up with. They might as well put out a May Day signal (which of course in its other meaning is the universal call for help, from the French *m'aider!*, which means 'help me').

May Day also has roots in far earlier festivals, for example Beltane, which marked the start of summer and was considered the best time for animals to be put out to pasture. Even today there is

Cherry blossom (*Prunus* 'Yoshino') in a shady corner of the Monks' Garden

a sense of relief that there is less mud, less heaving of water buckets and hay, fewer heavy gardening and farming chores, added to which the days are longer.

Fairies and witches are supposed to be very active on May Day but a number of trees are said to help repel them, such as hazel and particularly rowan (*Sorbus aucuparia*) which is also called the Witchbeam. Luckily, a number of groves still remain at Highclere, along with large amounts of hazel.

The Christian church annexed a number of ancient traditions and observances and used them to link May to the Virgin Mary as 'the Queen of May'. Many of these found renewed popularity during Victorian times and were in turn reimagined as a more contrived link to rural heritage. In some villages, the May Queen is still celebrated, as is the village Maypole, adorned with ribbons that are braided in dance.

At Highclere we have on occasion invited Morris Dancers to entertain us, which is another May Day tradition. They are a unique entertainment for unsuspecting visitors, with colourful costumes, bells on their shins and ribbons flowing from their hats as they dance a series of sets across the lawns. They hold and wield both large handkerchiefs and sticks, always ready to thwack each other's sticks in time to the music. Naturally we are delighted to pay the dancers today and know that the tradition dates back to at least 1448 when a similar payment was made. One year, however, it was relentlessly wet, so they danced for us all in the central Saloon of the Castle – which was unexpected perhaps but very entertaining and a reflection of the fun and revelry of May Day.

WOODS OF ENCHANTMENT

A Light exists in Spring
Not present on the Year
At any other period—
When March is scarcely here

A color stands abroad
On Solitary Fields
That Science cannot overtake
But Human Nature feels

It waits upon the Lawn
It shows the furthest Tree
Upon the furthest Slope you know
It almost speaks to you

Emily Dickinson, 'A Light Exists in Spring', 1890

HIGH ABOVE THE CASTLE, glades of beech have long rooted in the chalk soils. This is the queen of British trees and it creates a unique high leaf canopy. Walking along the ancient tracks, gazing up at the majestical cathedral height of the branches never fails to make me feel both humbled and at peace. I have read that it used to be said that no harm could befall a traveller who was lost and sought shelter under the branches of a beech, and equally that any prayers uttered under a beech should go straight to heaven. Certainly, talismans from beech wood were once carried to bring good luck and increase creative energy. The Anglo-Saxon word *boc* leads us both to the beech tree and to the word that later became book. In north European languages today, the words are closely connected: trees and wisdom.

Along the Wayfarers' Walk on a high chalk ridge south of the Castle, solitary oaks stand and fall in glades, mixed hedgerows mark the old trackways whilst stubble and beetle banks provide sanctuary belts amongst the crops. Every spring day offers new growth and new shapes and then, almost overnight, a sky-blue sea of bluebells overflows the ground, divided from azure spring skies by smooth grey trunks leaning across each other with lightly sunlit half-opened leaves.

Everywhere there is an infinite wash of colour and scent which fills in the time between the first warming of the soil and the closing of the woodland canopy above when the leaves fully unfurl. Just a humble woodland flower, the bluebell symbolises everlasting love and was beloved of England's patron saint, St George, and when it flowers en masse it takes the breath away. The poet John Keats called it the 'Sapphire queen of the mid-May'. Tennyson thought a mass of bluebells looked like 'the blue sky, breaking up through the earth', whilst Gerard Manley Hopkins wrote in his journal, in 1871, of 'the blue-buzzed haze and the waft of intoxicant perfume'. Like so many things it is now rarer than it once was and over half the world's bluebells are found in the UK. Drifts take between five and seven years to establish from seed to flower and are fragile: if you step all over them they can die, as the leaves cannot photosynthesise. Folklore holds that the flowers' bell heads could summon summer fairies to woodland gatherings and it is bad luck to bring a bunch into the house.

It is, however, very possible to plant bluebell bulbs – the native variety – under the spreading branches of a tree, perhaps in small irregular clumps. They need to be deep enough so the white base of the green leaves is covered by soil. Water well and they do ask for patience. Do not cut off the foliage and each year the bulbs will strengthen.

Bluebells often congregate in areas of ancient woodland which date back at least 400 years. These are species-rich habitats and today only cover about 2 per cent of the UK's land compared to double that amount before the Second World War. Relatively undisturbed by human development, unique, complex communities thrive in the undisturbed soils and accumulated decaying wood, along with fungi, invertebrates, insects, lichens and other plants. Unfortunately, these woodlands are being felled at a rate even faster than the Amazon rainforest is being diminished.

The poet Gerard Manley Hopkins was deeply observant of nature and struggled with Victorian industrialism, which he felt was both deeply damaging and taking away the time needed to wonder at the marvels of the natural world. He felt that he lived in an age of vandalism, both actual and spiritual, that did not understand 'the greater significance of the growing green'. In 1870, he wrote:

> I do not think I have ever seen anything more beautiful than the bluebell I have been looking at. I know the beauty of our Lord by it.

TREES OF GOD

We had better be without gold than without timber
John Evelyn (1620-1706)

RICHARD POCOCKE AND HIS COUSIN JEREMIAH were both taught by their grandfather, Reverend Isaac Milles, in the old rectory in Highclere Park alongside Robert Herbert of Highclere and his elder brother Henry Herbert (who later became the 9th Earl of Pembroke). As adults, between 1737 and 1741, they travelled through the Middle East, including Lebanon, and it was Richard who famously returned with the cones of cedar of Lebanon from which the first of Highclere's iconic trees descend.

Pococke kept a diary of his adventures, sending light, lively letters back to his mother (whom he addressed as 'Honoured Madam') every three weeks. One entry from 1738 describes the trees:

> They form a grove about a mile in circumference, which consists of some large cedars that are near to one another, a great number of young cedars and some pines. The great cedars, at some distance, look very like large spreading oaks; the bodies of the trees are short, dividing at the bottom into three or four limbs, some of which growing up together for about ten feet, appear something like thick Gothic columns, which seem to be composed of seven pillars, higher up they begin to spread horizontally: one that had the rounded body, tho' not the largest, measured twenty-four feet in circumference, and another with the sort of triple body, as described above, measured twelve feet on each side.

Cedars were venerated by ancient civilisations, recorded more than any other tree in the Bible, and it was from cedar that Solomon constructed both a temple and a palace. It was used to bury pharaohs, build ships and was deemed incorruptible because, although the wood is light-coloured, it is hard and utterly resistant to decay.

There are four *taxa* (family units) of cedar: Cedar of Lebanon, *Cedrus atlas* (also called *atlantica*) which has blue-tinged needles, *deodara* (meaning 'woods of Gods') which has a more slender silhouette, and lastly Cedar of Cyprus (*Cedrus brevifolia*) which grows slowly and is not so tall, more of a conical silhouette. The cedars admired by the two cousins used to form extensive forests in Lebanon, though these are now under threat. Some of the trees there are now called 'the survivors', as the thousands of trees have been reduced to groups of hundreds.

Thousands of miles from their native homeland, these trees provide structure and beauty throughout the year in the park. Highclere's records testify that cedar number one was raised in 1739 from:

> a Cone brought from Lebanon by Dr Pocock the oriental traveller, transplanted in 1767, when it measured 17 inches in Girth at a foot from the ground. By 1812 it was 6 Feet 10½ Inches and fifteen years later it was 8 Feet 11.

Brownlow North, Bishop of Winchester from 1781, was a frequent guest at Highclere and indeed his portrait still hangs here. Keen to acquire some cedars himself, he carried away so many of the young trees from Highclere that the driver of his post chaise was apparently almost entirely hidden by them. They were then planted out at Farnham Castle, one of the great medieval houses of England.

Many of these trees are over 250 years old and they provide welcome colour through winter months, framing the drives as you wind your way through the parkland, glimpsing and losing and gaining views of the Castle. 'How scenical, how scenical!' exclaimed Prime Minister Benjamin Disraeli, arriving for a weekend visit in 1866.

During our time here, Geordie and I have planted many new cedars to give pleasure to those who might walk under them looking for shade or shelter 150 years hence. This includes two more *C. deodora* to replace earlier ones.

THE ANCIENT ASH

THE CEDAR TREES, HOWEVER, ARE RECENT MAJESTIC ADDITIONS to the Highclere landscape. The famous English painter John Constable made some beautiful studies of ash and elm trees, writing in September 1821, 'I have done some studies ... particularly a natural (but highly Elegant) group of trees, Ashes, Elms, and Oaks ...' Equally they can inspire deep emotions – an American friend of the artist wrote: 'I have seen him admire a fine tree with an ecstasy of delight like that with which he would catch up a beautiful child in his arms.'

The Roman poet Virgil wrote his *Eclogues* some 2,000 years ago and described the ash as the most beautiful tree. His poems were performed with great success on the Roman stage, exploring all the usual political and romantic challenges, but above all described the exquisite beauty of the world in which we live. Ever since, the Arcadian landscape in which he set his stories has become ingrained in our drama and literature. Ash trees are part of the largest plant form, they are at the core of life on Earth, and in all cultures, they are, to a degree, surrounded by myth and fable.

In folklore, ash trees are often associated with the sacred. The Vikings believed that *Yggdrasil*, the World Tree, under which the gods held their councils, was an ash, whilst the Gaelic belief system also imbued it with powers of protection: of the five legendary guardian trees of Ireland, three were ash.

Ash wood is very strong and elastic, and it is said that a joint made of ash will bear more weight than any other wood. As a result, coach axles were made of ash as were oars, tool handles and archers' bows. The tree coppices well, giving strong, straight poles for bean poles after five years or oars after twenty. The density of the wood also makes it ideal for fuel – the Latin name *Fraxinus* means firelight – as it burns hot and long. It grows easily; if coppiced it springs back with enthusiasm and if an ash tree falls down through accident, it will try again.

A glorious red ash charms us every spring in the gardens to the south west of the Castle, and it is somewhere to sit today 'because' (as Warren Buffett remarked), 'someone planted a tree a long time ago'.

Sadly, ash dieback disease has now affected areas of ash on the steep chalk hillsides at Highclere and we are having to fell these trees and replant with other species. We hope for a new genetic variety which is resistant so we can plant these magnificent trees again for future generations.

Finally, as spring turns into summer, the chalk banks encourage the lilacs (*Syringa*) to flower. Whether primrose yellow or dark purple, white and all shades of pink, the scent lingers as the evening fades and perhaps it is best to follow the composer Ivor Novello's advice: 'We'll gather lilacs in the spring again, And walk together down an English lane', or at Highclere a path, as lilacs give way to wisterias with long racemes of purple and white which begin in spring and stay with us through early summer.

A HEALING HERB GARDEN

I know a bank where the wild thyme blows,
Where oxlips and the nodding violet grows,
Quite over-canopied with luscious woodbine,
With sweet musk-roses and with eglantine
William Shakespeare, *A Midsummer Night's Dream*

LACKING TODAY'S SUPERMARKETS AND GROCERS, for much of human history gardens have played a vital part in providing sustenance for daily life. The Bishops' gardens and farms at Highclere were no different. Fruit, vegetables and herbs were grown close by the buildings. Further afield, pastures provided fodder for sheep, cattle and horses, and crops such as oats were farmed on the arable land on the surrounding hills, really much as we do today.

Later, during medieval times, a walled garden was built on a south-facing slope to the south east of where the Castle stands today. The tall walls kept the wind out and the bricks retained warmth far better than stone. This may also have served as the location for the physic garden. Such a garden was central to every medieval infirmary and it would have been the most likely place for a community such as Highclere to have had one. Sage, hyssop, rue, chamomile, dill, comfrey and cumin ... all typical plants for such gardens and easy to grow on the chalk or alkaline soils found here. It is interesting to see how many of these are used for digestive complaints! I remember reading that it was not uncommon for medieval soldiers returning from battle, mentally shattered by all they had seen, to be offered work in monastic gardens and given herbs to encourage them to sleep. Nothing much changes in the turmoil of today.

In fact, even earlier, the Ebers Papyrus from ancient Egypt (c.1500BC) recorded over 850 plant medicines, including fennel and linseed which we still grow here, plus notes on treatments for trauma. Tutankhamun, now forever linked with Highclere due to the 5th Earl's role in the discovery of his tomb, was buried with garlic and onions to help his respiration and digestion in the next life.

Walking through the old walled garden today you can still see ancient foundations, the shadow of unused doors, coping stones which just extend out above the crab apples, figs and vines trained up the faded brick walls. Long beds of lavender grow in abundance whilst mulberry trees and a quince stand amidst green grass. We have also planted roses and other flowers for scent and beauty, but perhaps these also aid health by encouraging us to smile and feel happy.

The Monks' Garden, however, is a little distant from today's Castle, down an incline and along a gravel path. Reflecting on the history of herbs grown here, we have, in recent years, created a new, symmetrically planted, herb garden within a beech hedge near the Castle tearooms. In the middle is a modern sundial on which is inscribed 'Omnia tempus habent et suis spatiis transeunt universa sub caelo'. From the biblical book of Ecclesiastes, this translates as 'To everything there is a season, and a time to every purpose under the heaven'.

To my mind, nothing evokes the gardens of the past so much as herbs: overflowing mixtures of angelica, fennel, rosemary, borage, marjoram and violets. Both aromatic and pungent, they were the basis for medicine and health before the advent of modern medicine and many still play a recognised role today: plants form the basis of around a quarter of all modern western medicines and they must be treated with caution as different parts of plants may be toxic if used improperly.

Equally, vegetables and herbs were not differentiated from each other as they are today and all played their part in cooking – eaten raw, cooked or prepared as a tisane, tonic or as a flavouring to disguise the taste of rotten food. In addition, some herbs are essential companion plants if you grow vegetables, as they can improve the vigour of their neighbours and help to repel pests. Borage, for example, is an excellent companion plant to strawberries, whilst mint repels cabbage grubs and is also disliked by mice and rats.

Philip has worked in the gardens at Highclere for over 20 years and in particular he helps me look after the Monks' Garden, planting a traditional selection of herbs that we choose together. Some, such as bay, marjoram, rosemary, thyme and parsley, for example, are very familiar; others, such as sweet cicely, which appears early in spring, bergamot and angelica, less so.

Balm (Melissa officinalis) is a perennial which is easy to grow both in the ground or in a pot. Often called lemon balm for its scent, bees adore it: it is said if you plant lemon balm by a hive it will attract further colonies. It is also good for frayed nerves, possibly just by its scent alone, and was described by the seventeenth-century diarist John Evelyn as 'sovereign for the brain, strengthening the memory and powerfully chasing away melancholy'.

Lavender and rosemary are important structural elements in the herb garden

As usual, many of my choices are guided by association, and the angelica (*Angelica archangelica*) is planted for a great personal friend, Angeli Bolza. The name suggests heavenly associations and legend says it flowers on 8 May, the feast day of St Michael the Archangel, after whom the original Anglo-Saxon church at Highclere was named. It has tall, greenish-white umbels for much of the summer and was thought to offer protection against various diseases, especially the plague. Today the seeds are used in vermouth as well as in essential oils and as a cooking flavouring.

Another herb grown here is sweet woodruff (*Galium odoratum*), which when dried has the sweet smell of hay and honey – hence its name. Useful for scenting linen and warding off moths, it was also valued as a sedative and to help varicose veins. In Germany the herb is steeped in wine and drunk to celebrate May Day each year. We also have lovage (*Levisticum officinale*). Traditionally an aphrodisiac, it was grown and used by Greeks and Romans as well as in medieval times. All parts of the plant can be used: the seeds chewed to aid digestion; infusions used to help urinary problems, whilst the leaves have antiseptic qualities but can also be added to salads or soups. Another less usual herb is bugle (*Ajuga reptans*) which has astringent properties. The leaves, whether fresh or dried, have been used to treat wounds, throat irritations and mouth ulcers.

There is plenty of sage because, apparently, you will then never grow old, and also sorrel which aids digestion and cures liver problems, lavender for sleep, rosemary to promote energy and fennel and chamomile for teas.

Herb Broth

In my youth, I spent a few months in Germany learning the language and I well remember some of their culinary traditions, in particular the green herb broth. A special treat of early spring, it is associated with the Easter holidays and traditionally eaten on *Gruendonnerstag* (Maundy Thursday). Often it would have included some watercress or parsley but my recipe below is clearer in colour. The best thing to do is experiment. Whatever combination you choose, it is an excellent fillip for the immune system as we emerge from winter into spring.

2 onions, roughly chopped
1 bulb of garlic, peeled and roughly chopped
2 tsp apple cider vinegar
1 tsp whole black peppercorns
3 bay leaves
Large handful each of rosemary, thyme, sage and oregano
(and/or other herbs that smell good together)

Add all the ingredients to a casserole dish and add 4 litres (7 pints) of water · Bring to a boil, then reduce to a simmer and cook uncovered for 30–45 minutes until the liquid has reduced by a quarter · Remove as many of the solid bits as you can with a slotted spoon and allow to cool · Strain through a muslin-lined sieve to remove all the debris and either use or store in a sterilised container · Refrigerate (can also be frozen).

To forget how to dig the earth and tend the soil is to forget ourselves
Mahatma Gandhi

To everything there is a season and late spring is above all the time to plant, to scatter seeds in the vegetable beds or to pot up inside. Most of us have the space for a few pots of herbs.

SPRING HARVEST

IN THE SPRING SOMETIME in the 1240s 'the Garden was cleared of thorns, weeded with a harrow and planted as a curtilage with leeks, cabbages and other vegetables' along with substantial quantities of beans. In 1248–49 more than two acres were dug out and beans planted in two gardens. In 1262–63 the garden was again cleared of thorns and dug to plant beans, and likewise in 1265–66, 1267–68, 1268–69, 1270–71. Sadly, the records don't tell us what kind of beans were planted but they were clearly a staple foodstuff possibly for both humans and animals. Equally it is very clear that, just like today, there is a perennial battle to produce more plants than weeds.

Two spring-harvested crops that I am particularly keen on are rhubarb and beetroot (beets). Growing rhubarb gives you a splash of colour throughout the year and I was lucky to inherit some particularly vigorous plants in the garden. They have been subject to a quietly fought battle in recent years as a friend Genny and Philip the gardener consider how to harvest the stalks – whether you 'pull' or 'cut' and take all the plant or in sections.

RHUBARB

Rhubarb cannot be harvested until the plant has established itself properly – at least a year. Once it is established, it can be harvested once the stalks

of the leaves reach at least 25cm (10 inches) long. This will ensure that the plant has established itself well enough for the year to be able to tolerate being harvested. You could take some of the stalks earlier than this but if you take too many you will kill the plant. You also need to know when to stop. Whilst technically you can keep harvesting rhubarb until late summer, keep in mind that your rhubarb plant needs to store up enough energy to survive winter.

There are two ways to harvest rhubarb. One is to use a sharp knife to cut off the stalks, the second is to gently break the stalk off from the plant. Both have their proponents. Never harvest all the stalks of your rhubarb plant as you will kill it, and always throw away the leaves from the cut stalk as they are poisonous and should never be eaten.

BEETROOT

Beetroot can be boiled, steamed, roasted and pickled. Eaten hot or cold, blended into a soup or drink, red beetroots are ranked as one of the ten most potent antioxidant vegetables: a veritable titan of a superfood. Furthermore, it is easy to grow and ideal for anyone new to vegetable gardening.

Belonging to the same family as spinach, both the leaves and root can be eaten, although the leaves can taste quite bitter. Whilst so-called heirloom varieties like white and yellow beets are useful for making dishes look pretty, it is red beetroots that are the real powerhouses. They contain the cancer-fighting compound betacyanin and are also helpful in lowering blood pressure and improving digestive health as they are one of the richest sources of glutamine, an amino acid essential to the health and maintenance of the gut. They're also rich in fibre and anti-inflammatory.

For best results, sow beetroot little and often, harvesting the roots when they are young, tender and the size of a golf ball. If you grow varieties for winter storage, it is possible to have beetroot almost all year round, although it has to be admitted they are at their sweetest in June and July.

POTS OF FLOWERS

To get a continuous swathe of flowers in your pots, you need to plan your choice of bulbs. Succession planting in layers will allow a surprisingly large number of bulbs to be planted in each pot and produce a season-long display of blooms. At Highclere the gardeners fill all the pots in the courtyard and around the tea rooms with a carefully chosen mixture of daffodils, tulips and grape hyacinths (*Muscari*) to ensure that it always looks fresh and pretty for guests.

The key to the process is knowing the heights of the flowers and the bloom times, then there follows a certain amount of careful planning. Choose large, medium and small bulbs and layer them according to planting depth. The same effect can also be produced in your flower beds.

1. Prepare the flower bed by removing weeds and debris and working the soil deeply. Remove the soil to a depth of 20–25cm (8–10 inches) and put it to one side.

2. Mix some bulb food or bone meal into the base of the bed.

3. Take the largest bulbs, such as daffodils, tulips and alliums, and place them on the base of the dug-out area. Cover with a layer of soil.

4. Spread out the medium-sized bulbs such as the smaller tulip bulbs, grape hyacinths and Dutch iris. Again, cover with soil.

5. Lastly, spread out the smallest bulbs, such as crocus and anemone, and finish with the remaining soil.

With care and attention, the same principles can also be applied to seeds, although planning is even more essential here and definitely more patience.

SPECIALITIES

As with so many other estates, most of the specialist buildings from the past, from vineries to pinetums, orangeries and mushroom houses, sank into disrepair during the twentieth century. The growth in imported food, the lack of manpower following two world wars and changes in food fashions all led to their increasing obsolescence.

Behind the Monks' Garden lies a vinery. Whilst vines can survive much of the vagaries of English weather, the crucial time for the plants is late spring to mid-May. This is the growing time and sudden deep frosts can end all hope. The *Gardeners' Magazine* in 1834 explained the process at Highclere in some detail:

> The cuttings of the vines are first planted in very small pots, and shifted, as they advance in growth, into pots of larger size, till the latter are, at last, a foot in diameter, when they are placed in large saucers, and fed with liquid manure. The pots are placed at the back of the house, close under the glass, and the shoots are trained on wires down the slope, so as to give the leaves every advantage of sun and heat. It is expected that each vine will produce five or six bunches of grapes; those of Mr. Pillans, similarly treated, having produced 450lb. of grapes from seventy pots.

Another later article describes the vinery thus:

> In a small garden detached from the pleasure ground is a range of Vineries, in two divisions, each about 38 feet in length. The Vines have been planted by Mr. Phipps; one planted in the summer of 1854, has this season produced a heavy crop of Grapes of excellent quality. The other division was planted last summer - 1855 - and in this the rods are unusually strong.

The restored vineries now produce an abundance of fruit for us

Finally, in 1895, the garden accounts detail £226 to Boulton and Paul for a new vinery to produce table grapes. We have spent some time restoring these and, once again, they are producing grapes. Small and sweet, they remain a special treat for us today.

BRITISH WEATHER

HIGHCLERE IS SO-CALLED because the house has been built on a relatively high chalk escarpment for this part of England. As a result of the clear, unobstructed views the skies paint glorious backdrops in imaginative clouds by day, whilst sunset skies are shaded by all colours of red and then clear, dark heavens revolve slowly around.

Many of the cloud formations were named by an Englishman in Latin, of course, according to their height and shape. Clouds are creations of water particles and dust, ever changing in colours, shape and density. Beloved of landscape painters, they have a special beauty and lift the eyes except when they present grey sheets of never-ending rain.

From cirrocumulus to cirrostratus to large fluffy cumulus clouds that pop up on sunny days predicting good weather, there is no more sure topic of conversation than the weather. In spring there are myriad guides to the forthcoming year: 'If March comes in like a lion it will go out like a lamb.'

But to quote John Ruskin, 'There is no such thing as bad weather, only different kinds of good weather.' And thus spring becomes summer. ◇

SPRING COOKING

SPRING DAYS OFFER FIFTY SHADES OF GREEN AS TINY LEAF BUDS UNFOLD INTO a myriad of different shapes and tones. Cooking at this time of year is about welcome freshness: the delicious crunch of the first asparagus spears and fresh herbs offering varied flavours and tastes; the newest, smallest peas and beans which can be eaten raw, or Jersey new potatoes slowly savoured with bright yellow butter and green chives. There are few things better than picking and making wild green garlic pesto whether to accompany lamb or various pastas. Then, for a touch of sweetness, there are the pale pink stems of rhubarb growing in the garden which can be steamed with ginger or used in a crumble.

Omelette aux fines herbes

The 6th Earl of Carnarvon would sit at the head of the dining table at breakfast declaring that there was no better omelette in the world than the one his grandson of school age (Geordie) was just about to eat. The best eggs, the most perfect softly scrambled interior to the omelette and the excellent choice of the finest herbs in the country. No pressure for other cooks then!

This version is flavoured with finely chopped fresh herbs: parsley, chives, chervil and tarragon.

INGREDIENTS

6 large eggs
Salt and freshly ground pepper
2 tbsp (in total) finely chopped
  herbs such as parsley, chives,
  chervil and tarragon
25g (1oz) unsalted butter
Drizzle of olive/rapeseed oil

PREPARATION TIME 5 mins   **COOKING TIME** 5 mins   **SERVES** 2

Beat the eggs together with the salt, pepper and herbs.

Drizzle a little oil in a non-stick frying pan on a medium heat.
When hot, add the butter until it's foaming but not brown.

Pour in the egg mixture and swirl around the pan. Watch carefully as
the egg starts to cook. For the first 15 seconds, use a spatula to move
the egg from the edge of the pan to the middle, at the same time filling
the gaps by tipping the pan. Cook for a further 45 seconds until the egg
starts to firm at the edge.

Lift the pan from the heat. As it sets the omelette should be able to
move around freely in the pan. With a spatula, fold the omelette in half,
then slide from the pan straight on to a warm plate.

CHEF'S TIP

You can serve omelettes for breakfast, lunch or dinner.
Delicious with cheese, smoked salmon, ham,
chorizo, asparagus ... the list goes on.

Dressed Garden Peas, Broad Beans and Radicchio

*Everyone has always loved peas. Archaeological finds of peas date
from the late Neolithic era in the Middle East and peas were found in
Tutankhamun's tomb. You do not have to go far from Highclere to find
mushy peas on offer with fish and chips, but this fresh, pretty salad is an
uplifting way to greet the spring.*

INGREDIENTS

Half a bunch tarragon
500ml (17fl oz) vegetable stock
200g (7oz) broad beans
150g (5oz) garden peas
3 tbsp olive oil
Salt and freshly ground black
   pepper
1 tbsp sherry vinegar
1 tsp ginger, grated
Juice of half a lemon
2 sprigs mint, leaves chopped
Half a head radicchio, shredded
1 yellow grapefruit, segmented

PREPARATION TIME 10 mins   **COOKING TIME** 10 mins   **SERVES** 6

Put one sprig of tarragon and the stock into a saucepan and bring to
a boil. Tip in the beans and blanch for 2 minutes. Remove the beans and
plunge them into cold water.

Bring the stock back to a boil and blanch the peas for 4 minutes.
Remove them and add them to the cold water.

Finely chop the remaining tarragon leaves and drain the peas and beans.
Place them all in a bowl with half the olive oil and season well.

Combine the remaining olive oil with the vinegar, ginger, mint and lemon
juice. Stir in the radicchio, mixing thoroughly.

Mix the radicchio with the pea and bean mixture and transfer to a
serving dish. Garnish with the grapefruit segments.

Wild Garlic

Wild garlic is a heady, intoxicating promise of spring, the very essence of ancient shaded walks along still-damp tracks. The green leaves curl over the edges of ditches into the shade of wizened old trees. Sniff it and you can be sure you have the right plant, making it a good introduction to foraging. As it grows in abundance beside footpaths it is generally acceptable to pick a small amount.

It is an antiseptic and boiled leaves can be used as a disinfectant.

With its lighter flavour (compared to the more familiar bulb garlic) it can be made into a soup, used in a tomato salad, mixed into an omelette or simply mixed with olive oil and pounded into a pesto.

Wild Garlic Pesto

INGREDIENTS

150g (5oz) wild garlic leaves
50g (2oz) Parmesan, finely grated
1 garlic clove, finely chopped
Zest and some of the juice
  of ½ lemon
50g (2oz) pine nuts, toasted
150ml (5fl oz) good-quality
  vegetable oil
Salt to taste

PREPARATION TIME 15 mins   **MAKES** 1 jar

Rinse the wild garlic leaves thoroughly and roughly chop.

Using a blender, blitz the leaves, Parmesan, garlic, lemon zest and pine nuts together to form a rough paste. Season well and, with the motor running very slowly, add the oil, blending all the time.

Now taste, and add lemon juice or salt if required, before storing in a sterilised jar.

This will keep in the fridge for about 2 weeks.

Wilted Greens with Wild Garlic

I always bear in mind the value and taste of leafy green vegetables, which support our health and reduce the risk of a number of diseases as well as mental decline.

INGREDIENTS

1kg (2¼lb) spring greens,
  finely sliced
150g (5oz) wild garlic leaves,
  chopped
2 tbsp sherry vinegar
25g (1oz) butter
Salt and freshly ground
  black pepper

PREPARATION TIME 15 mins   **COOKING TIME** 5 mins   **SERVES** 6

Place the greens and the garlic in a saucepan with a splash of water and let the leaves wilt over a medium heat for 2–3 minutes, stirring occasionally.

Add the vinegar to the saucepan and continue cooking until the liquid is reduced to almost nothing.

Add the butter and season to taste. Toss the greens to coat with the butter and serve.

Asparagus

Emperor Caesar Augustus was a great connoisseur of asparagus and he actually organised elite military units to procure it for him. The famed 'Asparagus Fleets' brought back the best varieties to Rome. Furthermore, the fastest runners were hired to carry fresh spears high into the Alps, where it could be frozen for later use.

If you have neither fleets of ships nor speedy runners to hand, asparagus is surprisingly easy to grow, thriving on either well-drained soil or in raised beds. Asparagus plants are either male or female. Male plants produce more and better spears, so many modern cultivars are all-male. Any female plants can be distinguished as they produce orange-red berries. If you are growing an all-male cultivar, you will need to remove any female plants as well as any seedlings that appear.

Plant asparagus crowns in March, weed by hand (their roots are shallow), and use stakes and garden twine to make a 'fence' either side of the asparagus row for support, because during the summer the plants are tall and feathery. Allow the foliage of your asparagus plants to yellow in autumn before cutting down to soil level for the winter. Do not harvest for the first two years after planting. In the third year, harvest spears from mid-April for six weeks.

Asparagus Tart

INGREDIENTS

150g (5oz) plain flour, sifted,
plus extra for dusting
75g (3oz) butter, cubed,
plus extra for greasing
85g (3oz) Cheddar or another
hard cheese, finely grated

For the filling

5 eggs
175ml (6fl oz) milk
100g (3½oz) Cheddar or similar
hard cheese, grated
300g (10oz) asparagus, trimmed
and cut in half lengthways

PREPARATION TIME 30–40 mins   COOKING TIME 30–35 mins   SERVES 4

First make the pastry. Put the flour into a bowl, add the butter to the flour and rub in with your fingertips until it resembles breadcrumbs.

Add the grated Cheddar to the pastry and mix. Add 3 tablespoons of cold water and mix with a spoon or in a food processor until the pastry forms a ball. Wrap in cling film and chill for 5 minutes.

Butter a 20 × 6cm (8 × 2½ inch) deep loose-bottomed tart tin or a 35 × 12cm (14 × 4½ inch) rectangular tart tin.

Preheat the oven to 180°C/350°F/Gas mark 4.

Lightly dust the work surface with flour, roll out the pastry and line the tin with it. Chill in the freezer for 20 minutes.

Line the pastry case with baking paper, fill with beans and cook for 15 minutes. Remove the beans and paper, then return the pastry case to the oven for 10 minutes.

Crack the eggs into a jug, whisk, then add the milk and whisk again. Sprinkle half the grated cheese over the pastry case, then arrange the asparagus and pour over the egg mix and remaining cheese (if using a rectangular tin, you may not need all the mixture, so add it gradually).

Bake in the lower half of the oven for 30–35 minutes or until the egg mixture is set.

Asparagus with Parmesan

INGREDIENTS

Asparagus spears
Olive oil, for drizzling
Parmesan shavings
Sprig of thyme, to garnish (optional)
Salt and freshly ground
black pepper

PREPARATION TIME 10 mins   COOKING TIME 10 mins

Preheat the oven to 180°C/350°F/Gas mark 4.

Trim the ends of as many asparagus spears as you have (or want to eat – I can never have too much!). Lay them out on a foil-lined baking sheet.

Drizzle with olive oil and sprinkle over some crunchy sea salt and plenty of fresh pepper.

Roast the asparagus for about 10 minutes.

Grate or shave plenty of Parmesan over the top and serve immediately, maybe garnished with a sprig of thyme.

Bruschette with Broad Beans, Rocket and Feta Cheese

At its simplest, bruschetta is just grilled bread rubbed with raw garlic and topped with really good olive oil and a sprinkling of sea salt. Often topped with tomatoes, this is an alternative recipe that makes a delicious lunch.

INGREDIENTS

1 loaf ciabatta or sourdough
2 tbsp olive oil
1 garlic clove, peeled and cut in half
300g (10oz) fresh or frozen
  broad beans
A few leaves of fresh mint, chopped
Lemon juice
100g (3½oz) feta, cubed
2–3 large tomatoes, finely diced
Rocket leaves

PREPARATION TIME 10 mins   **COOKING TIME** 15 mins   **SERVES** 4

Slice the loaf into 2cm (1 inch) thick slices, drizzle with olive oil, heat a griddle pan and toast the bread until each side is gently grilled. Rub with the cut side of the garlic clove.

Boil the beans in a saucepan of water for 2 minutes, then rinse under cold water. Season and roughly chop, leaving some whole. Drizzle with any remaining oil. Mix in the fresh mint and lemon juice to taste.

Top each toast with the broad bean mixture, feta, tomatoes and rocket.

Watercress and Spinach Salad

Watercress grows wild in the Hampshire chalk streams and the local town of Alresford became the centre of the industry in 1865 when a railway line to London – the 'Watercress Line' – opened.

With its distinctive peppery flavour it has traditionally been used in salads and soups. It is recognised as a food with high nutritional value, and is packed full of nutrients including vitamins C and A, folic acid, iron and calcium.

INGREDIENTS

2 tbsp extra-virgin olive oil
Squeeze of lemon juice
1 large bunch watercress,
  stalks trimmed
100g (3½oz) bag baby spinach
  leaves, washed
1 small red onion, finely sliced
Salt and freshly ground pepper

PREPARATION TIME 5 mins   **SERVES** 4

Whisk together the oil and lemon juice and season well.

Combine the leaves and onion, drizzle over the dressing and toss together.

Celeriac Soup with Goat's Cheese Croutons

*Celeriac is a knobbly root vegetable usually with small roots attached. It
tastes like celery but the flavour is more intense, and can be eaten raw
(it is crunchy and best served thinly sliced), mashed, used in soups and
stews, and is easy to store for some months.*

INGREDIENTS

4 leeks, sliced into discs
50g (2oz) butter
1 tbsp olive oil
1 celeriac, peeled and diced
1·5 litres (2½ pints) vegetable stock
Salt and freshly ground
    black pepper
Slices of toasted baguette
Olive oil
100g (3½oz) soft goat's cheese
    with herbs

PREPARATION TIME 15 mins   COOKING TIME 40 mins   SERVES 6

Soften the leeks in a pan over a medium heat with the butter and
olive oil.

Add the celeriac and stock, bring to the boil and simmer for 15–20
minutes or until the celeriac is soft.

Drain, cool slightly and transfer to a blender, then blend until smooth.
Season well.

To make the croutons, preheat the oven to 200°C/400°F /Gas mark 6.
Dip each baguette slice in a little oil, toast in the oven for 5 minutes until
crisp. Spread the soft goat's cheese on top and serve with the soup.

Homemade Pea Soup with Garden Mint

INGREDIENTS

1 small onion, roughly chopped
1 medium potato, peeled and diced
1 garlic clove, crushed
850ml (1½ pints) vegetable
    or chicken stock
900g (2lb 4oz) young peas
    in the pod or 250g (9oz) shelled or
    frozen peas
4 tbsp chopped fresh mint
Large pinch of caster sugar
1 tbsp fresh lemon juice
150ml (5fl oz) buttermilk
    or soured cream
Salt and freshly ground pepper

PREPARATION TIME 10 mins   COOKING TIME 20 mins   SERVES 4

Put the onion into a pan with the potato, garlic and stock. Bring to the
boil and then simmer for 15 minutes or until the potato is very soft.
Add the peas and simmer for a further 5 minutes.

Stir in the mint, sugar and lemon juice, cool slightly, then pour into a
food processor or liquidiser and whizz until it is smooth. Stir in half the
buttermilk or soured cream, taste and season with salt and pepper.

To serve the soup cold, cool quickly, then chill. To serve hot, return the
soup to the rinsed-out pan and gently reheat. Do not let it boil or the
buttermilk or soured cream will curdle.

Swirl some of the remaining soured cream into each bowl when serving.

GARDENER'S TIP

Peas are also easy to grow from seed, from early spring into early summer.
They will need supports to scramble up but don't take up much space. If you
wish to start sowing earlier, begin indoors. Never sow into cold, wet soil. Make
a shallow trench, roughly 30cm (12 inches) wide and 5cm (2 inches) deep. Sow
in two parallel lines, about 10cm (4 inches) apart. Cover with soil, water well
and label before you forget and in ten days' time, you should see shoots appear.

Pan-fried Trout with Peas and Baby Broad Beans

Trout is very easy to cook and is an excellent source of the Omega-3 oils which are known to promote healthy ageing by reducing the risk of heart disease and stroke. Trout is also a good source of iodine and selenium as well as being one of the best foods for supplementing our vitamin D levels in the winter or early spring months. In today's world they are available all year round but spring was traditionally a good time to catch them.

INGREDIENTS

4 rainbow trout fillets
150g (5oz) butter
110g (4oz) peas
110g (4oz) baby broad beans
125g (4½oz) shallots, chopped
Handful of fresh parsley, chopped
Juice of 1 lemon
Salt and freshly ground
    black pepper

PREPARATION TIME 20 mins **COOKING TIME** 10 mins **SERVES** 4

Season the trout fillets, heat 50g (2oz) of the butter in a frying pan and fry the fish, skin-side down, for 2–3 minutes. When the skin is crisp and golden brown, turn the fillets over and fry for another minute or so until the fish is cooked through. Remove the fish and keep warm.

Add another spoon of the butter to the pan and tip in the peas and baby broad beans. Pour over just enough boiling water to cover the beans, return to the boil and simmer for 1–2 minutes until tender. Drain and set aside.

Add some more butter and the shallots to the frying pan and fry for 2–3 minutes until the shallots have softened and are golden brown and the butter has darkened in colour.

Return the beans, peas, half the parsley and the lemon juice to the pan and stir to combine. Season to taste.

Plate up the warm trout fillets and ladle over the pea and bean mixture. Garnish with the remaining parsley.

CHEF'S TIP

This is particularly nice served with purple sprouting broccoli and some new potatoes to soak up the lemony, buttery juices.

Poached Mussels with Shallots, Garlic and Herbs

Many people are put off cooking mussels because they are nervous about how to clean them, but it is really quite easy. There is no need to soak them before cooking; all you do is rinse them under cold running water and use a vegetable brush to scrub off any detritus on the shells, including the string or 'beard' that sometimes exists. If a mussel smells unpleasant, discard it, along with any that have cracked shells or shells with pieces missing. They should all be tightly closed before cooking.

INGREDIENTS

1½kg (3lb) live mussels
25g (1oz) butter
2 large shallots, finely chopped
2 garlic cloves, finely chopped
4 tbsp dry white wine
6 tbsp fresh lemon juice
3 tbsp minced fresh parsley
3 tbsp chopped tarragon
1 tbsp chopped chives
Salt and freshly ground
    black pepper

PREPARATION TIME 10 mins   COOKING TIME 10 mins   SERVES 4

Thoroughly wash and scrub the mussels (see note above).

Take a large lidded saucepan and gently melt the butter. Turn up the heat a little and add the shallots. Soften for 2 minutes without browning.

Add the garlic and cook for another 30 seconds. Then add the wine, lemon juice, parsley, tarragon and chives and bring to a boil.

Tip in the mussels, season then reduce the heat to low, put on the lid and cook for 3–6 minutes, depending upon the size of the mussels.

After 3 minutes, check to see if the majority of shells are still closed. If they are, re-cover the pan and cook for another 3 minutes, shaking the pan about halfway through.

Discard any mussels that haven't opened. Divide the mussels evenly between the bowls and pour over the sauce. Eat with fresh crusty bread and a side salad.

Eggs

Fritatta with Herbs

Given the quantity of eggs supplied by our assembled family of hens, we frequently rely on them when a quick and easy week-night supper dish is required and shopping is too much of a chore.

All our hens are named after Jane Austen heroines – the five Bennet sisters in Pride *and Prejudice;* Emma, Isabella and Mrs Weston from Emma; Anne from Persuasion; Catherine (Morland) from Northanger Abbey; Marianne, Eleanor and Fanny, (Mansfield Park); *and Charlotte from* Sanditon.

It is quite hard to tell the hens apart and I think Geordie feels the same about my favourite characters...

INGREDIENTS

30g (1oz) crème fraîche
2 tbsp chives, finely chopped
6 large eggs, lightly beaten
250g (9oz) parsley, finely chopped
250g (9oz) coriander,
  finely chopped
60g (2oz) dill, finely chopped
60g (2oz) tarragon, finely chopped
6 spring onions, sliced
4 tbsp olive oil
Salt and pepper

PREPARATION TIME 10 mins   **COOKING TIME** 20 mins   **SERVES** 4

Preheat the oven to 180°C/350°F/Gas mark 4.

Mix together the crème fraîche and chives in a bowl. Set aside.

In a separate bowl mix the eggs, the herbs, spring onions and half the olive oil. Season well.

Heat the remaining oil in an ovenproof heavy-based pan, pour in the egg mixture and cook over medium heat until the edges have just begun to set.

Transfer to the oven and bake for about 15 minutes until puffy and just set. Rest for 5 minutes and serve with the crème fraîche mix.

This can be made ahead of time and served just warm.

Baked Broccoli with Parmesan Eggs

Broccoli is in season through the winter and into spring. Renowned as cancer-fighting, laden with vitamins, minerals, phytonutrients and fibre, broccoli is packed with nutrients whether eaten raw or cooked.

INGREDIENTS

1 tbsp olive oil
1 onion, sliced
300g (10oz) broccoli,
  split into florets
3 tbsp freshly grated Parmesan
8 eggs
110ml (4fl oz) single cream
Sea salt and freshly ground
  black pepper

PREPARATION TIME 5 mins   **COOKING TIME** 15 mins   **SERVES** 4

Preheat the oven to 220°C/425°F/Gas mark 7.

Heat the oil in a frying pan and soften the onion for 5 minutes.

Meanwhile, blanch the broccoli in a pan of salted boiling water for 3–4 minutes. Drain well and add to the onions, stirring, and cook until slightly coloured. Stir in 2 teaspoons of the Parmesan and season well.

Divide the vegetables among 4 ramekins. Crack 2 eggs into each and season.

Spread half the remaining Parmesan over the bottom of a small baking sheet or cake tin and put into the hot oven for a couple of minutes until it has melted and browned (keep a close eye on it). Remove, let cool, break up roughly into crumbs and set aside.

Divide the cream between the ramekins, sprinkle with the remaining Parmesan, place on a baking tray and bake for 6–8 minutes until the eggs are cooked.

Serve sprinkled with the Parmesan crumbs.

Ham and Mustard Tart with Spring Onions

This is a delicious combination of favourite savoury foods. No one can resist the combination of ham and cheese, whether as a croque monsieur, or a tart such as here. You do not have to make the pastry – you can buy it and roll it out.

PREPARATION TIME 30 mins   **COOKING TIME** 30 mins plus chilling
SERVES 6

INGREDIENTS

300g (10oz) shortcrust pastry
300g (10oz) small new potatoes
3 large eggs
125ml (4fl oz) single cream
100g (3½oz) Cheddar cheese, grated
2 tbsp Cheshire cheese, grated
2 tbsp wholegrain mustard
Salt and freshly ground
    black pepper
200g (7oz) pulled ham
Bunch of spring onions, trimmed
    and halved lengthways
Flour, for dusting

Preheat the oven to 200°C/400°F/Gas mark 6.

Place a deep 23cm (9 inch) diameter fluted tart tin on a baking tray. Lightly flour a cool surface and roll out the pastry. Line the tart tin. Prick the base with a fork and chill for 20 minutes. Bake blind for 15 minutes and allow to cool slightly.

While the pastry is baking, cook the potatoes in boiling water for 15 minutes until tender. Drain, then once cool enough to handle, slice into 5mm (¼ inch) rounds and arrange in the bottom of the cooled tart case.

Beat the eggs, cream, cheeses and mustard together and season to taste.

Arrange the ham and spring onions over the potatoes. Pour over the egg mixture and cook for 15 minutes until set but still with a bit of a wobble. Stand for 5 minutes before serving.

Savoury Shortcrust Pastry

PREPARATION TIME 10 mins, plus 2 hours chilling
MAKES enough for a 23cm (9 inch) diameter dish

INGREDIENTS

120g (4oz) cold butter
200g (7oz) plain flour
1 egg yolk

Rub the butter and flour together in a large mixing bowl with the egg yolk using your fingers, adding maybe 4 or 5 teaspoons of cold water as necessary to properly incorporate all the ingredients and make a firm but still malleable dough.

Wrap in cling film and place in the fridge for at least a couple of hours before use.

Rack of Spring Lamb
with Anchovies and Gremolata

Anchovies impart a depth and saltiness to meats such as lamb.

My father was always keen on Gentleman's Relish – an anchovy paste enjoyed on hot buttered toast. He thoroughly enjoyed a walk across Green Park in London up to Fortnums on Piccadilly to potter round the food hall and make sure he had adequate supplies of this salty spread.

INGREDIENTS

30g (1oz) parsley
4 garlic cloves, crushed
4 anchovy fillets, roughly chopped
70g (2½oz) capers, drained
Zest of 1 lemon, finely grated
75ml (3fl oz) extra-virgin olive oil
1 × 8-bone French-trimmed
   rack of lamb

For the gremolata

Zest of 1 lemon
20g (¾oz) parsley, finely chopped
1 garlic clove, crushed
1 tbsp olive oil
Salt and freshly ground
   black pepper

PREPARATION TIME 10 mins, plus at least 3 hours for marinating
COOKING TIME 55 mins   SERVES 4

To marinate the lamb ...

Put the parsley, garlic, anchovies and capers in a food processor and blitz to make a paste. Add the lemon zest and olive oil and blitz again.

Rub the paste all over the lamb, cover and leave to marinate in the fridge for at least 3 hours or preferably for up to 24 hours.

When you are ready to roast ...

Preheat the oven to 130°C/275°F/Gas mark 1.

Place the lamb in a roasting tin. Roast for 50 minutes low and slow, then remove from the oven and place the rack skin side down in a cold dry frying pan (no oil) and gently bring to the heat, rendering and cooking the skin to a nice, crisp brown colour.

To make the gremolata ...

Put the lemon zest, parsley, garlic and olive oil in a bowl. Season with salt and pepper and stir.

Serve the lamb on a bed of gremolata.

CHEF'S TIP

Temperatures vary from oven to oven, so if you like your lamb pink, keep checking when cooking and trust your instincts.

Chicken with Peas, Lettuce and Artichokes

INGREDIENTS

4 large or 8 small chicken thighs,
  skin on and bone in
2 tbsp olive oil
1 large onion, chopped
2 garlic cloves, finely chopped
Sprig of thyme
50ml (1½fl oz) white wine
600ml (20fl oz) hot stock
1 tbsp butter
4 little gem lettuces,
  quartered lengthways
250g (9oz) peas
400g (14oz) can
  artichoke hearts,
  rinsed, drained,
  and halved lengthways
Juice of 1 lemon
1 tbsp chopped fresh
  flat-leaf parsley
  or picked thyme leaves,
  to serve
Salt and freshly ground
  black pepper

An all-too-familiar question is 'what's for supper?', to which, in a state of oh my goodness, the best answer may be 'a surprise'! Whether for family or for friends this is a good supper dish and much of it may be found in your pantry or kitchen cupboards.

PREPARATION TIME 15 mins   COOKING TIME 50 mins   SERVES 6

Season the chicken thighs. Heat the oil in a large casserole and brown the chicken thighs over a high heat.

Add the onion, garlic and thyme sprig and continue to cook for another 5 minutes. Add the white wine and cook for 1 minute.

Pour in the stock, bring to a simmer, then cover and cook for 30 minutes, until the chicken is completely cooked through and tender.

Add the butter, lettuce and peas and cook for 5 minutes. Add the artichoke hearts and cook for a final 5 minutes. Stir in the lemon juice and season.

Sprinkle the parsley or thyme over each portion as you serve.

Deconstructed Rhubarb Crumble

Rhubarb is a very easy plant to grow that simply keeps returning every year. To start with, plant dormant crowns in winter; it likes lots of manure and works well either in the ground or in a large pot. Not native to Europe, it was highly prized in the fifteenth century, but has become familiar through hothouse production. Never eat rhubarb stalks damaged by the cold, and never never eat the leaves.

Revered for its potential in treating ailments as diverse as dermatitis, pancreatic cancer and diabetes, rhubarb can apparently also lighten hair colour.

I always associate rhubarb crumble with my mother as it was one of her go-to puddings. It takes me back to childhood, to watching her make it and sitting at a table, in the safe nostalgic moments of memory. This is a different way to prepare it but my mother would have thoroughly approved of the suggestion of accompanying it with ginger ice cream …

INGREDIENTS

550g (1¼lb) rhubarb
85g (3oz) golden caster sugar
140g (5oz) self-raising flour
85g (3oz) butter, chilled
50g (2oz) light brown
   muscovado sugar
50g (2oz) walnuts,
   very finely chopped
   (optional if you are aware
   of any allergies)

PREPARATION TIME 10 mins   **COOKING TIME** 30 mins   **SERVES** 4

Preheat the oven to 200°C/400°F/Gas mark 6.

Rinse the rhubarb, trim the ends and cut into fingers. Place in a shallow dish, sprinkle over the sugar, mix thoroughly and spread into a single layer.

Cover with foil and roast for 15 minutes. Remove the foil. Give the dish a shake to distribute the sugary juices and roast for another 5 minutes until tender. Do not let it go mushy.

To make the topping, rub the self-raising flour and chilled butter together with your fingers until it is soft and crumbly.

Now add the sugar and the chopped walnuts, if using, and mix thoroughly.

Spread the topping over a baking sheet and bake for about 10–20 minutes until browned, checking frequently to make sure it doesn't scorch.

Serve hot with ginger ice cream or custard.

Pineapple Cake with Vanilla Icing

Christopher Columbus landed in America and one of the first meals he and his crew ate included a pineapple. The taste and delicious fragrance so excited them that its fame travelled back to Europe. It proved a challenging fruit to grow in the northern climes, though John Evelyn, the diarist, notes that one of the first pineapples was sent to Oliver Cromwell. Over time the Dutch developed the correct process – they needed an underfloor oven to heat the greenhouse which should be south-facing.

From 1750 until the twentieth century pineapples became a status symbol in any fashionable country house as a testament to the owner's wealth and to his gardener's skill and experience.

INGREDIENTS

250g (9oz) plain flour
400g (14oz) caster sugar
2 tsp bicarbonate of soda
2 eggs
1 tsp vanilla extract
300g (10oz) pineapple,
 fresh or tinned,
 approx. 1–2cm (½–¾ inch) cubes

For the icing

225g (8oz) cream cheese
110g (4oz) butter, melted
200g (7oz) icing sugar
1 tsp vanilla extract
Dash of lemon juice (optional)

PREPARATION TIME 15 mins   COOKING TIME 30 mins plus cooling   SERVES 6

Preheat the oven to 180°C/350°F/Gas mark 4.

Grease a square 20 × 20cm (8 × 8 inch) cake tin and line with baking paper.

In a large bowl, mix together the flour, sugar and bicarbonate of soda. Make a well in the centre and add the eggs, vanilla and diced pineapple. Mix well and pour into the tin.

Bake for 30 minutes or until a skewer inserted into the cake comes out clean.

To make the icing, beat together the cream cheese, butter, icing sugar and vanilla until it is creamy. If you like it to be slightly less sweet, add a dash of lemon juice. Spread on a warm but not hot cake.

As this cake contains fruit, it is best stored in the fridge – the flavours will only improve with time!

And so, with the sunshine and the great bursts of leaves growing on the trees, just as things grow in fast movies, I had that familiar conviction that life was beginning over again with the summer.

F. Scott Fitzgerald, *The Great Gatsby*

SUMMER

THE STILL WARMTH OF SUMMER AIR INVITES EVERY GUEST TO WALK BAREFOOT ACROSS the perfect flat green lawn, to tread gently and to feel the grass and earth beneath rolling, relaxed feet. If only summer at Highclere could always be like this – these hovering moments of happiness. In perfect weather the density of the summer air leaves time suspended, the sense of an idyll, languidly drifting over the lawns and gardens.

Summer afternoon – summer afternoon; to me those have always been the two most
beautiful words in the English language.
Henry James (1843–1916)

ENCLOSED BEHIND HEDGES DOWN BEYOND THE LAWNS, drifts of deep azure delphiniums, palest blush
roses, lavenders and clouds of crambe and gypsophilia, penstemons and geraniums dress the gardens.
Their colour and scent have the promise of celebrations and parties, taking their cue from the theatrical
set pieces which characterise the summer social scene, from racing at Royal Ascot, to concerts and opera
in gardens and halls, village fetes, the click of croquet mallets, cricket matches and tennis at Wimbledon.

Hopefully much of the food can be served outside, with picnics offering a wealth of small delights
to share, but the same themes can be brought inside as well. There's a wanton profusion of green vegetables and red-coloured fruits, an abundance of eggs and, if you wish, creams and ice creams, and don't
forget to make some water ices as well.

The eighteenth-century poet John Clare would spend hours watching beetles crawling up the
stems of wildflowers and 'bees lingering in generous sepals gathering their treasure', finding life in the
fields' edges and hedges as 'flower head swings to summer winds and insects happy wings'.

Being England, there may be summer rain, but it is nevertheless somehow different to other
seasons, refracting more light. Bees and butterflies begin to make themselves scarce when rain is on the
way but we all watch the clouds and the sky:

St Swithin's day if it do rain
For forty days it will remain
St Swithin's day if it be fair
For forty days will rain no more

Summer is always about hope. Hope for the perfect picnic weather and hope that all the earlier work in
the gardens will lead to a cascade of sensations with the faint recurring sound of lawnmowers and the
scent of cut grass which so embodies an English summer.

Jack Dows Castle, Highclere built by Hon Robert Herbert.

Stone Portico, Highclere Robt Herbert built this.

GEORGIAN HIGHCLERE

THE HONOURABLE ROBERT HERBERT was the younger brother of the Earl of Pembroke. He inherited Highclere Place House as a baby from his grandfather, Sir Robert Sawyer, in 1693.

A fastidious man, splendid in his dress and a somewhat fanciful character, Robert was nicknamed 'Amoretto' by Lord Chesterfield. At one dance, in the fashionable city of Bath in October 1734, 'he wore his gold laced clothes and looked so fine that, standing by chance in the middle of the dancers, was taken by many at a distance for a gilt garland'. He was renowned for clever similes and had a high regard for his own consequence as he graced the houses of various hostesses for breakfast, tea and dinner.

On one occasion, when Lord Chesterfield left Bath, he gave Robert a lift in his carriage, travelling back to London via Highclere where they were welcomed warmly by Mary Herbert. Robert's wife Mary was the daughter of the Speaker of the House of Commons and Lady of the Bedchamber to Queen Caroline, wife of George II. The politics of the time usually dictated that, as part of a Tory family, Mary would not be welcomed by the opposing Whigs, but this seemed not to apply to her. In fact, Mary had long been 'a personal and warm enemy' of Sir Robert Walpole and was 'so sensible, so well-bred, so handy, so cheerful and so agreeable' that the Queen showed special preference for her, meaning that she was often away from Highclere staying at Court.

Robert's own role as Groom of the Bedchamber to George I had ceased on the King's death but he did have a public role as Member of Parliament for Wilton, which was his brother's estate. Despite keeping his seat for 46 years, there is no record of his having made a single speech and, for most of his career, he held only minor government posts, voting for successive parliaments in all recorded divisions to the point where Rockingham (later Prime Minister) commented rather acidly that he would serve any administration. He was appointed Surveyor General in 1751 by the more assiduous and eminent politician Pelham, who wrote somewhat later that Herbert 'has been of the Board of Trade upwards of 20 years, tho' in it I believe not as many times', somewhat echoing Rockingham's assessment.

At this time Highclere Place was an attractive red-brick, L-shaped gentlemen's residence and right from the start of his tenure Robert was preoccupied with making it into the most charming estate, perfect for enthralling any prospective fair lady who caught his attention. As an inveterate traveller through classical Italy and Greece, Robert's brother was often called upon for architectural advice and Robert was keen to create a similar renown for himself in the realm of garden design.

Hon Robert Herbert

As a result, he was particularly concerned with improving the landscape around the house, creating an enviable 'Arcadia' with walks, parterres and 'wildernesses'. To the south east a diagonal beech avenue led to a mount adorned with a rotunda, whilst nearer to the house serpentine walks meandered through pleasure gardens in which 'eminences' – high spots or hillocks – often decorated with a statue, were scattered. Never satisfied with what he had achieved so far, he was always contriving some new project. By 1733 he had just completed a charming Octagon to complement the Rotunda in the Great Wilderness and was now considering a 'theatre in the woods' which would extend his walks, rides and viewing points.

There was always time available for a member of the landed gentry to explore the landscape, and the old chalk pit in Rookery Pit to the east of the house seemed a wonderfully secret glade, perfect to become a pleasure garden in the manner of the quarry garden that had been created in his childhood home, Wilton House. Stephen Switzer, the landscape architect and author of *Ichnographica Rustica* who worked at Wilton House, often advised his clients to create these little gardens a mile or two off from the main house to act as pleasant 'surprises' on rides out, not to mention providing the perfect setting for illicit assignations. In his diary, Jeremiah Milles, son of the classicist Reverend Isaac Milles, described it thus:

> At some distance from this in a little copse is a beautifull pitt, with a Tuscan Temple standing over the brink of it. Mr Herbert showed his taste in this improvement, which was nothing else but a deep chalk pit surrounded with a little scrub wood. He cleared & levelled the bottom of the pitt, & then turfed it over so that it appears like the Arena of an Amphitheater. One side over this arena is 40 feet perpendicular heighth out of which the bushes & briars grow in a very agreable wildness. The Tuscan Temple which is of wood, is an oblong square, & has 4 pillars in front supporting a triangular pediment. Opposite to this on the other side of the pitt is a seat, with a slope before it down to the arena, behind & all around it is a wood, thro' which there are serpentine walks.

Highclere was not built on the same scale as some of the huge Palladian palaces whose draughty rooms were cold and hard to live in and where small garden follies had become increasingly attractive options as they were cosy by contrast and provided an escape from grand formality. Nevertheless, with his smaller house and grand garden plans, Robert was hoping to have the best of both worlds.

In all aspects, this was an era of literary and classical reason and allusion and Robert referenced most of them. Along with his brothers, he had been educated under the auspices of the Reverend Isaac Milles, who had been given the Living of Highclere by Robert's grandfather. A much-admired classicist, Milles' influence was so highly regarded that Lord Pembroke had recommended his eldest son Thomas to Queen Anne to become the Bishop of Waterford and Lismore in Ireland.

With this pedigree, Robert happily mixed pagan gods of fields and nature with druids and ancient Britons and set them besides Roman and Greek gods. One of his main influences was the much-admired poet and celebrity Alexander Pope, many of whose works Robert had bought for the library at

Artfully contrived with much effort down the ages, views across the Highclere parklands nevertheless appear delightfully natural

Highclere. Although he is better remembered as a poet, Pope was also very interested in garden design, going so far as to claim that 'gardening is more antique and nearer God's work than poetry'. He worked extensively on his own garden at Twickenham where, amongst other artifices, he created a grotto.

In all, let Nature never be forgot.
But treat the goddess like a modest fair,
Nor overdress, nor leave her wholly bare;
Let not each beauty everywhere be spied,
Where half the skill is decently to hide.
He gains all points, who pleasingly confounds,
Surprises, varies, and conceals the bounds.

Consult the genius of the place in all;
That tells the waters or to rise, or fall;
Or helps the ambitious hill the heavens to scale,
Or scoops in circling theatres the vale;
Calls in the country, catches opening glades,
Joins willing woods, and varies shades from shades;

Now breaks, or now directs, the intending lines;
Paints as you plant, and, as you work, designs.

Alexander Pope, *Epistle IV*, 1731

Pope's influence was reasonably widespread and no less a person than Jonathan Swift described him as the 'master' and 'contriver' of the garden style that was more naturalistic than the endless symmetrical hedges and clipped parterres of the previously fashionable French style of gardens. As the eighteenth century progressed, landscape and gardens were thought of in increasingly poetic and painterly terms and the finest style of landscape was one in which artistic composition was translated not onto canvas but into the three-dimensional form of plants and trees and light and shade, dotted with ruins and temples.

Pope knew the Herberts and briefly stayed at Highclere. He also visited their neighbours, the de Lisle sisters, in nearby Crux Easton, in order to admire their famous seashell grotto. Sadly, nothing remains of this now but at the time it was quite an edifice. The front was of flint, the interior studded with shells, scoriae of iron ore, and other substances and it contained a seat for each sister, with a niche for the presiding 'magician'. Pope described the scene in an *Inscription on a GROTTO of Shells at CRUX-EASTON, the Work of Nine young Ladies*:

'Ere shunning idleness at once and praise,   Beauty which Nature only can impart,
This radiant pile nine rural sisters raise;   And such a polish as disgraces Art;
The glitt'ring emblem of each spotless dame,   But Fate dispos'd them in this humble sort,
Clear as her soul, and shining as her fame;   And hid in desarts what wou'd charm a court.

An inscription, dated 25 August 1733, also held to have been composed, extempore, by Pope is titled *On seeing the LADIES at Crux-Easton Walk in the WOODS by the GROTTO*:

Authors the world and their dull brains have trac'd,
To fix the ground where paradise was plac'd,
Mind not their learned whims and idle talk,
Here, here's the place, where these bright angels walk.

Robert Herbert and the de Lisle family enjoyed a longstanding relationship and in 1735, Robert presented the Living at Burghclere (a parish adjoining Highclere) to Dr Thomas Lisle, one of the brothers, who remained rector there until his death. Margaret, the youngest de Lisle sister, possessed a talent for painting and two of her portraits, depicting Sir Richard and Lady Kingsmill, who lived at Highclere before the estate was bought by Robert's grandfather, can still be seen at the Castle today.

Despite everything he did, sadly Robert was really never quite satisfied with his efforts, always feeling that he lacked sufficient eyecatchers that would make his garden – and thus himself – famous. In his quest for the same credentials as Pope, he never stopped adding to his plans or showing off his latest improvements to friends and acquaintances, in particular by creating picnics and al fresco entertainment outings so that he could display his landscape in the best possible light.

During the course of the assorted circular walks on offer, various 'stands' would mark places where visitors could pause to admire a particular view or effect. Sometimes rustic benches were permanently installed at these points and on other occasions chairs and tripod tables would be carefully placed for a 'nuncheon' (now called luncheon), with food appearing from baskets. This often took the form of a cold collation: cold ham and chicken, even a small venison pie, followed by a syllabub or an ice cream from the dairy. Alternatively, '*Pique Niques*', a French term which conveyed the idea of small dishes to 'pick' or 'peck' at whilst the rhyming addition '*nique*' suggested a 'thing of little importance', a mere 'bagatelle', became a popular choice. Even then, it seems they appreciated that food eaten outside often tastes better than food inside.

By the end of his life in 1769, Robert Herbert had witnessed the accession of three kings: George I, II and finally, in 1760, George III. He built ever more 'eyecatchers', developed longer rides and walks and, given the topography at Highclere, some beautiful retreats. Using the Rotunda as a clock face, he led both his visitors' eyes and footsteps to the follies Heaven's Gate (1737) and Dan's Lodge,

the theatrical temple in Rookery Pit, the Temple of Diana, Jackdaw's Castle (1743) and, finally, a walk around Milford Lake with its villa at one end. Thus, his friend and erstwhile fellow student Jeremiah Milles would write in his diaries:

> Mr Herbert's house ... lies at the bottom of Sidedown Hill, from whence an avenue of beeches leads to it, it is near half a mile long. This house, which was a very good one in the ancient taste, has been so much alter'd and improved by the present worthy Possessor that it is for its size one of the most beautifull and elegant houses in England. It has besides a good old Gothic front, which faces the stables, two other modern ones, the Principal one towards the hill, the other towards the garden which is laid out in grass.

FOLLIES

MARY HERBERT DIED BEFORE HER HUSBAND, in 1757, and as they had no children, Robert left Highclere to his nephew, Henry Herbert, who also became MP for Wilton. Now in the possession of charming estate and thus a most eligible bachelor, Henry ambitiously applied for the hand of Lady Elizabeth Wyndham, daughter of the 2nd Earl of Egremont, who lived at Petworth House in Sussex.

Time moves on and fashions change. Lord Egremont had been one of the first to commission that great landscaper Capability Brown to redesign his parklands and, not to be left behind, Henry in turn commissioned Brown to draw up a plan for his park, with a new lake and a new house in the modern style to replace the old Highclere Place House.

When he visited Highclere in 1770, Brown found agricultural buildings clustered on the north-west side, an old cemetery within a brick wall and large groups of trees which, to his mind, cut off any views or sense of space. They would all have to go and thus, in a relatively short space of time, much of Robert's great vision and hard work was swept away as if it had never been. The classical references exhibited in his follies were magnified into a new Palladian-influenced style of house, and the gardens smoothed and extended to create a neverending Arcadia.

Of the follies, Andover Lodge, a small triangular folly marking a view point en route to Heaven's Gate, remains where it was, as does Heaven's Gate at the top of Siddown Hill, although it is no longer approached by its great double avenue. However, you can still gaze up towards the archway and thence to the Castle and the far distant hills leading towards Oxford. The Etruscan Temple no longer stands in its glades and amphitheatre but is now repositioned to look south across Capability Brown's undulating endless pasture, whilst the Rotunda and Octagon were simply removed altogether, as were the parterres and careful tessellation close to the house.

The two largest of the eighteenth-century follies are still in situ and remain fabulous locations for a picnic. The nearest to the house, 100 yards across the east lawns, is a classical temple that now stands some 12 feet above the current level of the lawns, although when it was built, it would have been level with the long gallery or library which faced it in the eighteenth-century building, Highclere Place House.

It is called Jackdaw's Castle, perhaps for the simple reason that there used to be an avenue behind it in which jackdaws used to roost. Its history, though, is somewhat grander. The pillars used to stand as part of the portico of one of the smartest houses in London: Berkeley House. Built in the reign of Charles II – around the time of the Great Fire of London in 1666 – it was later bought and renamed Devonshire House by the family of the same name, but sadly it burnt down whilst being refurbished in 1733. The columns were presumably deemed no longer needed and sold off. Robert Herbert bought them and had them transported to Highclere by horse and cart.

Once roofed, today it stands open to the elements but the proportion of the columns follows the harmonious classical principles so much admired by eighteenth-century architects and intellects. The Corinthian, the most ornate of the classified orders of columns, is charac-terised by slender columns and elaborate capitals decorated with acanthus leaves and scrolls. The 'capital', derived from the Latin *caput* or 'head', forms the topmost part of the column and mediates between the column and the load thrusting down upon it by broadening the area of the

OPPOSITE, FROM TOP
The Temple of Diana
Andover Lodge
Winchester Lodge
Beacon Hill Gate
Heaven's Gate

column's supporting surface. This is not, in fact, needed here but might have been in the earlier building of which the columns were part and would have been very important to Robert as a representation of heritage, culture and classical architectural fashion.

Despite its now raised setting, Jackdaw's still retains Robert's vision, giving definition and a viewpoint both from the Castle and from itself looking back at the Castle, as well as long, framed views into the parkland and ancient trees.

The Temple of Diana is further away and is now only seen by visitors as they leave the estate. Overlooking Dunsmere Lake, and part of the Capability Brown remodelling of the park, it may originally have been Robert's 'rotunda', though that is not entirely clear from the records. It too has a classical form, this time with plain Ionic columns. Later on, in 1838, the architect Charles Barry raised the height of the dome, added 16 urns and altered the interior, giving it greater height and more authority as a building in its own right. The artist George Frederick Prosser, who often drew views of the Estate, wrote:

> The effect of this temple is exceedingly good, not only from the approach but from every other part of the grounds. Its architecture is faulty, inasmuch as its colonnade is interrupted and the wall which supports its dome is not shown above its entablature, but these faults are lost in the feeling of gratification experienced on observing such an object placed in so fitting a situation.

All of these observations reinforce the suggestion that the Temple might have begun life elsewhere, then been repurposed and adapted.

It is not possible today to use the interior of the temple but the exterior has been repaired and is now enjoyed once more. It is a beautiful setting. Just down the slope are some magnificent ancient cedar trees whilst the unusual soils and landscape provide a site of special scientific interest whose lichens, fungi and gentians are gaining in robust strength every year.

ABOVE
Jackdaw's Castle
RIGHT
A pyramid orchid in front
of the Temple of Diana

PICNICS

DURING THE EIGHTEENTH CENTURY, letters and diaries were as likely to be written in French as in English and our archives reflect the esteem in which the French language, customs and culture were held at that time. The formality of English gardens reflected the French example, as did the idea of picnics. Jean-Jacques Rousseau, for example, would dine with friends '*tête à tête en pique-nique*'.

Following the French Revolution in 1789 and the consequent arrival of French émigrées in London, a club was founded in 1801: The Pic Nic Society. Members dined in extravagant luxury and expense, drank far too much, gambled and even enjoyed amateur dramatics. Perhaps as a result of their association with such excess during this time, picnics were regarded with considerable suspicion in nineteenth-century France.

The picnic's slightly mixed reputation was used by Jane Austen to pen a keenly observed portrait of a rustic picnic on Box Hill, Surrey, in *Emma* (1816). It was a painfully embarrassing scene and a vivid turning point in the book. However, with the advent of trains, bicycles and motor cars, British families from all walks of life soon adopted picnics with enthusiasm and by the time Mrs Beeton was listing the 'bill of fare for a picnic for 40 persons' in her *Book of Household Management*, they had become an essential part of British life.

This is both slightly odd and rather ironic as the British weather is nothing if not variable. Straddling the latitudes, and being in the path of the jet stream circling across the Atlantic Ocean, unsettled weather in all its variations can be enjoyed in just one day in most parts of the country. Nevertheless, despite the certain inconsistency of the weather, an extraordinary number of casual and formal social events revolve around picnics during the British summer.

Simple mown
paths through the
Wildflower Meadow

Picnic lunches, picnic teas, cocktails outside on a summer evening which are no different from the roving picnic of light snacks in the eighteenth century, concerts outside with picnic suppers, picnics for sports day, picnics for Royal Ascot, and always the question: what shall we do if it rains? Nevertheless, we all carry on and pray for fine weather, agreeing with the novelist Somerset Maugham's view that 'there are few things so pleasant as a picnic lunch'.

Undoubtedly British, I very much enjoy planning picnics for friends in the gardens. In addition, Highclere offers concert and picnic teas and picnic tea boxes for guests. Somewhat to the surprise of the warm-weather-loving Portuguese butlering team of Luís and Jorge, spring walks and picnic teas and lunches may well begin here as early as March, but the main season for picnics is the summer.

Most of the time, picnics are simple and fun – an al fresco meal which is above all the sense of being with, and taking time out in, nature. The celebrated English novelist Evelyn Waugh's *Brideshead Revisited* (1945) includes a description of such an impromptu meal:

> I've got a motor-car and a basket of strawberries and a bottle of Château Peyraguey – which isn't a wine you've ever tasted, so don't pretend. It's heaven with strawberries.

Finding some shade and 'a sheep-cropped knoll under a clump of elms', the characters eat the strawberries, drink the wine and gaze up at the trees. The picnic described in *The Wind in the Willows* (1908) was slightly more extensive, with 'a fat wicker luncheon basket' packed with 'cold chicken ... cold tongue, cold ham, cold beef, pickled gherkins, salad, French rolls, cress sandwiches, potted meat, ginger beer, lemonade and soda water', which led to a congenial summer's day eating, chatting and snoozing. Perfect happiness all packed up in a hamper. Equally, I have walked with my husband accompanied just by a Thermos flask of soup, a couple of fresh crusty bread rolls and some water and simply found a tree stump with a view. At other times there is a more organised approach where, unknowingly, I have taken up the pleasure of the eighteenth century with a meandering walk with friends followed by a rustic-styled al fresco lunch.

Then there are the fairytale moments from an evening dinner on a warm June evening sitting at a long table in the Temple, to wandering across the lawns to Jackdaw's for cocktails and canapes before dinner in the Dining Room. The grass smooth underfoot, the gigantic cedars and the old walnut tree gentle in the evening breeze, new exotic species to be admired nearby, and all casting drowsy shadows as guests and friends enjoy a mellow golden hour.

A Summer Picnic

PIQUE-NIQUE TECHNIQUE

Planning, preparation and allowing time make all the difference. You will need a wicker hamper (it puts you in the mood) in which you pack ...

· plates and glasses
(preferably not glass or china)
· knives, forks and spoons
· bottle opener/corkscrew
· small chopping board with
bread knife/second knife
· napkins and kitchen roll
· bin bag
· table cloth

Then, in a tote bag ...

· sun hat and cream
· book to read
· insect repellent
· bite/sting spray

Someone capable will be needed to convey ...

· rug/throws/cushions
· a fold-up table and chairs if you prefer

And last but certainly not least, don't forget ...

· a cool box
· ice packs or a bag of ice
to keep food and drinks cool
· plenty of water
(and an extra bottle or two of rosé)

SUMMER

Heritage Tomato Tart

Geordie and I are passionately devoted to our 'heritage' here at Highclere, so, of course, we use these tomatoes — varieties that have been grown without crossbreeding for 40 or more years. They also have the added advantage of coming in lots of different colours, so they make the tart look really pretty as well as tasting wonderful, and they contain lycopene, one of the most powerful natural antioxidants.

INGREDIENTS

200g (7oz) heritage tomatoes
125g (4½oz) soft goat's cheese
150g (5oz) ricotta cheese
1 tbsp milk
Small bunch of chives, chopped
1 tsp finely grated lemon zest
20cm (8 inch) ready-made
   shortcrust pastry case
   (or to make your own,
   see page 70)
½ tsp dried oregano
1 tbsp olive oil
Salt and freshly ground
   black pepper

PREPARATION TIME 10 mins   COOKING TIME 15–20 mins   SERVES 6

Preheat the oven to 200°C/400°F/Gas mark 6.

Slice the larger tomatoes, cut the small ones in half and place to one side.

Mix the goat's cheese, ricotta and milk together until smooth. Add a good pinch of black pepper, most of the chives and the lemon zest and mix again.

Spoon the cheese mixture into the pastry case. Arrange the tomatoes on top then sprinkle with a little oregano, the remaining chives, salt and a drizzle of oil.

Bake in the oven for 15–20 minutes until the tomatoes start to soften.

Remove from the oven and allow to cool for at least 10 minutes before cutting into slices.

Potato Salad with Lemon and Chives

*Prayer for peace and grace and spiritual food,
For wisdom and guidance, for all these are good,
but don't forget the potatoes.*
   John Tyler Pettee (1822–1907)

INGREDIENTS

1kg (2¼lb) potatoes, skin on
Zest and juice of 1 lemon
2 tbsp olive oil
½ tsp caster sugar
50g (2oz) mayonnaise
60g (2oz) soured cream
50g (2oz) chopped chives, plus extra
   to garnish
2 large celery stalks, finely chopped
Salt and freshly ground
   black pepper

PREPARATION TIME 25 mins   COOKING TIME 30 mins   SERVES 8

Cook the potatoes in a pan of boiling water until soft. Drain.

Whisk together the lemon zest and juice, olive oil, sugar and ½ teaspoon salt.

Add the hot potatoes to the lemon mixture and stir gently to coat. Let the potatoes cool at room temperature for 30 minutes, stirring occasionally.

Stir together the mayonnaise and soured cream until smooth. Mix in the chives and celery and season to taste. Add the mayonnaise mixture to the potatoes and stir gently to coat well. If not serving right away, cover and refrigerate. Garnish with extra chopped chives.

97

Burrata with Roasted Tomatoes, Basil and Olive Oil

INGREDIENTS

400g (14oz) cherry tomatoes, halved
1 garlic clove, sliced
5 tbsp olive oil
2 tbsp balsamic vinegar
Handful of fresh basil leaves
Zest and juice of 1 lemon
2 tbsp pine nuts, toasted
200g (7oz) burrata (or mozzarella if you prefer, in which case, tear or slice)
Salt and freshly ground black pepper

PREPARATION TIME 15 mins   COOKING TIME 15 mins   SERVES 4

Preheat the oven to 180°C/350°F/Gas mark 4.

Put the tomatoes and garlic on a baking tray, drizzle with olive oil and season with salt and black pepper. Roast for 15 minutes, drizzle with the balsamic vinegar and leave to cool.

Blitz the basil, lemon zest and juice and remaining olive oil together and adjust to taste.

Fill a serving bowl with the roasted cherry tomatoes, top with the toasted pine nuts, basil oil and burrata (or mozzarella) and black pepper.

Crayfish and Avocado Salad

INGREDIENTS

PREPARATION TIME 10 mins   SERVES 6

For the dressing

100ml (3½fl oz) olive oil
1 lemongrass stalk, bruised
1 shallot, finely sliced
1 tsp dill, finely chopped

For the salad

200g (7oz) crayfish
Juice of 1 lemon
Mixed salad leaves,
   including baby spinach
2 ripe avocados, sliced
1 lemon, sliced, to garnish
Salt and freshly ground
   black pepper

To make the dressing ...

Place the olive oil and lemongrass in a small pan over a low heat and let them infuse gently for about 20 minutes.

Remove from the heat and add the shallot. Allow to cool, then add the chopped dill.

To assemble the salad ...

Toss the crayfish gently in the dressing and put to one side.

Now take the dressed, washed salad leaves and arrange the sliced lemons around the bowl.

Toss the avocado slices in lemon juice with salt and pepper to save them from going black. Mix with the crayfish and serve.

Smoked Salmon Roulade

INGREDIENTS

20 smoked salmon slices
200g (7oz) raw baby spinach
500g (1lb 2oz) hot-smoked salmon
250g (9oz) cream cheese
Juice of 1 lemon
200ml (7fl oz) double cream
Pinch of cayenne pepper
1 tbsp dill, chopped
1 tsp chives, chopped
Salt and freshly ground
   black pepper

PREPARATION TIME 30 mins, plus chilling   SERVES 4

On a clean table, spread out a sheet of cling film and onto this lay out the smoked salmon slices, with a slight overlap, covering an area of 15 × 30cm (6 × 12 inches). Now line with the spinach.

Put the hot-smoked salmon (and any smoked salmon trimmings), the cream cheese and the lemon juice into a food processor and blitz to make a smooth purée.

Add the double cream and cayenne and whiz again briefly, being very careful not to overwork the mixture. Add dill and the chives and season to taste.

Spoon the mixture over the spinach and start to roll up into a cylinder shape, then tightly roll up the cling film, twisting the ends to keep the roulade tight, and chill in the fridge for a minimum of 6 hours.

When ready to serve, unwrap the rolls and slice with a very sharp knife.

Wilted Spinach with Toasted Pine Nuts

INGREDIENTS

50g (2oz) pine nuts
1 tbsp olive oil
500g (1lb 2oz) bag fresh spinach
Zest and juice of 1 lemon

PREPARATION TIME 5 mins   COOKING TIME 5 mins   SERVES 4

Toast the pine nuts in a dry pan until just golden. Shake frequently to make sure they don't burn.

Heat the oil in a wok and tip in the spinach. Cook for a minute.

Add the toasted pine nuts and lemon zest and juice and stir to mix.

Serve immediately – this goes with almost anything!

Pepperonata

INGREDIENTS

4 tbsp vegetable oil
250g (9oz) red onions, sliced
2 garlic cloves, crushed
2 bay leaves
4 red peppers,
   sliced into fine strips
2 yellow peppers, deseeded,
   sliced into fine strips
Pinch of caster sugar
Salt and freshly ground
   black pepper

PREPARATION TIME 25 mins   COOKING TIME 45 mins   SERVES 4

Heat the oil in a large frying pan over a medium heat. Add the onions, garlic and bay leaves and fry gently for about 5 minutes, stirring occasionally.

Add the peppers, then cover and cook gently for 10 minutes. You may need to cook the peppers in batches initially until the volume has shrunk a little.

Season well with salt, pepper and sugar. Cook, uncovered and stirring frequently, for 30 minutes or until the mixture is thick.

Remove the bay leaves and check the seasoning. Serve hot or cold.

Roast Beef Salad with Homemade Horseradish

This can be cooked up to two days ahead and the beef carved four hours in advance, giving you more time with your friends before eating.

INGREDIENTS

6 small candy beetroot (beets)
5 tbsp olive oil
500g (1lb 2oz) potatoes
4 red onions, cut into wedges
700g (1½lb) fully trimmed
   beef sirloin
200g (7oz) green beans
Cherry vine tomatoes
   (5 on the vine per person)
3 tbsp balsamic vinegar
1 tbsp wholegrain Dijon mustard
Salt and freshly ground
   black pepper

GARDENER'S NOTE

Horseradish is the perfect foil for beef and thought to help rheumatism and increase circulation.

It is easy to grow and easy to make. It has a clearer taste than the shop-bought variety. You just need to grow one or two plants; they are tough and spread so you may choose to confine them in a pot.

PREPARATION TIME 25 mins   COOKING TIME 50 mins   SERVES 6

Preheat the oven to 200°C/400°F/Gas mark 6.

Lay out the beetroot (beets) on a sheet of baking parchment and sprinkle over 1 tablespoon of the oil and a little water, then fold it up into a sealed parcel. Roast for about 30 minutes until tender. Remove, cut the beetroot in half and keep warm.

Peel and cut the potatoes into chunks, then parboil for 5–6 minutes. Place in a roasting tin along with the onions and 2 tablespoons of the oil and cook for 30 minutes until golden. Turn off the oven and leave the vegetables inside.

Season the beef and rub over 1 tablespoon of the oil. Heat a large pan over high heat and brown the beef all over to seal it. Put it in a roasting tin and roast for 15–20 minutes (rare), 20–25 minutes (medium rare) or 25–30 minutes (medium) ... and no longer!

Remove the beef, cover with foil and rest for at least 20 minutes.

Cook the beans in boiling salted water for 3 minutes (best served al dente). Drain.

Roast the vine tomatoes in the oven for no more than 5 minutes and season with salt and pepper.

Whisk together the vinegar, the remaining tablespoon of oil and the mustard and season well, then use this to dress the beetroot and beans.

Arange the potatoes, onions, beetroot, green beans and tomatoes around the carved beef for people to combine as they prefer, with homemade horseradish sauce on the side.

Horseradish Sauce

INGREDIENTS

15g (½oz) horseradish,
   freshly grated
1 tbsp white wine vinegar
Pinch of English mustard powder
Pinch of caster sugar
150ml (5fl oz) double cream,
   lightly whipped
Salt and freshly ground
   black pepper, to taste

PREPARATION TIME 30 mins   SERVES 4-6

Soak the grated horseradish in 2 tablespoons of hot water for 30 minutes.

Drain, squeeze dry and mix with all the other ingredients. Serve in a bowl.

Tarte aux Fraises

Fresh strawberry tarts really sum up an English summer. When my son was little, a visit to the local strawberry farm was wonderful entertainment on a warm afternoon. An hour or so could be whiled away picking the fruit with a contented boy who probably ate more than he put in his basket.

INGREDIENTS

125g (4½oz) unsalted butter
85g (3oz) icing sugar
1 egg
200g (7oz) plain flour,
   plus extra for dusting
100g (3½oz) good-quality
   strawberry jam
500g (1lb 2oz) strawberries
   (simply hull small ones;
   slice larger ones)
2 tbsp apricot jam
1 tbsp lemon juice

For the crème pâtissière

300ml (10fl oz) milk
150ml (5fl oz) double cream
1 tsp vanilla extract
3 egg yolks
60g (2oz) caster sugar
3½ tbsp cornflour
50g (2oz) butter, cubed

PREPARATION TIME 40 mins   COOKING TIME 45 mins, plus chilling time
SERVES 10

Preheat the oven to 200°C/400°F/Gas mark 6.

Grease a 23cm (9 inch) diameter tart tin.

Gently beat the butter and icing sugar together until smooth but *not* fluffy. Mix in the egg then add the flour.

Push it together into a ball of dough, wrap in cling film and rest in the fridge for 20 minutes.

Dust a surface with flour and roll out the pastry into a circle 3cm (1 inch) bigger than the tin. Line the tin with the pastry, leaving an overhang. Prick the base with a fork and chill again for 30 minutes. Line the pastry case with scrunched-up baking paper, cover with baking beans and cook for 15 minutes. Remove the baking paper and beans and cook for a further 15–20 minutes until crisp and golden. Leave in the tin to cool.

To make the *crème pâtissière* ...

Put the milk, cream and vanilla in a pan over a medium heat and bring up to a simmer, stirring occasionally.

Whisk the yolks and sugar in a bowl for 3 minutes until pale, then stir in the cornflour until combined.

Pour a quarter of the hot cream over the egg mix, whisking continuously, then pour the warm egg mix into the pan with the rest of the cream. Stir over a medium heat for 5–8 minutes until the mixture thickens. Transfer to a large bowl and cool for 15 minutes, whisking occasionally.

Gradually whisk in the butter until smooth, cover and refrigerate until needed.

Beat the strawberry jam to loosen it, then spread over the bottom of the pastry case. Spread the *crème pâtissière* over the jam and arrange the strawberries on top in a pattern.

Heat the apricot jam in a small pan with the lemon juice and gently brush over the top of the strawberries.

Homemade Lemonade (TWO WAYS)

The expression 'making lemonade from lemons' denotes turning something sour or pedestrian into something delicious or useful: not everyone may see this opportunity but life is good if you can find a way to be positive about what it has dealt you. Lemons, however bitter, taste wonderful if you are creative with them. Likewise, if we take the time and look, it is amazing what we can see and achieve.

The first recipe below is my own, a balance between the tart, refreshing taste of the lemons and the sweetness of sugar, perhaps flavoured with a little mint as well. The required balance of the two is up to individual taste, so there is no one correct answer. What is more, it needs continual adjustment depending on the juiciness of the lemons.

INGREDIENTS

6 lemons
150g (5oz) caster sugar
A few torn mint leaves
1·4 litres (2½ pints) water

PREPARATION TIME 20 mins, plus overnight chilling

Scrub the lemons in warm water and put the water in a pan over high heat to boil.

Pare the yellow zest from three of the fruits using a potato peeler or zester (avoid the white pith, which is bitter).

Pare a fourth lemon and keep the strips to one side.

Squeeze the juice from all the lemons into a large bowl, add the sugar, pour in the boiling water and throw in the torn mint leaves.

Add the zests, stir well, cover and leave overnight in a cool place.

Next day stir again, taste to check and add a little more sugar if needed.

Highclere Chef's recipe

This is the way our chef Paul Brooke-Taylor makes it.

INGREDIENTS

Zest and juice of 4 large unwaxed
    lemons
150g (5oz) caster sugar
1·2 litres (2 pints) water
    (still or fizzy)
A few sprigs of mint

PREPARATION TIME 20 mins, plus overnight chilling

Mix the lemon juice and zest with the sugar and stir until the sugar has dissolved.

Add the water and stir. Pour the mixture through a sieve to remove the zest.

Serve with sprigs of mint.

For Blueberry or Raspberry Lemonade, gently crush a handful of your chosen fruit with the back of a spoon, place in the jug with the lemonade, stir and serve.

THE WILDFLOWER MEADOW

THE EIGHTEENTH-CENTURY *PARTERRES* that used to exist to the south of the earlier house were dug up under the guidance of Capability Brown. Instead, a curved bowl of lawns was scooped out of the chalk to guide the eye towards distant views of carefully placed trees on the horizon. In the parkland, to the west of the house, the great dark spreading cedars of Lebanon were planted, casting long afternoon shadows on a summer evening whilst the pale trunks and light-lit leaves of English beech and lime drew the eye east towards the monumental escarpment of Beacon Hill.

In a past world the sloping ground below the lawns would have been mown but Geordie and I chose instead to create a wildflower meadow. Many chalk species meadows in southern England have been lost over the last 70 years, so the chance to recreate one was a challenge we could not resist. We began over ten years ago, taking time to harrow the ground for two years to break up the existing grass so that the wildflower seeds could establish themselves with less 'aggressive' competition. The mixes of seeds chosen were geared towards traditional Hampshire chalk grassland species, and over the years it has developed, changing in colour and variety so that every year brings a new depth of diversity.

Wildflower meadows are no less work than a traditional border but require a very different approach. Most projects at Highclere tend to be on a large scale but you can create a wildflower area anywhere. The key is a sunny spot with poor soil and no competition to the wildflowers. The first task is to remove the top three or so inches of topsoil and dig out and remove the weeds. Use a hoe and keep working the soil to break it down. Lay down some black plastic to stop any remaining seeds germinating. Patience at this point gives you a much better chance of success before seeding, which is best done either in the autumn or in March. Scatter the seeds in all directions making sure you don't miss any ground and then gently walk across them so they are pressed into the soil. Water it in the first year. If it suits your garden better, another option is to scatter your wildflower seeds in a selection of different-sized pots.

Weeds are flowers, too, once you get to know them.
A.A. Milne (1882–1956)

As to what variety to plant, all advice is to focus on native species. A particularly good one is yellow rattle which helps reduce fertility, but on land similar to Highclere's you should be able to encourage field scabious, bird's foot trefoil, harebell, vetch, eyebright, corncockle, lady's bedstraw, milkwort and British orchids. The very names of the plants recall earlier traditions as well as medicinal purposes. For example, scabious (scabies) seemed to help with healing boils and skin maladies. Lady's bedstraw was a popular choice for bedding, thanks to its soft and springy quality and pleasant scent (when dried it smells of hay). Furthermore, it has astringent properties and was thought to repel fleas.

Orchids are usually associated with the spectacular colours of far-flung lands but there are 52 species of native British orchid. They were nearly collected to extinction in Victorian times but reappear if given space and peace. Pyramid orchids are plentiful in the Wildflower Meadow whilst the rarer bee orchid can be found on the chalky soil in the dappled glades around the edges.

Wildflowers also provide shelter and food for a number of pollinators, including bees. There are over 250 species of bee in the UK and they play a vital part in supporting the ecosystem. They attract butterflies and other insects which in turn encourage birds, bats, amphibians, reptiles and small mammals, all of whom contribute in turn.

Sir David Attenborough commented that three-quarters of the UK butterflies are in decline and one-third in danger of extinction. Butterflies and insects are a key indicator of the health of the land-scape, of nature. They are often quite precise in their food source, for example, Common Blue and Adonis Blue both rely on vetch or bird's foot trefoil, whilst the Large White likes cabbages or nasturtiums, Small Tortoiseshells like nettles, and Red Admirals or spectacular Peacocks like buddleias.

Walking slowly along the winding mown path which meanders diagonally through the meadow is glorious, addictive and restorative. As summer progresses it becomes ever noisier with the wealth of insects – the hum of their wings an extraordinary testament to its success. Finally, the flower heads will turn brown but still, I think, rather beautiful. They give height and texture, gently falling down the slopes as the shadows lengthen and ochres become the colour of the season. There are many good moments in life but often the simplest ones are the most satisfying. Then, in late September, when the hollow-stalked flowers and grasses start to shed their seeds, we cut the meadow, saving the seeds to sell in the gift shop whilst the remainder of the 'hay' is baled and removed to maintain the low fertility of the ground. Paul and his garden team will then scarify (rake over) the entire area.

BEES

THE WORD 'MEADOW' is derived from the Anglo-Saxon *maed*, which is written today as mead. Traditionally this is an alcoholic beverage created by fermenting honey with water, sometimes with various fruits, spices, grains or hops, although it has rather fallen out of fashion these days.

Bees have been part of Highclere's farming landscape for centuries: in fact, the Highclere Anglo-Saxon charter of 749 AD refers to *Hunig-weg* (Honey Way), which defined one boundary of the estate. Honey and bees were as prized 1,200 years ago as they are today. Wherever you lived in whatever rank in society, beekeeping was essential to farming and practically every other area of life, from the mechanics of pollination to the use of honey as a sweetener, an antiseptic, for making candles and furniture polish. Of all these practical uses, it is their role in pollination that is most vital. Bees pollinate 70 per cent of the crops that provide 90 per cent of food in the world and a strong colony, around 60,000 bees, flies the equivalent distance of the Earth to the Moon every day.

Despite their importance, bees have experienced an almost catastrophic decline in recent years. Their population in the UK alone has reduced by 75 per cent in the past century. The reasons given are fast-changing environmental factors: pesticides, loss of habitat and stress. What we do at Highclere is not in any way significant but we have tried to do our bit to help. As well as planting our Wildflower Meadow, we have instituted wide wildflower margins around the arable fields and kept expanses of open undisturbed hillsides.

Highclere's apiculture expert is Mike Withers, who has kept bees on the estate for over 50 years. Now in his eighties, his fascination and passion continues unabated. I watched Mike one day carefully trying to collect a swarm in a 'skep'. Straw skeps were first designed in the time of Alfred the Great, over 1,000 years ago, and have not changed very much since. Once you have collected up the bees, making sure you have the queen, you then 'run' them over a board into their new hive. This is the crunch point, as there is a chance of the swarm absconding, but Mike is hugely experienced. The Queen Bee went in over the workers and, once she was ensconced, the moment of concern passed.

Bees build their honey stores throughout the summer. Orchards are often an ideal setting in which to place hives, where bees have always been found valuable both for the essential pollination work they do and as a deterrent to scrumpers. They thrive on the blossom of fruit trees, but equally they are very partial to blue coloured plants, such as the generous panicles of the buddleia shrubs along the edge of the Wildflower Meadow, the lavender borders in the Monks' Gardens, the borage in the Healing Herb Garden, and also the sweet chestnut trees and blackberry bushes in the wider estate. Such plants help them produce sugars which will remain runny in the comb over the winter months.

Honey itself is something of a miracle food: complex, nutritious and antibacterial, it contains 24 different sugars as well as small amounts of plant enzymes and proteins. It is the only food that includes everything that is needed to sustain life.

A useful piece of advice is that bees are less likely to sting you if you wear light-coloured clothes. You should never swear in front of them, do not try to deceive them and you should tell them everything about your life as they are excellent listeners:

> Marriage birth or burying
> News across the seas
> All your sad or marrying
> You must tell the bees.

THE LIME AVENUE

WALKING TOWARDS THE GARDENS on the eastern side of the Castle, the scent in the air tantalises and draws you towards the avenue of lime trees planted some 200 years ago. Interestingly, the scent is stronger at a distance, sweet and aromatic, fading as you get closer and you notice that the trees are humming with bees in the dappled light. Honey from lime trees is one of my favourites. The age and habit of the trees encourages not only bees but diverse quantities of other wildlife as well: moths, aphids and birds.

The small-leaved lime (*Tilia cordata*) dates back to the Ice Age when it was common throughout Europe. Popular from the Romans onwards, most parts of the tree had, or still have, a use. They coppice easily to provide sticks and fuel, and even today Morris Dancers (English folk-dancing teams) use sticks made from lime to thwack against each other in their traditional dances. The flowers were dried and used to make a tea, considered an efficacious treatment for headaches, insomnia and a nervous disposition, whilst the fibrous layer under the bark was used to make and weave baskets, shoes and nets. In France flowering branches are still cut down and fed to cattle, in the belief that this will improve milk production, although I think we have moved on from the other superstitions such as that just sitting under a lime tree might cure epilepsy and other nervous illnesses.

The wood itself is pale and soft and thus valued for carving. Some of the most exquisite wood carvings by Grinling Gibbons in the late seventeenth century were done in lime wood, the trees appear in medieval poems, whilst in Germany generations of legal judgements would be given *sub tilia*.

With deep and spreading roots, lime trees can live for over a thousand years, providing us with anchors of reference and contributing not just scent but to well-being and art.

THE WHITE BORDER

IN HIGH SUMMER, one of the most sheltered and tranquil garden walks lies between the southern soft faded wall of the Monks' Garden and a very tall, thick, dark yew hedge which runs parallel with it. It was not always so tall but during World War Two there were too few gardeners to keep it under control.

It is a long, slim, rectangle shape and my parents-in-law decided to utilise the space by creating a single, deep, white border there, beginning by planting six equidistant, ornamental, pale grey weeping pears. One of the most famous and quintessentially English gardens was begun by Vita Sackville-West at Sissinghurst Castle, Kent, in 1930. She wrote in a newspaper of 'a pale garden, next summer that I am now planting under the first flakes of snow'. Only the colours of white, green, grey and silver were to be allowed in this new garden, thus creating the first White Garden, which remains so much an inspiration to gardeners today.

Each distant end of the border is supported by Yucca, *Romneya coulteri* (Californian poppy) and sage, with buddleias giving height and crambe (a favourite of my mother-in-law and a huge blowsy relation of cabbage) making a spectacular display in the centre.

Sadly, not so long ago we lost the pear trees to honey fungus but we have recreated the height by putting tall green obelisks in their place which have white roses and clematis trailing over them.

Geordie and I each have our favourites, from gaura to lilies, white agapanthus, anemones for later, white tulips planted for May, scented nicotiana and gypsophila with its cloud of white, the velvety grey of lychnis, veronicastrum, gillenias for beautiful contrasting stems in autumn, paeonies, white lilies, the redoubtable hydrangea 'Annabelle' and campanula, all of which crowd the border whilst *Wisteria sinensis* and *Hydrangea petiolaris* paint the wall in white hanging tendrils and flower clusters.

Every year we experiment with shapes and groupings, always trying to imbue the walk further with enduring interest and different moments of pleasure.

Halfway down the border, in the centre of the ancient wall and under a brick arch, lies a wrought-iron frost gate. These days it is helpfully signposted for visitors but nevertheless it still induces the anticipation of wondering what you might find as you pass through it. Commissioned in 1962, this is 'The Secret Garden', the work of renowned plantsman and garden designer James Russell.

THE SECRET GARDEN

THE BLACK-SCROLLED GATE OPENS without a squeak. The first thing you notice is a faint scent, a reminder of warmer climes. Either side of the entrance are two *Libocedrus decurrens* – also known as incense cedars – whilst facing you is the first of a series of cherry trees.

James (Jim) Russell was at school with my father-in-law (the 7th Earl) and a lifelong friend. Most of Jim's clients came through friendship and consequent referrals and he had already worked at Highclere creating an extraordinary garden around Milford Lake, an eighteenth-century villa on the Estate. Letters recall, however, that he found the autocratic 6th Earl somewhat challenging to deal with: apparently, he would be stood in a line with the gardeners and be barked at on a regular basis.

Russell was, above all, a plantsman, and his skills were both practical and aesthetic. His personal enthusiasms were for rhododendrons and the old shrub roses in which his Sunningdale Nursery, in Surrey, specialised. Given the soil for the new garden at Highclere was on chalk, it needed some work as it was on the side of the wall that had been used as a rubbish pit by centuries of earlier gardeners. Using a beech hedge to give definition to the far side of the garden, Russell filled the curvaceous deep borders with his favourites, such as lilacs, hydrangeas, hostas, dogwoods, *Eucryphia* 'Nymansay' (brush bush) and old

roses. Cherry trees provided structure and height and his plan shows monardias, potentilla, salvia, agapanthus, fuchsia and campanula creating drifts nearer the front of the borders.

Jim Russell was very good company and over time he became ever more adept at dealing with his friend's father, who was the opposite of shy and, as such, liked everything large, colourful and immediate in his new garden. He remained a frequent guest at Highclere, staying for both parties and gardening projects. The 'improvement' and new plantings at Milford Lake House garden exhibit exceptional merit and class in their own right, and the heritage and specimen value of the rhododendron gardens, which were developed over many years, are of great significance. The renewal of the landscape by the 7th Earl over his 25 years of collaboration with Russell, and the importance of this plantsman's garden, reinvigorated longstanding horticultural traditions at Highclere which we continue to build upon.

According to notes from a talk Russell gave in the USA, he spoke of gardens as 'akin to paintings – or to sculpture, since they involve different angles of viewing; they also share elements of the temporal arts such as music, drama, and novels', which is perhaps an echo of Robert Herbert's desire to translate eighteenth-century paintings into the landscape. In 1968, the Sunningdale Nurseries in Surrey were removed to Castle Howard, in Yorkshire, where Jim Russell's work is very well known and this major figure in twentieth-century horticulture sadly died in 1996.

We have developed his deep shrubberies and out of one corner have created a new walk leading to a scented glade, which begins with lily of the valley, wallflowers and continues towards pots of gardenia installed after frosts and sweet peas growing up metal frames.

From either end of the Secret Garden, paths and beech arches extend into the Wood of Goodwill. The western end unwinds through the dark high juniper plantings into the entry to Robert Herbert's eighteenth-century beech avenue on the one side, whilst at the other end a curvaceous walk up offers a sunlit stroll through the Wildflower Meadow. The borders retain the hydrangeas, roses and a few of the original cherry trees. Given Highclere's now longer opening periods, we have introduced more spring plants. Tulips and penstemon, architectural plants such as *Mahonia japonica* and Christmas box and a collection of buddleias form backdrops in front of which the wealth of colour and scent of annuals and perennials are better highlighted. Climbing roses, clematis and honeysuckles scramble up against the old walls. The disintegrated cherry trees have been tidied up but the trunks left for other plants to

climb over and we have created new heights using groups of shrubs such as Pineapple plants (*Cytisus battandieri*), with their bright golden-yellow flowers aptly named for their delicious scent so popular with bees and other pollinating insects. The scent of philadelphus ('Lemoinei', 'Avalanche' or 'Beauclerk') is mesmerising, although much of the year they wait in the background with little to mark them out. It is, however, very possible to grow a clematis through them to add a different season of interest. *Hydrangea* 'Annabelle' returns in this garden as a reliable summer extravagance, draping itself behind garden benches whilst other varied hydrangeas wander out into the Wood of Goodwill.

It is one of the ironies of Highclere that the film *The Secret Garden* was shot here in our own Secret Garden and starred Maggie Smith who, some years later, was once again filmed here when it doubled as the garden of the Dower house in *Downton Abbey*. In this latter case, it was the hydrangeas that took a starring role, tumbling in glory around the bench on which she sat.

The central strength of the garden remains the late-summer planting. The shapes and textures as well as colours flow, still reflecting the original design. However, every garden reflects the times and we have gradually developed the planting into longer drifts of colour and genus in the mode of renowned garden designer Gertrude Jekyll. Whilst she was a genius and able to advance colours through the season with great precision, we find the weather and other challenges leave us having to acknowledge a life imper-fect. Geordie and I hope to achieve impact and avoid clashes but it is also about putting plants where they are likely to grow well.

The penstemons introduced in the top border in the Monks' Garden and the salvias from the Peach House bed are both repeated here in different colours. The delphiniums are planted together in banks, which allows us to better stake them, lupins stand against them in the front whilst later on daylilies and foxgloves (*Digitalis*), which need no such help, take over.

Later in August, goldenrod, black-eyed Susan and anemones offer new colours and lead the eye whilst Geordie then turns his focus to groups of dahlias in some of the herbaceous beds and I to crocosmia and fuchsias which drift out into the Wood of Goodwill.

The scale of Highclere always calls for teams to curate and create, to dig and to mulch, to plant and to prune. We were lucky to have Don Dowsett as a gardener here for 42 years, full of stories and knowledge. Never knowingly optimistic, he would always hope to keep the size and shape of the garden as it was when he started. Very fond of Don but nevertheless undeterred by his protestations, the garden grew by perhaps 30 acres in his later years with us. He was unique and our annual planting plans followed his vision. He would walk round with each of us, discuss and listen to our ideas and then plant everything according to his own plan as well as adding some orange clashing colours in the wrong place just to wind us up. It would inevitably lead to an argument between Geordie and I, as clearly the communication at the core of every marriage is often inconsistent. The result was that Geordie and I would creep back in at weekends and move plants around, which used to wind Don up.

Over the years we have planted and moved colours and textures around, learnt a huge amount and, working with the current gardening team, become more coherent. Part of the romance of every garden is finding something new; new combinations and new spaces and views. What is not new is the belief in the importance of nature.

The English Romantic movement, led by Coleridge, Keats, Shelley and Wordsworth, believed that society should see nature as its most valuable asset and remember the immense benefits derived from it. Wordsworth, in particular, believed that people dissipate too much energy on material things instead of being closer to nature where we would find more happiness in our lives.

From the Wildflower Meadow to the tranquillity of the White Border, the order of the Monks' Garden to the romance of the Secret Garden and through the trees and glades of the Wood of Goodwill, there are paths to engage the senses and find the concord that William Wordsworth proposes in order to enjoy life to its fullest, if only we can live in harmony and agreement with nature:

The kiss of the sun for pardon
The dong of the birds for mirth
One is nearer God's heart in a garden
Than anywhere else on earth
Dorothy Frances Gurney, 'God's Garden', 1913

ROSES

So MUCH OF THE OLD GARDENS have been swept away at Highclere through various re-modelling exercises, the exigencies of two world wars and the resulting depleted labour force here, that a significant amount of what you walk through today has really evolved during Geordie's and my 'tenancy' of Highclere. Some of the areas of the gardens, such as the azaleas on the east lawns, have just been brought out of hibernation, whilst other areas – 'rooms' – have developed as we have linked walks together. The result is that much of it is relatively 'young'.

Each project we take on tends to be based on the landscape, in garden heritage and emotional connection. Given there is no formal rose garden here and that I had always dreamed of one, I thought a good compromise was a rose arbour, one you could walk through and where you could enjoy the scents and colour from every angle. My motivation was my mother ('Life doesn't come with a manual; it comes with a mother'). Her kindness, her courage and her sense of humour have sustained me through her memory as well as my childhood spent with her. I am one of six sisters and our mother, Frances, died too young. We miss her every day although, just like others, we have all learned to continue to live each day.

With a dream and a passion, I embarked on this project to mark visibly my mother's love into my life. Having found a flat area, which was not perhaps ideal given the lack of protection from the prevailing wind, but otherwise possible, I embarked. Ever optimistic, I found my eyes had thought it was more flat than it was and it needed to become level. Luckily I had not set a budget – everything at Highclere brings surprises and this way I do not exceed any budget.

Rusty in the art of higher mathematics, the simplest plan seemed to be to copy the size of the metal arches from the yew walks in the Monks' Garden. The circumference of the circle was made by standing in the middle of level ground holding a piece of string which would mark the inside diameter. It seemed sensible to leave four gaps in the archways at the points of the compass which could be joined by a paved pathway with small gaps in between the stone slabs in which to plant chamomile. It would crunch under foot in summer and contribute a scent to every step.

Roses do not necessarily need rich soil but like every plant they will grow better if planted properly in well-prepared soil. The choice of climbing roses to scramble over the walkways was the fun part. One consideration for me was that the Castle and gardens are open throughout the summer, so roses offering long flowering periods would be a bonus, scent was a must and a colour scheme would give coherence. In this case, thinking of my mother, I focused on roses in shades of white through pinks to deep reds. 'Paul's Himalayan Musk', for example, is very fragrant, pale pink and reasonably tough, so it was ideal to cope with the less-protected side of the arbour. 'Zephirine Drouhin' has continuously flowering deep pink blooms whilst 'Etoile de Hollande' has larger red blooms. 'Aloha' has larger mid-pink flowers whilst 'Chateau de Clos Vougeot' is more sprawling but highly scented. Not all of them worked and each year we see what might be better to replace. In fact, we have added in a new endeavour to our portfolio: a Lord Carnarvon climbing rose which is fuchsia red touched with white and, of course, scented.

My preference is to plant bare-root roses, which need to go in between November and March. There is a process to aid success: leave the roots in a tub of water for at least two hours before you plant them. Meanwhile, dig over the soil, not forgetting to dig beneath where the roots will sit in order to allow enough root space – roses are deep-rooted plants. Add some compost to the bottom of the hole, place the rose in and back fill so that the stem base lies just below the surface of the soil. Step around it to firm the soil and finally water it. It is better not to crowd a rose: leave space so it is not competing with other plants. This also helps combat disease.

In the case of climbing roses, you need to help support them with either wire if they are on a wall or by tying them in to the pergola or archway. As they grow, gradually tie more of the stems onto the supporting structure, in this case the arbour. If you tie them horizontally it will encourage flowering shoots to form low down. Encourage the side shoots by fanning them out left and right into the available space, tying in as you go, and the result will be a mass of roses everywhere.

Over time, keep an eye out for weeds and remove them by hand-fork rather than using a hoe as roses produce some roots near the soil surface which will otherwise be damaged. The trick is to cover the soil with a thick layer of mulch - composted manure, and other organic and natural fertilisers once a year. In fact, if you use tree bark on the very top it should suppress weeds, which saves you a job.

Some of the huge variety of roses cultivated at Highclere, some in formal settings, others dotted through the landscape. The new shrub rose 'Lady Carnarvon' is shown CENTRE BOTTOM

Roses live for years. They are best pruned in January and February and in terms of climbers you want to encourage strong growth from the base of the plant. In every case remove dead, dying, damaged and diseased stems. It is also best to remove any remaining leaves to reduce the risk of disease spores being carried over to another year. Joyously, if you cut a little too much, they will still grow back.

Shrub roses are scattered throughout the gardens and walls. Rosa 'Compassion', with creamy apricot tinged blooms, is a stalwart, the pale pink 'Wildeve' and 'Princess Anne', a fuchsia

and white rose, never fail. Scottish ground-cover roses such as 'Dunwich Rose' and 'Stellata' flower continuously over months. Meanwhile, rugged roses such as 'Wild Edric' and 'Roseraie de L'Hay' (an old highly scented type) survive outside the fenced areas as they seem to be left alone by the rabbits and deer.

Never quite content, like any other gardener, I have now expanded the design of my rose arbour. We have removed the turf left inside the arbour, marking out four quadrants divided by small pathways and leaving a circle in the middle. These have been filled with bare-rooted shrub roses and the pleasure of ordering these involved more research. My mother was a very kind and diplomatic person, so I have planted the rose 'Tranquillity', an excellent large white rose with dark green, glossy foliage, along with 'Emily Bronte' (soft pink), 'Gabriel Oak' (fuchsia), and 'Eustacia Vye' (soft apricot pink) – three literary characters referencing books much enjoyed by my mother. I then added 'Mme. Isaac Pereire', a classic rose from 1841

with large, showy, intensely fragrant blooms of deep crimson, 'Queen of Denmark' (from 1826), also a classic with paler pink blooms, and finally a new shrub rose, 'Lady Carnarvon', which is cream with a hint of apricot and scented.

We hope our work over the winter will bear success with all the promise of heady scent and colour to linger through the summer. In and around the shrub rose are rosemary, lavender, 'Johnson's Blue' geranium and froths of *Alchemilla mollis*. Each has a purpose. Rosemary is both ornamental in that it can be clipped into dome shapes but also has culinary and medicinal uses. It is also said to protect against the evil eye, which is always useful. Lavender was introduced into Britain by the Romans, who used it in bath water: to heal cuts, repel fleas and nits, to promote sleep and to relax the body. In concentrated form it is an antiseptic and is often used to combat clothes moths. Lavender still edges the ancient walls of the Monks' Garden today, takes a central space in the Healing Herb Garden and now is in the rose arbour as well. It is a reminder of sunny moments – just plant a large pot and keep it by a sunny window.

SUMMER FRUIT AND VEGETABLES

I have lived temperately, eating little animal food, and that not as an aliment, so much
as a condiment for the vegetables, which constitute my principal diet.
Thomas Jefferson (1743-1826)

NOTHING SAYS 'SUMMER' quite so much as a flourishing vegetable garden full of blossoming plants ready
for harvest. There are so many advantages to growing your own vegetables and, if you stick to the easier
varieties, of which there are plentiful options, it really isn't too much of a chore. Home-grown vegetables
are better flavoured, bursting with nutrients and often cheaper than those bought in the shops. If it is
more challenging to live the 'good life' from the garden through the winter, there is no such excuse in the
summer and there are few more balancing and rewarding ways to spend an hour or two a week than
growing even a few of your own vegetables.

A little time spent pottering in the longer evenings will enable you to keep the weeds down,
look out for pests and indulge in a little watering as necessary. The smell of the ripening plants can be
intoxicating, and where would summer be without fresh tomatoes off the vine – the two go hand-in-hand.
A vegetable garden also has the potential to feed the soul, making sure you have fresh air, exercise and
a chance to experience nature at work first hand.

As usual with gardening, creating a vegetable bed is all about preparation. The first step is to
decide where you want your beds to be. Consider the size, shape and location of your garden in order to
work out what would best suit you. Vegetables need a good, deep layer of fertile soil and the fastest way to
achieve this is with raised beds which can be infilled with compost. Avoid planting in square patterns or
rows and instead, stagger the plants by planting in triangles. By doing so, you can fit more plants into each
bed, although be careful not to space your plants too tightly or you will strangle their growth.

Likewise, succession planting allows you to grow more than one crop in each space over the
course of a growing season so that you can get three or even four harvests out of it. Lastly, by keeping
your plants warm by using mulches, cloches, row covers or even cold frames, you can add a few weeks
to each end of the growing season. This buys you some more time to harvest yet another succession crop,
for example, early lettuces near the beginning of the season and kale towards the end.

At Highclere, we have spent this last winter creating some new vegetable beds behind the Monks' Garden. For years this area had been dominated by looming shadows of dark tangled laurels which had been allowed to run riot for decades. They covered the most extraordinary amount of space and we have been able to push them back to reveal a really quite large space without disturbing what they look like from the other side. Here we have built a whole series of raised beds using the surprisingly fertile soil we have found there, from earlier vegetable efforts that have been augmented with a lot of well-rotted compost.

The final trick is to go vertical. A surprisingly large number of vegetables, and not just beans, can be grown 'upwards' over supports, which can be as ornamental as you require them to be. In a small space, this has the added advantage of making what is essentially 'a working garden' also look decorative.

PLANTING IDEAS FOR SUMMER VEGETABLES

Winter seed catalogues are an excellent early source of inspiration, but garden centres and supermarkets have a straightforward selection of seeds or smaller plants, too. Look for easy-growing, disease-resistant varieties and then work out a succession planting that suits you. To avoid a total glut with some of the prolific vegetables, space out planting the seeds at two-week intervals so that you can extend availability throughout the whole season. For an example, the following fruits and vegetables will be ready over the summer months:

- Beetroot (beets), broad beans, broccoli, cauliflower, chicory, chillies, courgettes (zucchini), marrow, potatoes, runner beans, sorrel, summer squash and Swiss chard.
- Cucumber, lettuce, peas, peppers, radishes, rocket, spring onions.
- Blackcurrants, gooseberries, raspberries, redcurrants, rhubarb, strawberries.

As the warmth develops you can enjoy:

- Blueberries, fennel, French beans, garlic, samphire and tomatoes.

It is not just us, vegetables also have personal preferences about who they prefer to be in bed with. There are a few key ones to remember:

- Tomatoes are best kept apart from potatoes.
- Strawberries and raspberries do better apart from potatoes and all brassicas (i.e. cabbage, cauliflower, etc.).
- Almost everyone likes beetroot, except for runner beans. ◇

SUMMER COOKING

WARM FINGERS OF SMILING SUMMER LIGHT CURL ROUND SHUTTERS or curtains early every morning. Each day promises a new adventure just because the sun is shining. Walking the dogs and oneself before breakfast is simply fun, and then breakfast is so easy: melon or a juice of whatever is lying around – perhaps spinach, apple and fresh ginger – with some live yoghurt, or mango or blueberry and perhaps some chia seeds or flaxseeds for added health. Drink them or eat them in a bowl outside. Or try avocado on toast with a splash of unpressed green olive oil, sliced fennel or a poached egg.

Good-for-you Granola

Granola is the more American version of muesli and each dish claims health benefits. It does incorporate some excellent nuts and seeds but the yummy elements, such as maple syrup and honey, require good walks after breakfast to work off. It is delicious and I add a little kefir or live yoghurt and some blueberries.

INGREDIENTS

2 tbsp coconut oil
125ml (4fl oz) maple syrup
2 tbsp honey
1 tsp vanilla extract
300g (10oz) jumbo rolled oats
50g (2oz) sunflower seeds
4 tbsp chia seeds
50g (2oz) pumpkin seeds
100g (3½oz) flaked almonds
100g (3½oz) dried berries of
    your choice
50g (2oz) coconut flakes

PREPARATION TIME 10 mins   COOKING TIME 30 mins
MAKES approx. 15 servings

Preheat the oven to 150°C/300°F/Gas mark 2.

Mix the oil, maple syrup, honey and vanilla in a large bowl before tipping in all the remaining ingredients, except the dried fruit and coconut. Stir in thoroughly.

Tip the granola onto two baking sheets and spread evenly. Bake for 15 minutes, then mix in the coconut and dried fruit and bake for a further 10–15 minutes. Remove and scrape onto a flat tray to cool.

The granola can be stored in an airtight container for up to a month.

Chilled Cucumber and Mint Soup

The TV series Jeeves and Wooster *(from the books by P.G. Wodehouse) was filmed at Highclere nearly 30 years ago. The inimitable Jeeves always remained cool as a cucumber in the face of the antics of Bertie Wooster and friends. They might eventually have tired of cucumber sandwiches for tea, but they would undoubtedly have enjoyed this soup. It could not be simpler and I use bio yoghurt, which has plenty of good bacteria to help digestion.*

INGREDIENTS

3 cucumbers,
   plus extra to garnish, diced
350ml (12fl oz) natural yoghurt
2 garlic cloves
2 tbsp chopped mint leaves,
   plus extra sprigs to garnish
Zest and juice of 1 lemon
Handful of ice cubes
Drizzle of olive oil
Salt and freshly ground
   black pepper

PREPARATION TIME 5 mins plus chilling time   SERVES 6

Peel two of the cucumbers, leaving the third *au naturel* to give a good green colour, then chop them all roughly.

Blitz the cucumber with the yoghurt, garlic, mint, lemon zest and ice until completely smooth. If it is too thick, add some more ice.

Add the lemon juice and salt and pepper to taste. Chill.

To serve, stir gently and pour into bowls, adding a drizzle of olive oil and a sprig of mint. If you like, you can also sprinkle over some extra finely diced cucumber for a bit of crunch.

Crab, Cucumber and Passion Fruit Tian

A 'tian' is French cuisine's 'Classic vessel' – in this case a ring that we use to add shape to this dish, creating elegant, individually plated servings ... but it's just as enjoyable on the table as a single, coventional free-form salad.

This dish is all about the 'mise en place' – the term used by professional chefs to describe preparation before building a dish.

INGREDIENTS

For the dressing

3 passion fruits
1 red chilli, deseeded
   and finely sliced
1 tsp caster sugar

For the salad

200g (7oz) picked white crab meat
Zest and juice of 1 lemon
3 tbsp natural yoghurt
1 small cucumber
1 grapefruit
4 sprigs of samphire
Salt and freshly ground
   black pepper

PREPARATION TIME 20 mins   SERVES 6

Prepare the dressing ...

Cut the passion fruits in half and carefully scoop out the seeds into a small pan, making sure to get all the juice. Add the chilli, sugar and one or two teaspoons of water and warm gently.

Fill the passion fruit shells with the mixture and save the rest of the dressing to drizzle when plating.

The *mise en place* ...

Season the crab meat with salt, pepper, lemon zest and a little juice to taste.

Now mix in the yoghurt, making sure the mixture does not become too loose to hold its shape.

Finely slice half of the cucumber and set aside.

Peel and deseed the other half of the cucumber, and dice the flesh. Mix with the crab.

With a sharp knife, remove all the peel and outside membranes from the grapefruit, then cut segments of flesh free from between the inner membranes.

Poach the samphire in a little boiling water for 1 minute then immediately chill it under cold running water to fix its brilliant-green colour.

Assemble the salad ...

For each guest, place a tall-sided pastry cutter on to a plate. Fill with a portion of the crab mixture and carefully remove the ring.

Garnish the top of each crab serving with some grapefruit segments and cucumber slices.

Place a passion fruit half beside the crab.

Divide the samphire between the plates and drizzle with a little of the reserved dressing.

Holy Mackerel with Lemons
from the Highclere Greenhouses

'Holy Mackerel!' is an exclamation of surprise that dates back at least 200 years and is perhaps a reference to Catholics eating fish on Fridays. The North East Atlantic mackerel has been overfished for the Scandinavian and European markets. Perhaps now, after so many arguments, fishing can be properly managed and a sustainable quantity of fish caught and eaten in the UK.

June, July and August are the months to forage on tidal mudflats for samphire, also known as Saint Peter's herb, after the patron saint of fishermen. In the USA they call it 'sea beans' and in Canada 'sea asparagus'. Whatever the name, it needs to be thoroughly washed and although you can eat the tiniest tender stems raw, you can also boil or steam them for a couple of minutes and serve with a drizzle of melted butter and even a squeeze of fresh lemon juice.

INGREDIENTS

2 tbsp creamed horseradish (from a jar is fine, but if you would like to make your own, see page 102)
Salt and freshly ground black pepper
150g (5oz) Greek yoghurt
1 tsp English mustard
Zest and juice of 1 lemon
1 tsp red wine vinegar
3 sprigs of flat-leaf parsley
300g (10oz) washed, picked baby spinach
3 mackerel (1 per person)
Handful of samphire
2 tbsp finely diced cucumber
2 lemon wedges

PREPARATION TIME 10 mins   COOKING TIME 15 mins   SERVES 3

Preheat the oven to 180°C/350°F/Gas mark 4.

Combine the horseradish and yoghurt and season with salt and black pepper.

Mix the mustard with the lemon juice and vinegar and stir in the lemon zest. Stir this mixture into the yoghurt.

Roughly chop the parsley and spinach and add to the yoghurt mixture.

Fill the washed, cleaned mackerel with the yoghurt and herb mixture.

Place in the oven for 15 minutes or until cooked, test at the back of the head or top of the fish spine with the tip of a knife to see if it's hot.

While the fish is cooking, if your samphire is not already tender to the bite, boil it for a couple of minutes in salted water.

Now dress the mackerel on a plate with the cucumber, samphire and lemon wedges.

Any unused yoghurt mix can be served on the side.

CHEF'S NOTE

Some people serve four fish as 'Bread and Fishes' – in the shape of a cross with a mixed green salad and crusty bread.

Scallops, Samphire, Ginger and Spring Onions

Scallops are rich in protein and nutrients such as magnesium and potassium, all of which support heart and brain health. As with all other fish there are times to catch them and times to leave them in peace, and dredging is best limited in time or sea area, with diver-caught scallops the most sustainable of all. They are always a treat, with each bite to be savoured.

INGREDIENTS

1 onion, julienned
A little plain flour
1 tbsp olive oil
15 scallops
2 knobs of butter
1 red onion, finely diced
4 spring onions, trimmed and sliced
1 tsp fresh root ginger, grated
2 garlic cloves, crushed
100g (3½oz) samphire
1 tbsp sherry
3 tbsp soy sauce
3 tsp clear honey
2 tsp sesame oil
Flesh of 1 tomato, diced
Salt and freshly ground
  black pepper

PREPARATION TIME 10 mins   **COOKING TIME** 10 mins   SERVES 3

To make crisp onion strips, roll the julienned strips in seasoned flour, and cook in a pan with the olive oil over a medium to high heat. When crisp, remove from the oil and transfer to kitchen paper to dry, sprinkling with a little salt if required.

Pat the scallops dry with kitchen paper and heat the first knob of butter in a large non-stick frying pan.

Place the scallops into the pan working clockwise around. Add the second knob of butter, together with the red onion, sliced spring onions and grated ginger. After 1 minute, turn the scallops over and cook for a further 1 minute.

Add the garlic and samphire and cook for another minute or until the scallops are just cooked. Remove from the pan and set aside.

Add the sherry, soy sauce and honey to the pan, and simmer until reduced by half. Now add the sesame oil and the tomato flesh. Pour over the scallops and serve immediately.

Highclere Orange and Lemon Chilli Chicken

Chicken remains a favourite supper dish in every season and combining it with the taste of citrus and a little chilli in the sauce gives it a piquancy which is refreshing. Serve with new potatoes and green beans.

INGREDIENTS

PREPARATION TIME 20 mins   COOKING TIME 40 mins   SERVES 6

For the chicken

1 tbsp vegetable oil
Zest of 1 lemon
Zest of 1 orange
½ tsp fresh or dried tarragon
½ tsp thyme
½ tsp parsley
400g (14oz) chicken thighs,
   boned, skin intact
Salt and freshly ground
   black pepper

For the sauce

150ml (5fl oz) lemon juice,
   plus zest from the fruits
250ml (8fl oz) orange juice,
   plus zest from the fruits
2 tsp grated ginger
1 tsp red chilli, finely chopped
1 tsp caster sugar, to taste
1 tbsp cornflour

Preheat the oven to 180°C/350°F/Gas mark 4.

Mix together the oil, zests, herbs and seasoning and rub thoroughly into the chicken pieces.

Put the chicken on some non-stick baking paper in a baking dish and cook for 30–40 minutes until the skin is golden and crispy and the juices run clear.

For the sauce, put all the ingredients except the cornflour into a heavy-bottomed pan and gently bring to the boil. Allow to cool slightly.

Mix the cornflour with a splash of cold water to make a thick paste. Add to the saucepan and bring to the boil whilst whisking to thicken the sauce. Allow to cool and adjust the seasoning and sugar as required.

Place your cooked chicken thighs on a plate and pour the sauce around (so as not to ruin the crispy skin), sprinkle with a little salt and enjoy!

Slow-baked Lamb
with Anchovies, Garlic and Herbs

Slow roasting ensures that the meat falls apart and the dish can be placed in the middle of the table to share.

INGREDIENTS

4 sprigs of rosemary,
  leaves finely chopped
4 garlic cloves, crushed
1 tbsp capers, finely chopped
3 anchovy fillets in oil,
  drained and finely chopped
2 tbsp olive oil
2 lemons
1½kg (3¼lb) shoulder of lamb, on
  the bone
2 red onions, cut into wedges
Small glass of white wine

PREPARATION TIME 10 mins   COOKING TIME 4 hours   SERVES 6

Preheat the oven to 160°C/325°F/Gas mark 3.

Mix the rosemary, garlic, capers, anchovies and olive oil with the zest and juice of 1 lemon, reserving the squeezed lemon halves.

Make 3–4 slashes across the top of the joint of lamb and rub the mixture all over.

Scatter the onions into the base of a large roasting tin. Cut the remaining lemon in half, squeeze the juices into the tin, and place all the used lemon halves in the tin with the onions. Place the lamb on top and roast for 1 hour.

Pour in the wine and roast for a further 3 hours until the meat is really tender. Leave to rest for 15 minutes, pull into chunks rather than carve, and serve with the pan juices.

Risotto with Lemon and Aubergine

Aubergine (eggplant) is such a versatile vegetable. Grilled, fried, baked, stuffed or roasted, it has a creamy texture which absorbs other cooking flavours and thus it is often also used in curries. The name comes from the Arabic al-bādinjān, which evolved into the Spanish alberenjena. This etymology is a reminder of its origins in warm, southern climates, and thus the subsequent need to offer the plants protection when grown in northern winters. It works very well in a risotto and the lemon offers a crisp balancing taste in summer.

INGREDIENTS

150ml (5fl oz) olive oil
2 large aubergines (eggplants)
2 tbsp butter
1 medium red onion
2 large garlic cloves
200g (7oz) risotto rice
125ml (4fl oz) white wine
750ml (1¼ pints) stock
Zest and juice of 1 lemon
50g (2oz) Parmesan, grated
Generous handful of fresh
    basil leaves, chopped
Salt and freshly ground
    black pepper

PREPARATION TIME 25 mins   COOKING TIME 30–40 mins   SERVES 4

Heat 2 tablespoons of the live oil in a shallow pan over a medium heat. Place the whole aubergines in the pan and quickly rotate them to get a little oil all over. Char the aubergines until the skin is blackened and the flesh is soft and smoky, about 15 minutes. Keep turning them to blacken all over. Leave to cool.

Scoop out the flesh and chop into medium-sized dice. Fry the flesh in 1 tablespoon of butter for several minutes, turning continually until crisp and golden. Strain the fat and set the aubergine on kitchen paper to drain.

Fry the onion and the garlic in the remaining olive oil until translucent. Add the rice and stir to coat it in the oil. Fry for 2 or 3 minutes then pour in the wine, turn up the heat so the wine evaporates.

Reduce the heat and begin to add the hot stock to the rice a ladle at a time. Ensure the previous liquid is absorbed before adding another ladle. When all the stock has been added, remove the pan from the hob.

Add the lemon zest and juice. Stir in the aubergine and the remaining butter. Season with salt and pepper and add Parmesan to taste. Serve in individual bowls with extra Parmesan, topped with basil.

Lemon Syllabub

During the leisure time of the aristocracy in the eighteenth century, there
was nothing more fashionable than a cold meal prepared in great style to
be enjoyed in the countryside. A syllabub was without doubt included to
demonstrate that the owner was quite à la mode.

INGREDIENTS

PREPARATION TIME 10 mins   SERVES 4

284ml (10fl oz) whipping cream
60g (2oz) caster sugar
60ml (2fl oz) white wine
Zest and juice of ½ or 1 lemon
   (depending on how juicy it is)

Whip the cream and sugar together until soft peaks form.

Stir in the wine and the lemon zest and juice to taste.

Spoon into glasses.

This is lovely as it is, but you could serve with berries on top, or some
almond biscuits on the side ... or both!

Best Lemon Curd

Lemon curd is so simple to make: you just need to whisk eggs, butter,
sugar and lemon juice in a pan on the stove for a bit. The result, however,
is excellent; Geordie loves it on toast but I think it is sometimes useful as
part of a pudding, tangy and full of summer.

INGREDIENTS

PREPARATION TIME 30 mins   MAKES 1 jar

Zest and juice of 3 large lemons
225g (8oz) caster sugar
60g (2oz) unsalted butter
2 eggs

Mix the lemon zest and juice, sugar and butter together in a pan over
a low to medium heat. Stir gently until the sugar has dissolved.

Beat the eggs in a bowl until light and fluffy. Remove the lemon mixture
to a large bowl and add the eggs a little at a time, whisking constantly.

Return the mixture to the pan over a medium-low heat and stir gently
until it begins to thicken. Allow to come to the boil and keep on a medium
simmer for 3-4 minutes until the curd is sufficiently thick.

Remove the pan from the heat and put the curd in a pre-prepared
sterilised jar. Allow to cool before sealing and storing in the fridge.
The mixture can be stored in this way for up to 3 months.

Lemon Meringue Tart

This is one of my husband's favourites, but oh my goodness can it go wrong! Geordie likes to dig a large spoon into this quite ostentatious pudding, which has risen proudly in the dish and been gently caramelised on the top in the oven. It is neither hot nor cold and small individual tarts will not do. The cream jug follows the tart around and I always feel nervous in case it has a soggy bottom (never!) or the top has been scorched a little too far. But it is a bit of zesty magic and worth the stress.

INGREDIENTS

120g (4oz) unsalted butter
200g (7oz) plain flour
1 tbsp iced water
2 large eggs
1 jar homemade lemon curd
   (see page 144)
Salt

For the meringue topping

4 large egg whites
85g (3oz) caster sugar

PREPARATION TIME 20 mins
COOKING TIME 30–40 mins, plus chilling time   SERVES 6–8

Preheat the oven to 190°C/375°F/Gas mark 5.

Rub the butter into the flour until you have a fine breadcrumb mix. Add a little pinch of salt.

Mix the water with the eggs and add to the flour mixture. Bring the ingredients together with your hands and shape into a smooth ball. Cover and chill in the fridge for at least 1 hour.

Roll out the pastry to fit a tart tin. Prick the base all over with a fork, place a sheet of non-stick baking paper over the pastry base, fill with baking beans and bake for 15–20 minutes. Leave to cool.

Fill the pastry case with the lemon curd.

For the meringue topping ...

Reduce the oven heat to 180°C/350°F/Gas mark 4.

Beat the egg whites until very light and fluffy. Add the sugar gradually, continuing to beat until all the sugar has been added and the meringue forms stiff peaks.

Spoon the meringue over the surface of the lemon curd. Bake for 10–15 minutes until the meringue is lightly golden. Allow to cool before serving.

Crème Brûlée

Oscar Wilde commented that he could resist everything except temptation, and this is indulgent and very tempting, with a rich, creamy base oozing out from under the crunchy sugar topping. These puddings must be made ahead in order to chill them thoroughly before 'burning' the top, which then forms a crisp, caramelised sugar layer.

INGREDIENTS

420ml (14fl oz) double cream
100ml (3½fl oz) milk
1 vanilla pod
5 large egg yolks
50g (2oz) golden caster sugar, plus
    extra for the topping

PREPARATION TIME 50 mins   **COOKING TIME** 30–40 mins   **SERVES** 4

Preheat the oven to 180°C/350°F/Gas mark 4.

Sit four 175ml (6fl oz) ramekins in a deep roasting tin at least 7·5cm (3 inch) deep, one that will enable a baking tray to sit well above the ramekins when laid across the top of the tin.

Pour the cream and milk into a medium pan.

Lay the vanilla pod on a board and slice lengthways through the middle to split it in two. Scrape out all the tiny seeds and put them into the cream mixture, along with the pod. Set aside.

Put the egg yolks and sugar in a mixing bowl and whisk until pale and fluffy.

Heat the cream until it is almost but not quite boiling. As soon as you see bubbles appear around the edge, take the pan off the heat.

Pour the hot cream into the beaten egg yolks, stirring continuously.

Pour the mixture through a sieve to remove any lumps. Scoop away all the foam from the top of the liquid and discard. Pour the cream mixture into ramekins.

Pour enough hot water into the roasting tin to come about 1½cm (¾ inch) up the sides of the ramekins. Put the roasting tin into the oven and lay a baking sheet over the top of the tin so it sits well above the ramekins and completely covers them. Leave a small gap at one side to allow air to circulate.

Bake for 30–35 minutes until the mixture is softly set but still has a bit of a wobble. Cool slightly, then put in the fridge to set completely.

When ready to serve, wipe round the top edge of the dishes and sprinkle 1½ teaspoons of caster sugar over each ramekin. Spray with a little water using a fine spray (the sort you buy in a craft shop) just to dampen the sugar then use a blow torch to caramelise it. Hold the flame just above the sugar and keep moving it round and round until caramelised. Refrigerate for an hour and serve.

Pannacotta
with Gooseberry and Elderflower Compôte

My mother loved gooseberries – from fools to compôtes, in crumbles or just for breakfast.

A perfectly set, slightly wobbly pannacotta is the perfect spring pudding, especially when served with some not-quite-sweet gooseberry compôte which cuts through the creaminess. The fragrance from white, lacy elderflower heads not only makes delicious summer cordials but is always useful as a sweet balance in puddings.

You will need ramekins or dariole moulds, lightly greased with a mild vegetable oil.

INGREDIENTS

6 leaves gelatine
250ml (8fl oz) double cream
200g (7oz) caster sugar
1 vanilla pod, split lengthways,
    seeds scraped out
550ml (19fl oz) full-fat milk
2 tbsp clear honey for the
    pannacotta, plus 1 tbsp
    for the compôte
150g (5oz) gooseberries
3 tbsp elderflower cordial

PREPARATION TIME 50 mins, plus overnight chilling   SERVES 8

To make the pannacotta ...

Soak the gelatine according to the packet instructions until soft.

Heat the cream, sugar, vanilla pod and seeds in a pan over a low heat until the sugar has dissolved. Take off the heat.

Squeeze out the water from the gelatine and then stir the leaves into the cream mixture until the gelatine is completely dissolved.

Leave to cool, then add the milk and honey. Strain through a fine sieve into a bowl to ensure there are no lumps. Keep stirring for the next 10 minutes as the mixture thickens to make sure that no lumps form.

Pour into the greased ramekins or dariole moulds, and leave in the fridge overnight to set.

To make the compôte ...

Heat the gooseberries with the elderflower cordial and honey until the fruit softens and begins to fall apart. Add more honey if necessary to sweeten it. Mush it together until the fruit is completely crushed.

To serve, turn out the pannacottas onto serving plates and put a dollop of the compôte on top of each one.

GARDENER'S TIP

Gooseberries are easy to grow and prefer a sunny site, whether planted as a bush trained against a wall or in a container. Despite my best efforts I cannot usually keep up with the generosity of their harvest and diligently top and tail them for freezing. First lay them out on a tray in the freezer and then scoop them into a bag for use throughout the year.

Chocolate Cake with Strawberries and Cream

Who does not anticipate strawberries every summer? – strawberries and cream whilst watching tennis at Wimbledon or sweet, ripe, chopped berries filling an irresistible cake.

This is a very indulgent cake for a special occasion, very moist and rich and a little goes a long way. It looks amazing but is surprisingly simple to make. The mixture itself is quite thin so it is important to use old-fashioned sandwich tins rather than springform tins which will probably leak.

INGREDIENTS

225g (8oz) plain flour
350g (12oz) caster sugar
85g (3oz) cocoa powder
1½ tsp baking powder
1½ tsp bicarbonate of soda
2 eggs
250ml (8fl oz) milk
125ml (4fl oz) vegetable oil
2 tsp vanilla extract
250ml (8fl oz) boiling water

For the filling

200ml (7fl oz) double cream
1 punnet strawberries, plus extra to
   decorate the top of the cake

For the icing

200g (7oz) plain chocolate
200ml (7fl oz) double cream

GARDENER'S TIP

Strawberries are easy to grow and like the English summer. There are early or mid/late varieties or a type called Everbearers, which grow well in containers and keep producing bunches for you to pick. They need rich, fertile soil and a sunny position ... and don't forget to water.

We have to keep our strawberry pots quite high up on tables as our Labradors compete to pick them when they are just perfectly ripe.

PREPARATION TIME 30 mins, plus 1–2 hours chilling
COOKING TIME 45–60 mins   SERVES 6–8

Preheat the oven to 180°C/350°F/Gas mark 4.

Grease and line two 20cm (8 inch) diameter sandwich tins.

For the cake ...

Place all of the cake ingredients, except the boiling water, into a large mixing bowl. Beat the mixture until smooth.

Add the boiling water, a little at a time, until the mixture is smooth and sloppy.

Divide the mixture between the sandwich tins and bake in the oven for 25–35 minutes or until the top is firm to the touch and a skewer inserted into the centre of the cake comes out clean.

Remove the cakes from the oven and leave them in their tins to cool completely.

For the filling ...

Whip the cream until it is reasonably stiff but be careful not to over beat it.

Cut the strawberries into quarters or reasonably small bits and gently stir into the cream. This will stiffen the cream a bit so be careful.

Remove the cold cakes from their tins and place one on a serving plate. Gently spread the cream and strawberry mix over the plated cake and position the other cake on top.

For the icing ...

Break up the chocolate and heat it and the cream in a saucepan over a low heat until the chocolate melts. Remove the pan from the heat and whisk the mixture until smooth, glossy and thickened. Set aside to cool for 1–2 hours, or until thick enough to spread over the cake.

Carefully spread the icing over the top and sides of the cake and decorate with a few more strawberries or slice them thinly and arrange over the top of the cake.

Summer Suppers

THE ART OF ENTERTAINING

At a dinner party one should eat wisely but not too well,
and talk well but not too wisely.
W. Somerset Maugham (1874–1965)

GOOD FOOD, GOOD WINE AND CONVERSATION are essential ingredients in life, the highlights and the memories. The current dining room is a rarity – a room that is both impressive and warm in terms of colours and light. It is nevertheless situated on the north side of the Castle and has one small radiator, so warm, rich, velvet evening wraps or dresses for the ladies work as well in summer as in winter.

In earlier centuries, however, the dining room was on the south side of the Castle. Either way, it is not desperately convenient for the kitchens. Originally, in Highclere's earliest incarnations, everyone would have eaten together in the great medieval hall, seated at long trestle tables with large logs offering welcoming warmth in the old fireplace. Given the number of people, it would have been a bustling scene. This was some distance from the kitchens, which were housed in a separate building in order to minimise the risk of fire, given that cooking was conducted over open fires. Unlike the dining room, which swapped sides, the kitchen has remained in the same place for centuries with the same inconvenient issue of the hot food courses having to travel some distance from oven to plate.

It was the 2nd Earl of Carnarvon who moved the dining room to its current location, which previously had been a statue gallery. Two hundred years later, my mother-in-law refurbished the rooms with wonderful yellow silk wall-hangings, which prove an excellent foil for the paintings. For the most part, these are portraits which, in true Victorian fashion, testify to the importance of the Carnarvon family, their taste and style, thus creating a backdrop in which to entertain royalty, prime ministers, pioneers of technology, archaeology, music, art and diplomacy. Ironically, to today's eyes, in the majority of the portraits the men have even longer flowing hairstyles than the women, but each one tells a story, a reference to their lives and history as well as that of Highclere Castle. However, the room is dominated by the great Anthony Van Dyck portrait of King Charles I on horseback which was painted in about 1633.

Dinners are a chance to enjoy the drama and civilisation of this grand room. Sitting in front of a beautiful polished table, the flowers, silverware and glimmering candlesticks merge to create a remarkable and unrepeatable atmosphere. Beautifully presented food, accompanying wines in gold-edged glasses, conversation, debate and laughter allow each guest to step into the theatre of the evening.

In many ways it is comparable to theatre. Geordie and I plan who to ask and then agree the placements, Luís and his butlering team set the table, each course is carefully chosen and the wines deliberated on and selected. Such high drama creates memories and a date in the diary to look forward to.

Lunches and walks or cocktails and dinner, music and dancing – it is all the colour of life.

THE COOL, CLEAR SCENT OF A CHANGING SEASON IS THE REWARD OF AN EARLY autumn morning: angled blades of grass hung with pearls of dew and threads of silver string spun by busy but shy spiders in the dark-green-leaved shrubs beside the Castle lawns.

The autumn months are a time of gifts, abundance and rich colours, of russet and gold foliage throughout the various gardens and woodlands. The ochres of an autumn sunlight are quite unlike other months: they have a dappled, subdued golden light that intermittently fades over the weeks as it begins to abandon us to the oncoming winter.

AUTUMN

A SECOND SPRING

'AUTUMN IS A SECOND SPRING WHEN EVERY LEAF IS A FLOWER' (in the words of Albert Camus) and, unlike in spring, the flowers, plants and fruits all deepen into jewelled colours. During these glorious weeks, the fruit trees ripen, slowly reaching the point where each plum, pear or apple needs only a gentle twist to be added to a fruit bowl, or stored or cooked. Looking beyond ourselves, however, an orchard is also a gift for nature as it turns uniform grass into an ecosystem of many heights and colours.

Over these weeks, autumn transforms the world around us into flame reds, burnt ochres and translucent gold as leaves, cones and seeds scatter lightly to the floor or are windblown into hedges. The grass becomes a rustling, dying carpet as this brilliant season fades into the pale monochrome of winter. As the year and the light fades, this ripe time nevertheless explores some of the loveliest weeks of life in the gardens and woods.

Late flowers provide a final pitstop for the bees, and beekeeper Mike Withers has to judge how much longer he can take honey from them in order to ensure they have their own supply for the winter months. In early autumn, departing wild birds circle the tower of the Castle, from warblers to flycatchers, nightjars and swallows. They will all head south in the haze of an autumn evening.

Simon Andrews, Highclere's farm manager, and the farm team have been working long hours harvesting whenever the weather was in their favour and are now storing and loading up the crops which are ready to be sold, lorries arriving almost daily and leaving full to the brim.

Meanwhile, the huge red Harvest Moon hangs over us, sunset approaching ever earlier around the time of the autumn equinox. It seems bigger than the summer moon and, from thousands of miles away, reflects the ruddiness of the Earth's colours. September's Harvest Moon is followed by the Hunter's Moon in October and the so-called Snow Moon in November. Even with all the scientific explanations of the tilt of the Earth and particles in the air, it is the most romantic, mystical sight.

A touch of cold in the Autumn night –
I walked abroad,
And saw the ruddy moon lean over a hedge
Like a red-faced farmer ...
T.E. Hulme, 'Autumn', 1609

H A R V E S T

For everything there is a season,
and a time for every matter under heaven:
a time to be born, and a time to die;
a time to plant, and a time to pluck up what is planted.
Ecclesiastes, ch. 3, vv.1–2

FOR 800 YEARS the buildings and farms at Highclere were owned by the Bishops of Winchester, producing cattle and dairy products, goats, sheep and wool, corn, oats, hay, venison and rabbits, pigeons and peacocks, hens and eggs, fish, autumn fruits, honey, vegetables, herbs, cider and mead. In fact, in many ways, it was far more diverse than today's harvest.

Once we all lived directly off the land but nowadays, for many of us, it is courtesy of myriad intervening grocers, butchers, bakers, supermarkets and food-processing factories. However, walk through the brown-hued autumn fields, 'the stubble-plains with rosy hue', hear the rustling of leaves under your feet in a wood or glance round a groaning orchard, either in your imagination or in real life, and you understand where the produce actually comes from.

Autumn is not just about collecting in the harvest or the bounty from the orchards. It is also the season to forage from the pasture and woods, although Keats' 'mellow fruitfulness' needs the sharpness of later frosts to sweeten the sloes and hips in the hedgerows for winter use. This is all part of the food larder and, during the autumn, the major question has always been, and still is, how to store it.

Over the centuries Highclere has remained a living landscape engaged in the daily work of nurturing and collecting food from the land around us and it is a unique experience to live in an environment which has such a coherent and meaningful sense of place.

THE MEDIEVAL BARN

Bumpy grey tarmac and a collection of large sheds and spaces lie nestled in the lea of a hamlet three miles east of the Castle. The farmland around here is deeper and more productive than that of the high chalk downlands and, as with many farms, the machines and sheds are collected together in an incongruous mix of old and new. Nearby, over to the west, late lambs graze fields that once hosted medieval homes.

Diagonal ridges and bumps are all that remain of them, along with a dew pond in one corner field, but the ancient aged oak barn from that era has survived. Wedged within and surrounded by subsequent farm storage, it is obscured by the enormous brightly coloured machines that sit next to it. Tractors with wheels taller than I am and air-conditioned cabs with complicated consoles are parked alongside the lively yellow and green of the combine harvester. It has such wide wings that they have to be furled together just like a metal butterfly. Every machine is full of GPS algorithms, all tuned to be super-efficient in terms of both economics and nature conservation, plotting careful courses across fields to cause the least-possible damage.

Walk across the scuffed, much-used modern surfaces and you reach a tall entrance tucked back between grey sheds. The slatted, wood-framed opening is stained a drab off-black but inside is another world both in space and time. The structure of the barn feels more akin to that of a cathedral. The dendrology tests suggest it was built in about 1438 and the footprint has an unusual width as well as length. It's possible that the Bishops employed carpenters who were also working on jobs in Winchester Cathedral and in Oxford, which would account for this.

The principles and construction of the barn are certainly akin to a church. It has eight bays with great oak trusses which span the width. Each truss has a king post at either end and queen posts which link to the curved trusses thus creating the shape of an arch, whose compressive stress gives maximum strength and support to the building. High up in the roof every truss is notched as if ready for a purlin but they have been left unused, suggesting that the foreman and carpenters changed their minds and divided the top supports into thirds rather than halves to use two levels of purlin support. The result is a cathedral-like interior which maximises space. The oak timbers came from trees felled at Highclere, as would have the majority of any other materials needed.

This barn replaced a smaller one which had most likely already been there for many centuries, since this had always been the main post Roman area for farming enterprise at Highclere. In 1348, however, and then again in 1361, the English population was decimated by the Great Plague which swept through Europe. As with the entirety of Britain, whole villages around Highclere disappeared forever and, due to the resulting lack of manpower, some fields ceased arable production altogether. Very little building work took place at this time and it wasn't until the administration of Bishop William of Wykeham that any new investment was made in the lands and buildings of Highclere when fields were re-organised and new tenants found.

Just 50 years later, in the 1430s, a further crisis occurred with another outbreak of the plague and a series of hard winters. Wheat, barley and oats were scarce, prices steadily rose and efficient storage became quite literally the difference between life and death. Given that tenants remained hard to find, the then Bishop of Winchester, Cardinal Henry Beaufort, took back responsibility for the buildings and began again to carry out some investment in the land and buildings. His successor, Bishop Wayneflete, continued to take an interest in Highclere and completed the rebuilding of Manor Farm Barn.

Nearly 600 years later we are again restoring it, augmenting the trusses, leaving visible the structure, using oak as needed, though sadly not from the estate, and marvelling at our predecessors' skills and abilities. It is a masterpiece of carpentry which we only really began to appreciate when we restored one third of the building using just oak and the original techniques to join the great pieces of wood. It is still used for agricultural storage whilst nearby sheds continue to store the harvest from crops to haylage.

Despite the fact that the landowners were Catholic bishops, superstition and witchcraft remained widespread in the countryside. Drawn high on an oak beam guarding the entrance to the main transverse doorway is a witch's mark, a hexafoil (below). It would have been put there to protect inhabitants, visitors and, most importantly, the harvest stored within the barn, from all witches and evil spirits. The large opening across the middle bay of the barn would have provided enough space to allow horses to pull in a cart carrying the harvest and wait there whilst it was unloaded before walking on and leaving via the other side, which made it the ideal position for the mark.

Such protection symbols or 'apotropaic' marks have been found in many historic buildings, from medieval churches to private houses, as well as in barns. It is a daisy wheel, the theory being that the witch's eye will be transfixed following the endless wheels around and around, therefore rendering them incapable of casting spells. Curiously, the hexafoil design is not limited to witches' marks: it is incorporated within much Gothic architecture and is also used in cloisters and in the stained-glass windows of cathedrals such as Salisbury as well as many others in France and Germany.

To the north-east of the barn lies a field called Horse Meadow and at one time it must have been the centre of what used to be the village of Old Burghclere. Over the centuries, its use has not changed and our horses and sheep still graze the pasture. On the north side there is an extensive array of earthworks which are the remains of a medieval settlement of five crofts. Pottery fragments found in the flint rubble attest to the remains of homes whilst the ditches, ridges and flattened areas point to the farming activities. From the landscape records it is clear that, at one time, this part of Hampshire must have been heavily settled and farmed, which was why such a huge barn was required.

Harvest required co-operation, mutual reliance and good organisation through the local community each and every year.

The crops were similar to those produced today: wheat, barley, oats and pannage for the pigs. In addition, 'beremancorn' was also grown, which was a particular blend of barley wheat used in the medieval period for baking and brewing. Apples were collected for the cider presses; cheese was made from the dairy and eggs collected throughout the year.

Highclere had an additional contribution to the routine diet of the past: fish ponds. The engineering effort and expense to create these was considerable, but making several smaller fishponds rather than just one large one meant that each could be regularly maintained and cleaned out without disrupting availability. A seventeenth-century document refers to collecting rent for the Highclere Mill at Milford, seemingly placing the mill there along with a string of five fish ponds; old maps show two more ponds existed where the larger lake, Dunsmere, sits today, plus there was at least one pond at Redpools which lay more in the centre of today's park at Highclere.

In those times, the farm was measured in term of 'hides'. Unlike today, land measurement was linked to practical considerations: one hide was considered sufficient to feed a family, a furlong was the distance that could be ploughed by oxen before they needed to rest, and an acre was the amount of land that could be ploughed in one day. It was the latter consideration that gradually led to the development of longer arable strips so that fewer turns of the plough, always the challenging part, were needed. Taxation was levied on each hide, initially in the form of food and later on in money. In 1086, the Domesday Book recorded that there were seven and a half hides at Clere; in addition the priest Aluric 'holds of the Bishop a church with one hide'. However, the real difference to today is not so much in the measurement of land as in the style of ownership. As the ultimate owner, the Bishops of Winchester simply collected rents from their tenants whereas today we farm and manage the land ourselves.

Views of Dunsmere Lake, today and from the archives — always a wild and evocative place

Today, autumn remains one of the busiest periods in the farming calendar, though it requires far fewer people than in previous times. Following the harvest, the key preoccupation remains that of processing and storage followed by preparation of the soil for the next crop and its autumn planting. The word harvest is derived from the Anglo-Saxon word, *Haerfest*, which means autumn; in turn *haerfest-lic* means harvest-like, autumnal. Whilst the harvest is primarily gathered in over the summer, it is really in the autumn that we are storing, sorting, planning and offering thanks.

AUTUMN TASKS

Much of the world thinks they have considerably more certainty over food supplies than our ancestors had, but perhaps it should not be taken quite so much for granted. 'Farming looks mighty easy when your plough is a pencil and you're [sitting in an office] miles away from the corn field,' said General Eisenhower, 34th US president.

Highclere farms all of its own land, which allows a 'holistic' approach, integrating the needs of the crops with an appreciation of the land, nature and wildlife. Simon has been here for over twelve years and his experience and deep love of this part of Hampshire is apparent. Neither Geordie nor I usually drive the tractors or combines, as Simon and his team are far more skilled. One day, however, I did clamber up into the driving seat of the combine and lurched off along a track in the field. It was not something I advised Geordie of in advance but it did bring to mind The Wurzels' song from my childhood (it actually topped the charts!) which began 'I've got a brand new combine harvester and I'll give you the key ...'

Looking across the rolling earthen fields in the ochre autumn sunlight the very air smells different and the roughened bareness is interspersed only with the last tall yellow stacks of straw ready to be collected for use by the cattle or horse industry. The haylage is already wrapped and stored from earlier in the year. Making haylage for use in the autumn is something of an art. The sugars in each of the square haylage bales need to be just right and there is much anxiety about the precise pattern of weather for

optimal results. After it is cut, it is partly left to dry before being baled in the field, brought back and wrapped to seal out the oxygen. Once safely stacked in the yard, there is a collective sigh of relief all round.

By September the barley, wheat and oats are stored in sheds. The winter barley tends to be collected very soon after harvest and loaded into lorries. Meanwhile, the wheat is dried as necessary and stored whilst we wait for the results of the Hagberg tests, the protein tests and the weight per volume. All of these standards identify the dough-making quality of the harvest and whether the wheat can be sold for bread, which attracts a premium price. Otherwise, it will all go into the animal food economy: to feed cattle, chicken and pigs. The harvest depends on the weather, on considered and swift decisions from Simon and my husband, as well as prayers and a certain amount of crossed fingers.

The oats go through a completely different process. Much of Highclere's oats are sold into the performance horse world as an essential food of the highest quality. The dry oats are separated into large and average sizes, then put through a cyclone cleaning process to get rid of dust, before clipping and polishing. The spinning equipment takes off the outer sharper edges either end and, depending on the market, the grains are then either rolled or bruised before being put into bags. Next to the oats business are banks of solar panels which help power the process before the excess is returned to the national grid.

During autumn, Simon and his team also cultivate and prepare the ground for drilling for the following season. The Romans followed a simple field rotation plan of food, feed, then fallow, but at Highclere we follow a more extensive rotation between different arable crops, grass leys, grazing livestock and beans. Such combinations help to support increases in small mammals, pollinators and farmland birds. Turnips are sown into fields as winter feed for the sheep as they contribute up to 35 per cent of the soil's organic matter. This in turn contributes vital nutrients to spring-sown crops and supports organisms which make for a healthy soil. Where possible we avoid deep ploughing, as a minimal till leaves the soil less disturbed.

In the past we have sown oilseed rape (canola) but not at the moment as we can no longer protect the seed against a rather irritating periodic beetle attack. The Cabbage Stem Flea Beetle is a serious pest in brassica-type crops. Rapeseed has been a popular crop for bees due to its rich source of pollen and nectar. Instead, this year winter linseed has been added to the rotation, which might be used for animal feed or specialist oils as well as our usual winter wheat, barley and oats. In late October the tiny black linseeds are harvested with painstaking care from the fields between Beacon Hill and Manor Farm Barn. Linseed has the most beautiful blue flowers in summer but by now they are long gone. The seeds are a superfood: high in fibre, vitamins and minerals such as magnesium, zinc and iron, which has many benefits, including helping to support a healthy nervous and cardiovascular system. It is also fed as a supplement to animals, and at Highclere we have combined it with our oats to create a nutritious food for performance horses. On an entirely different tack, linseed oil is a traditional method of treating wood and so, in all of our restored ancillary buildings, where possible, we leave the ancient beams to play their part visibly within the architecture of the rooms, conserved once more with linseed oil. It is a key ingredient in more environmentally friendly paints which, in fact, last longer on wooden windows than more conventional ones, and it is also used in linoleum floor coverings.

Just as in past centuries farming practices evolved to suit the land, the weather and the demand, so does the farm today. It may be described as a science but it is also about culture in its broadest sense, about growing and the cycle of the seasons.

ORCHARDS

IF MANY CREATION STORIES begin in paradise and a garden, they often end in an orchard with an apple. The Roman writer Plutarch eulogised in 100AD: 'No other fruit unites the fine qualities of all fruits as does the apple. For one thing, its skin is so clean when you touch it that instead of staining the hands it perfumes them. Its taste is sweet and it is extremely delightful both to smell and to look at. Thus, by charming all our senses at once, it deserves the praise it receives.'

The Bishops' Rolls in Winchester are an extraordinary record of medieval life spanning 500 years from 1208. The manorial accounts include Highclere and depict the detail of life here from the crops to the weather and include the seemingly never-ending repairs which are still so much a part of our life here today.

As a result, we can trace the story of Highclere's walled gardens over a span of some 800 years. The earliest recorded fenced gardens at Highclere were built before 1200AD and were to the east of a collection of buildings which stood much where the Castle is today, whilst the first record of an orchard stems from 1218 when a new garden was constructed at Highclere and planted with 61 young fruit trees. Later there were better fences made, more trees planted or replaced and cabbages and leeks planted as well. Cider apples were grown there between 1246–47 and 1290–91, and again in 1320–21 and 1325–26 but, somewhat strangely, no fruit is recorded as being produced in 1300–01 and for most of the fourteenth century.

Productivity was essential in order to provide food for the dark, cold months of the year in a world without supermarkets and refrigeration, and by 1400 Highclere was considered a fine example of a medieval bishop's palace, with inner and outer courtyards, a chapel and hall, chambers and out-buildings, stables, a hay grange, orchards, gardens, an 'ashe' park, deer park, farms and barns. The courtyards, orchards and gardens lay across what are now the east lawns whilst the farm and barn stood to the north. Walls were likely to be built from flint, stone and a chalk and clay mix but fencing could be as basic as simple piles of brushwood.

Old documents suggest that by the late fourteenth century a covered colonnade led from what was now described as a medieval palace to the orchards and gardens. The inspiration for the symmetry and covered walk may well have been an unconscious tribute to traditional Roman gardens which were *hortus conclusus*, enclosed beautiful areas, although the height of the walls would have been more modest compared to later generations of walled gardens. The orchards themselves were designed in the shape of a cross and included a sheltered spot to grow herbs as well as the fruit trees.

Over the following century, the fortunes of Highclere fluctuated as it was increasingly tenanted out before eventually passing into secular hands with the dissolution of the monasteries. Records from this period are sparse, but in 1679 Sir Robert Sawyer, a successful lawyer, bought the estate with its farms, orchards and house for himself, his family and descendants who still possess and steward the estate today. The document (below) lists the farms, fields and rents, all of which would produce a good harvest not just in terms of arable crops but also in terms of the orchards and kitchen gardens.

Sir Robert Sawyer was described as 'a proper comley gentleman, inclining to the red; a good general scholar... inclined to be pedantic'. Reverend Isaac Milles, the Rector at Highclere, admired 'his principles and chearful Temper' whilst Samuel Pepys noted 'my old chamber fellow ... does very well in the world and is married and hath a child'. He was buried in 1692, in the church which he had rebuilt on top of the earlier one, and from what records he left it would seem he did make some distinctive changes to the park and gardens. Thus the formal ecclesiastical entertaining space of the medieval Highclere began to contract into a more traditional gentleman's residence. Today, the walls and quadrangle still remain but the original stone and flint walls are now taller than they once were. The lower parts of the walls are still irregularly ancient but they were increased in height by the 2nd Earl of Carnarvon, with additional courses of bricks and coping stones to make it all slightly grander. Old doorways were blocked up and new, more symmetrical ones created.

Robert Sawyer also began to remove the more functional elements of the gardens and to create the avenues and grandiose schemes which would be so dramatically extended by his grandson, Robert Sawyer Herbert. The large walled courts of orchards, vegetables and herb gardens listed amongst the sale particulars to the east of the site of the Castle were reduced and eventually demolished as succeeding generations increasingly focused on the aesthetics of gardens rather than their productive use. As a result, walking across the East Lawns today, there is a somewhat artificial flatness, although slight intriguing bumps and changes in grass quality still hint at the past.

A Particular of the Manors of Highclere and Burghclere in the County of South'ton

The mannor howse called Highcleer place howse very handsome & ye front double built with brick & coyned wth free stone built 1616 with a large Gatehouse & stables.

A fair garden containeing an Acre of ground & upwards & two kitchen gardens.

One great Orchard well planted wih good Apple peare & wardens upwards of fower acres.

One Lesser Orchard well planted wth summer apples & peares & quinces and One acre of meadow called the Ash Park adjoining to them.

One larg pigeon howse well stocked.   — *All valued at p ann. £40.*

The ffarms of Highcleere with the Down & Appertnances the ffarme howse in good repair with a brew howse & a howse to dry malt on a new built large barne tyled being 9 bayes of building and two double porches a carter's stable with severall other outhouses and other lesser barnes Let to a good Tennt.   — *Rent p ann. at £1181*

THE MONKS' GARDEN

HIDDEN BEHIND A SCREEN OF SHRUBS AND TREES, the south-facing flint and brick-walled garden from 1218 still survives, tucked away by the natural slope of the land. It still welcomes visitors but is now called, in respect to its heritage, 'the Monks' Garden'. However, the productive vegetable and fruit gardens which the monks had tended to for so long were relocated by the 2nd Earl's father into the huge new walled gardens designed by 'Capability' Brown in 1771, which lie to the north-west of the Castle, some distance from the house.

His daughter Harriet wrote in 1831, 'My father is looking remarkable well and in high spirits ... and will soon begin his Italian garden about which Emily (younger sister) was so anxious last summer.' Italian garden style is about order and balance, both borrowing from the surrounding landscape for maximum visual impact, but also creating lines of demarcation. As part of this restyling, the 2nd Earl created the nine arches in the western side of the wall enclosing the Monks' Garden which opened it up. He likely also introduced an amount of statuary (sadly no longer present) and created a fountain in the centre (also long gone) with the yew tunnels planted as an axis.

As each successor added in his changes, gradually this walled garden became the more ornamental garden it is today, merely alluding to its fruitful history in the crab apples growing against the walls, fig trees nestling in the warm, mellow brick corners, a mulberry and quince taking centre stage and lavender growing around the walls. It remains a 'hortus conclusus', an enclosed beautiful area framed by flint and stone and brick walls, imperfect coping stones and tendrils of plants growing out of blown lime mortar. Foundations and walls built up in layers, it is a garden of time.

FIGS AND OTHER FRUITS

Fig trees (*Ficus*) come in a huge variety of perhaps more than 750 different types but our climate is somewhat borderline in terms of the sun they require. Hence the most consistent crop is found in a now ancient fig tree nestled in each corner of the south-facing walls by the Orangery where warmth accumulates on a summer's afternoon. The delicious fruits are irresistible and hard to pick without just eating them. It was under a fig tree in the sixth century BC that Prince Siddhartha sat and meditated. He received enlightenment and was thereafter called Buddha, but I doubt those who planted the trees realised this.

Meanwhile, the native British crab apple *Malus sylvestris* – forest apple – is the ancestor of all our cultivated apples. The long-lasting scented flowers appear before the hawthorn in the spring and up to 90 types of insects are known to congregate around the boughs. Above all, bees love the nectar held within the white petals with golden stamens as they produce up to ten times as much pollen as standard apple trees. As crab apples age, they become more gnarled and bent and by autumn, when the oval leaves turn

yellow, the lichen-dressed branches with spiky twists become more apparent. They produce colourful fruits which often last into winter and it is well worth while, if a little fiddly, to make crab apple jelly. Birds such as thrushes rely on their fruit, although they seem to leave them until last. If they blow over, they can regenerate and sprout again and their year-round interest and compact size makes them a useful garden tree, for example *Malus* 'Gorgeous', 'Everest' or 'Jelly King'.

The medlar trees grow along the eastern wall and have the benefit of being both disease- and pest-resistant, plus you can collect the fruits long after other fruit trees have finished. They need two frosts, the key to the fragrance and taste, before the fruit is ready, which makes a delicious ruby red jelly. Pear trees are espaliered behind the garden sheds and bothies on the south-facing wall and mellow the stones and bricks as well as offering fruit which tastes perfumed and juicy, entirely different to shop-bought offerings.

Not far from this original medieval orchard, we have planted more fruit trees: an apple, pear and quince among others, around the Walnut Walk in the Wood of Goodwill. A small orchard does best with five different trees and wildflowers and herbs underneath to attract the pollinators. Each tree has its own space, and is mulched and wood chipped around the stem of the tree to draw back the competition. Really anyone can plant an apple tree, and the spring blossom and the autumn fruit harvest contribute to every garden. Evenly spaced mulberry trees stand in the centre of the lawns and their fruit makes a delicious jam (see page 233).

Visiting today, the Monks' Garden retains its sense of antiquity and harmony but also gives a sense of well-being through the scent and colour of various flower beds: 'Happiness is to hold flowers in both hands.' And, to quote Lady Bird Johnson, 'Where flowers bloom, so does hope.'

Spring begins with the pale abundance of the *Clematis armandii* covering the wall to the left of the main entrance. Then, where once there were vegetables, there are scented roses, both climbing and shrub – 'Albéric Barbier', 'Gertrude Jekyll', 'Blairii No.2', as well as *rugosas* and *Rosa* 'Red Coat'. Around them are pink and white penstemon, which flower through much of the summer whilst blue agapanthus offer height later. Echoing the colour of the agapanthus, a mixture of *Geranium* 'Johnson's Blue' and froths of *Alchemilla mollis* cover the soil, and we have planted more clematis and the peach sorbet rose 'Compassion' on the side of the arched views back up towards the Castle.

Within the Monks' Garden the 4th Earl of Carnarvon built a Peach House with a series of bothies behind it, in front of which is a long, narrow bed planted anew for texture and colour. Along the length are *Euphorbia palustris* with its lime-green heads, and *polychroma*, again lime green but the flower has a more strongly defined sepal. At either end are yuccas and then along the bed are clumps of Russian sage, *Cirsium atropurpureum* (deep-red plume thistle) and bronze fennel. Tall blue delphiniums, deep red lobelias and late dahlias such as the 'Bishop of Llandaff' with its deep chocolate-coloured foliage and strawberry red blooms provide bursts of colour later on in the season. Deep-blue salvias ('Amistad') never fail and astrantia (such as 'Claret' and 'Bess Ross') give pops of colour at the front of the border.

The earlier fountain has long since been filled in and its footprint planted with *Rosa bonica* whilst the west and east walls are planted with lavender, thus offering both symmetry and a nod to the part that herbs played in medieval treatments for ailments.

Interest in walled gardens declined following the First World War but they have once more made a comeback – albeit often in a number of different guises. Of course, there is always a deep pleasure in growing and picking fruit and vegetables, but orchards have fared better, not least perhaps because their advantage is that once a tree is established, it provides fruit year after year for decades, requiring little other input except pruning (once a year).

If you are thinking of planting an orchard then deciding which trees to plant is the most important decision. Consider what fruit you enjoy and what it is hard to buy. A mulberry has delicious fruit and astonishing blossom whilst a Victoria plum is tough and the fruit tastes so much better than the ones you can buy. Two apple trees (check they are pollination compatible) should be included for all the advantages listed above, and perhaps a medlar. Plan where you will put them and mark the ground with sticks to think about the view. When you first plant the trees, clear a space around each one to allow it to establish itself without competition. Later on, plant flowers around each tree to attract pollinators, as well as being even more pleasurable for you to look at.

A NEW WALLED GARDEN

WALK DOWN THE HILL FROM THE CASTLE in the direction of Highclere Village for about half a mile, passing by a few traditional brick-built cottages and, settled behind high mellowed walls, turn past what used to be the parking place for a hayrick and into a partially walled entrance yard. An unassuming, faded, rain-washed, blue wooden door stands in the corner. Push it open, cross over the lintel and it is another enchanted world.

For much of my time at Highclere this has been an overgrown, abandoned yet magical space, sloping south-west with the promise of adventure, secret paths and treasure. Once it would have been a hive of ordered seasonal hard work, a place of endeavour and abundant productivity from the time it was first built all the way up to the end of the Second World War. It is such a size that it is obvious it was built a long time ago in a period of confidence, power and personal ambition.

Covering well over four acres it is, in historical terms, a relatively recent walled garden, dating from 1771 according to the inscription on a lintel and as drawn in Capability Brown's plan. This was Highclere's 'supermarket', making localism very precise and providing abundant produce for the large house, owners and staff throughout the year.

At the end of the eighteenth century, the 1st Earl of Carnarvon commissioned Capability Brown to help him create an outstanding parkland, a world apart to impress friends and neighbours as well as highlight the topography around the house for his own pleasure and enjoyment. The essential components were swiftly added, sweeping vistas with careful

planting, a lake, a kitchen garden and all the modern elegance and commanding approach to the landscape that Brown could bring.

A new and grander walled garden was called for and an area away from the house was created to provide a truly productive garden that was also a feast for the eyes, a *ferme ornée*. The walls were higher and longer than around the original walled garden, the yard for the dairy herd was built next door, pigs kept nearby and all designed so that the busy activity of the gardeners would not disturb the family and guests. Situated on sloping ground, it had in and out water from the start. Its large size reflected the fortunes of the family and a visit to the garden was a required outing for all guests.

The walls were constructed from brick that absorbed the day's heat whilst nails driven into the lime mortar hosted a firm framework of wires which held the espaliered trees. Bricks were an expensive material to use as they were both taxed and handmade (mass production only began in the reign of Queen Victoria, some 50 years later), so they too were a symbol of wealth.

Glass houses on the south-facing walls enabled exotic fruits to be offered at dinners and these were supplemented by a series of greenhouses behind the garden where pineapples and melons were grown. The lower part of the garden where there was a natural spring became the orchard, whilst the more northerly side was used for potatoes. The garden slopes downwards offering natural shelter from the north and east winds, but an additional shelter belt was planted to the south and east as that is the direction from which the prevailing winds at Highclere come.

In its heyday, the walled garden employed a veritable army of gardeners led in the late nineteenth century by the bearded head gardener Mr Pope, who was succeeded in 1908 by Mr Blake. Neat beds jostled with fruit cages whilst cordoned trees stood guard over lettuces and brassicas. Crop rotations were rigidly followed (essential for a successful vegetable garden) and planting was staggered to provide a long productive period.

Early each morning one of the gardening team would be found standing outside the kitchens waiting to tell the cook what was looking promising and to collect a list of the vegetables and fruits required for luncheon or dinner. Cap in hand there was always the hope of a freshly baked biscuit or cake whilst they waited before making their way swiftly back to pass on the list.

Whilst Highclere was at this point in time a home and not a business, it still required precise communication and organisation. Just as they do now, the gardeners had a number of pests and mites to contend with, one of them being birds, in particular crows, so scarecrows were dotted round the beds,

As more food started to be imported during the 1920s, and labour became scarcer, the number of gardeners declined. The walled garden became something of a luxury and there was neither the need for such a huge area nor the finances to maintain it.

By the outbreak of the Second World War, towards 90 per cent of the UK's basic ingredients were imported and vegetable and fruit gardens were on the decline. There was a resurgence between 1939 and 1945, following the Government's 'Dig for Victory' campaign. 'Land girls' arrived to help in the gardens and on the farm at Highclere but, once the war and rationing were over, this again declined.

In the walled garden at Highclere nature gradually took over, the buildings becoming ever more dilapidated with self-seeded buddleia and other plants, even trees, growing out of the walls. Saplings and scrub bushes took over the once neat beds and, since it was no longer financially possible to keep a dairy herd at Highclere, nor any pigs, their old yards slowly declined as well. It became an abandoned scene and, as in previous centuries, old walls and buildings were taken down and redeployed elsewhere.

In the meantime, the original walled medieval garden close to the Castle remained productive with working glass houses, useful ancillary storage sheds and a mushroom house, although it too gradually changed focus to become a cutting garden, and a space for recreation. Whilst the orangery continues on a small scale to produce oranges and lemons for the Castle, most of the greenhouses there are now used to grow flowers and indoor plants with which to decorate the Castle rooms.

In the last ten years or so, though, life has returned gradually to the big walled garden. First to move in were our chickens, happily living amongst the remains of greenhouses. Visits every day led first to the doors and gates being mended and then some of the coping stones and lime mortar in the walls alongside the chickens. Nettles were strimmed, broken glass cleared out and fallen trees cut up and taken away.

In the centre of the wall at the bottom of the sloping land lies a frost gate which has now been reinstated anew, with our initials woven into the wrought ironwork. It now opens into what once was Mr Pope's prized orchard. There is always such delight in rediscovering the old fruit trees dripping with

made from old clothes and sacking. Considered to be one of the most intelligent birds, these opportunistic creatures live in large groups and there is an oft-repeated anecdote that they are bright enough to count to four or five, use basic tools and both hide and store food. In medieval times, crows were thought to live abnormally long lives. They were also thought to be monogamous, able to predict the future, to predict rain and reveal ambushes, though I doubt the gardeners who work here today would agree with that useful assessment.

Just behind the walled garden is a further smaller walled garden crested by a long, low row of brick buildings, the western part of a rectangle completed by the further walls of a collapsed greenhouse. These used to be melon houses, whilst the brick buildings with slatted shelves were used to store roots and fruits. It is the late apple varieties that store best and each apple was carefully wrapped in old newspaper before storing in the cool.

By the Victorian era, the British had developed some of the finest walled gardens in the world, and with advances in science and technology, could introduce and grow rare species of flowers and plants collected from around the world. As a result, the position of Head Gardener was very important.

William Pope was Head Gardener at Highclere for 25 years (1882-1908) and by the end he had 100 staff working for him. He lived in a rose-covered cottage in the centre of the park with his wife Maria and their ten children who survived childhood. Highly regarded, he was a fellow of the Royal Horticultural Society as well as a member of the Fruit and Vegetable Committee of the same society. He exhibited all around the country and, both of them being keenly competitive, Lord Carnarvon would hire a train to transport all the produce, with the return journey bringing in a large number of trophies. He was an excellent fruit grower, showing 30 varieties of apple, and after he retired, he became a judge at many shows.

At the outbreak of the First World War, Lord Carnarvon lobbied to keep the gardeners on an exempt list so that the walled garden could keep going: it was the source of food for the wounded soldiers in the Highclere Hospital which had been set up in the Castle by his wife Almina. In addition, he had bought quantities of tea and cheese for all at Highclere to ensure they could be reassured by their favourite drink and thinking that the cheese would store well.

Sadly, some of Highclere's gardeners did go to war. Cecil Pope, William's sixth child, died in 1916 and the Roll of Honour testifies that too many Highclere families lost their beloved sons in the hot sun-stroked battles of Mesopotamia (modern-day Iraq) as well as other fields of battle.

Painstaking garden accounts kept by William Pope, Highclere's pre-war Head Gardener

deeply coloured fruits and this hidden gem is an irresistible draw during autumn. Guests to Highclere such as Benjamin Disraeli might describe 'ripe pears and famous pippins ... and plums of every shape and hue'. We have introduced British Lop pigs to find sheltered places in which to rotavate the ground, in between lying down on top of each other and snuffling out food, and, over time, we can begin to see what we have found.

A century ago, more than 200 varieties of fruit could be found growing in a single orchard and each village would have had their unique varieties of plums, damsons, cherries and apples. However, half of Britain's pear orchards and two-thirds of Britain's apple orchards have disappeared since 1970. There are 2,300 known varieties of apple but it is the Cox and the Bramley which dominate Britain's orchards these days.

Meanwhile, we have moved on to the garden itself. Simon and the farm team have used a small tractor to harrow the ground, rubbish and detritus have been removed and the old paths and quadrants from 1771 have gradually been revealed, complete with a water pipe running through the middle. Today's world, however, is far removed from the vanity projects or productive imperatives of the past and we needed to wait for the right idea to germinate in order to decide how to best use this space whilst in the meantime quietly clearing the walls and turning the soil.

PLANTING A FUTURE

HIGHCLERE CAN BE UNDERSTOOD not just through layers of history but also geology. Sitting and sharing a glass of champagne with our friends and suppliers of special vintage Champagne, the Joseph Perrier family, we began to wonder if the geological strata which runs from Champagne, under the English Channel and emerges here in chalk soils and clay caps, with rugged flints, could become a vineyard if it had a large walled garden to help retain the heat of the sun and ripen the grapes.

It has taken the last four years to test the soil, consider the temperatures and consult an expert. As a result, Chardonnay grapes are planted in the top two quadrants and pinot noir in the lower two. Hopefully, we will be able to pick and make a small quantity of our own wine in years to come, with a balance of minerals, crispness and sweet grapes to create a special glass of sparkling wine - or champagne as Joseph Perrier might call it, although we will not be allowed to do so, being quite some distance from the actual region of Champagne in France.

Like any farming activity there is permanent worry about the weather, late frosts (we have purchased a machine which should blow hot air around if the temperature drops), pruning and, like any garden, weeding.

Chickens, pigs, a new vineyard and a revitalised orchard are the first steps in what we hope will be a new life within these walls. Capability Brown's principle of design was to make a thing of beauty out of a productive farm and vegetable garden. With perseverance this beautiful walled space has a role once more. I always loved Frances Hodgson Burnett's book *The Secret Garden* and the magic of that hidden space: 'It was the sweetest, most mysterious-looking place anyone could imagine', and I'm hoping that we are creating just such a different magical world here.

An Autumn Picnic

Field Mushroom, Roast Vegetable and Gruyère Quiche

Geordie enjoys going for a morning run and during early autumn often reappears with his breakfast – field mushrooms collected en route. They seem to literally emerge overnight and are a perfect breakfast ingredient, or of course work beautifully in a quiche partnered with cheese.

INGREDIENTS

For the pastry

175g (6oz) cold butter, cubed
225g (8oz) plain flour,
   plus extra for dusting
1 egg, beaten

For the filling

2 onions, quartered, then each
   quarter halved lengthways
200g (7oz) baby courgettes
   (zucchini), halved lengthways
1 small aubergine (eggplant),
   cut into small chunks
1–2 tbsp olive oil
125g (4½oz) field mushrooms, sliced
300ml (10fl oz) double cream
4 eggs
180g (6oz) Gruyère cheese, grated
Salt and freshly ground
   black pepper

PREPARATION TIME 30 mins, plus 20 mins chilling
COOKING TIME 1½ hours   SERVES 8 generously

First make the pastry ...

Rub the butter and the flour together to form breadcrumbs. Add the egg and 1 tablespoon of cold water and mix.

On a lightly floured surface, roll the pastry out into a big enough circle to line a 27cm (10 inch) diameter quiche tin, leaving a generous edge to allow for shrinkage during baking. Prick the base and chill in the fridge for 20 minutes.

Preheat the oven to 180°C/350°F/Gas mark 4.

Line the pastry case with baking paper and fill with baking beans. Bake for 10 minutes. Remove the beans and paper and bake for another 10–15 minutes. Set aside to cool.

Meanwhile roast the vegetables ...

Raise the oven temperature to 200°C/400°F/Gas mark 6.

Put the onions, courgettes and aubergine (zucchini and eggplant) on a baking tray, drizzle with olive oil, season and roast in the oven, turning occasionally, for 30–40 minutes, or until tender and golden brown.

Remove from the oven and reduce the temperature to 180°C/350°F/ Gas mark 4.

Place the mushrooms in a heavy-bottomed frying pan, add a flash of oil and some seasoning and gently cook for 3–4 minutes. Remove and place on some kitchen paper to soak up the excess oil.

Whisk together the cream, eggs and half the cheese and season well.

Now assemble the quiche. Sprinkle the remaining cheese onto the base of the pastry case, spoon in the roast vegetables and the mushrooms so that they are evenly distributed then pour over the cream mixture.

Bake for 25–35 minutes or until the filling is set and golden-brown on top. Leave to cool slightly before removing from the tin. Serve warm.

WOODS AND GARDENS

IF WE ARE DEDICATED TO GATHERING AND COLLECTING through the autumn months, in contrast, the woods, the shrubs and flowers are scattering and throwing their seeds into the winds. The results are spectacular.

'I came from Burghclere,' writes Cobbett in his *Rural Rides* (c. 1830): '... on an early November morning, through Lord Carnarvon's park. The oaks are still covered, the beeches in their best dress, the elms yet pretty green, and the beautiful ashes only beginning to turn off. This is, according to my fancy, the prettiest park that I have ever seen: a great variety of hill and dell a good deal of water. I like this place better than Fonthill, Blenheim, Stone, or any other gentleman's grounds that I have seen. The trees are very good.'

William Cobbett does not enthuse over all the trees but does mention the beech: 'A part of these downs is covered with trees, chiefly beech, the colour of which, at this season, forms a most beautiful contrast with that of the down itself, which is so green and so smooth.'

Sadly, thanks to the terrible bouts of tree disease that have afflicted the English countryside during the last 30 years, Highclere has lost all of the elm and most of the ash that was so admired 200 years ago. The beech thankfully remains and is continually replanted on a regular basis to make sure it survives long into the future.

A beech avenue traverses the Wood of Goodwill and on its western side the planting is dedicated to autumn colours which make the most of the season's afternoon and evening sunlight, fingering the silver grasses and setting lights through nature's rich paintbox. The older beech trees offer natural seats on their twisted high roots whilst the dogs love to drink from puddles between them. Beech trees are not as long-lived as other species but when the canopy first opens in spring, with tendrils of light filtering through the leaves, or when as now they contribute to the glory of the

Beeches of many kinds provide the most dramatic turns of autumn colour all over the Estate

painted autumn landscape, they take one's breath away. They are gregarious trees, growing best planted in groups, relying on their mycorrhizal fungi to create partnerships and anticipate natural challenges.

In some ways this is the time of year that nature issues its final invitation to us all to walk and admire. The planting here is relatively recent, as is the reinstatement of this whole part of Highclere's gardens, and the scale and planning of shapes, textures and colours sometimes feels overwhelming. At first, Geordie and I just stood wondering and then we began.

Some years ago, in autumn, I was walking around the gardens at Milford Lake with my father-in-law. I still remember the beauty of a clearing of *Parrotia persica* and thus, a few years after his death, I began with a group of five of these ('Horizontalis') and, despite the fact that they lack appreciation for the soil here, they have developed and are a lovely reminder of my walk. They lie just to the side of the beech where they have air and space to stretch out.

Around them are a *Liquidambar styraciflua*, a sorbus, an *Acer cappadocicum* 'Rubrum' and *aureum* and an *Acer davidii*, all flanked by groups of smoke bushes (*Cotinus*). A path is fringed by *Euonymus europeaus* 'Cascade', cotoneasters, *Rhus typhina* (which has the softest grey stems and vibrant colours), autumn viburnums for dark green contrast, *Nyssa sinensis*, pale grasses, *Cornus kousa* and a burning bush (*Euonymus alatus*), whilst, scattered around, beds of rose- and red-coloured hydrangeas ranging from 'Wims Red' to 'Eugen Hahn' and 'Julisa' mix with crocosmia along with some of my favourite geraniums, 'Johnson's Blue', creeping underneath.

Glancing across up to the Castle, the Wildflower Meadow has turned to shades of disintegrating russet and browns and, in a few weeks, Simon will organise for the meadow to be brush harvested and will then package the seeds for sale. In the meantime, insects of all sorts are busily collecting what foods they can.

> ... Decidedly, in our opinion, there is no place in England where so much dignity of character, so much elegant variety, and so much cultivated beauty, is preserved throughout a place of such great extent ... against the natural beauty of the grounds, and the judicious disposition of the woods, groups, and scattered trees. We know no place in which the trees are as well disposed over so great an extent of surface ... We noticed *Diospyros virginiana*, *Nyssa aquatica*, *Negundo fraxinifolia*; *Liquidambar*, both species; *Dirca palustris*, 3 ft. high, with a stem 6 in. in diameter; *Rubus nutkanus*, which has the habit of the Virginian raspberry, and bears an eatable fruit, resembling the cloud-berry.
>
> John Claudius Loudon

EYECATCHERS SCATTERED THROUGH THE WOOD OF GOODWILL echo the late borders within the Secret Garden. Flourishes of asters, Michaelmas daisies, fuchsias, crocosmia and schizostylis wander between the borders and the woodland areas. The orange colours contribute a vibrancy and energy as well as warmth, whilst the blue is much liked by late bees. It is in the late afternoons, when the days are imperceptibly shortening into the low-level ochre haze of autumn evenings, which is the best time to walk here. The air feels saturated with an inexpressible transience and even now, in the infancy of its creation, this corner reflects a mood, a scent and colour.

The idea of walks and arboretums is not new. In Victorian times, the man most responsible for this craze among the upper classes was a Victorian Scottish writer and landscape designer, John Claudius Loudon. He was a prolific writer on horticultural design and communicated many of his ideas through his own *The Gardener's Magazine* which he started in 1826. In particular, he liked the idea of arboretums as public places. A man of strong opinions and criticisms, Loudon nevertheless wrote glowingly of Highclere.

However, showcasing autumn in a relaxing, tranquil environment is only one facet of the season. It is also a time of increasingly intemperate weather and cold winds. Outside the UK, autumn and fall become interchangeable descriptions of the season. The term 'fall' is probably a deviation from the Old English words *fiaell* and *feallan*, both of which mean to fall from a height. A theory goes that by the 1500s, some English began describing the seasons separating summer and winter as either 'spring of the leaf' or 'fall of the leaf'

(spring and fall in short) and that this was exported to the new world with the colonists. Back in England, spring remained but autumn, from the Latin *autumnus*, took over as the standard description of this time of year. Another theory is that the falling leaves and worsening weather references the fall from grace in the Garden of Eden, a reminder of the temporary nature and fragility of life.

Over these few weeks, the deciduous trees will take in and absorb all the sunshine they can before they seal off the end of their twigs from the leaves. This is essentially a survival mechanism to ensure there is less expanse of canopy to catch the winter storms which might otherwise bring them down. Some also use this time of year to create tiny buds, which otherwise uses a lot of energy when their resources are most impoverished following the winter months. Likewise, small mammals spend their time collecting nuts and provisions, preparing to hibernate, birds fatten up on available seeds and berries and, of course, we are all also out foraging ...

FORAGING

Ye elves of hills, brooks, standing lakes and groves,
And ye that on the sands with printless foot
Do chase the ebbing Neptune and do fly him
When he comes back; you demi-puppets that
By moonshine do the green sour ringlets make,
Whereof the ewe not bites, and you whose pastime
Is to make midnight mushrooms ...
William Shakespeare, *The Tempest*

LOOKING FOR WHAT CAN BE PICKED 'FOR FREE', straight from nature's bounty, somehow makes one far more observant and every walk a little different. The generosity of nature and its harvest at this time of year extends from fields to woods, trees and hedges.

On the lawns around the Castle a number of large old tree stumps are slowly subsiding into the earth. They provide a wealth of sustenance for a subterranean world we cannot see as they slowly disintegrate over decades, and childhood walks were filled with imaginative stories of the fairies who lived in such mounds and roots. British fairies are tiny whimsical creatures who can be quite mischievous and tend to live for a long time as you never really hear that they die. They live in an enchanted land near ours (but not ours) and you must not interfere with them or you will be subject to their pranks.

It is in the autumn that fairy rings magically appear in the fields, marked either by darker grass or by mushrooms and fungi. It was thought that this was where the fairies would dance and that they were a gateway to their world which was only visible at a certain time. You must never step inside one and only walk round one in a clockwise direction. Neither should any animal graze inside the ring.

Mushrooms and fungi are part of a different world, using the soil and all that is below to grow and survive. They require none of the sunlight and chlorophyll which is needed by most plants but are an essential ecosystem for animals, plants, trees and soil.

We buy and cook chestnut mushrooms which taste woody like the tree of the same name, large field mushrooms tasting of the earth and porcinis and oyster mushrooms growing upwards in a delicate fan. The best recipe is often the simplest: tossed in a large frying pan with herbs, butter and some crushed garlic and allowed to cook in their own juices.

Mushroom houses were first built in the early nineteenth century. French gardeners used large underground quarries and caverns with great success, whilst the English gardener Oldacre, who learnt his skills from earlier German success, pioneered them in England. Within a short time, no kitchen garden was complete without a mushroom house and they had huge advantages, as when they worked well, the produce was available for most of the year. They could be grilled, baked, served with a gratin, made into a soup, added to stews, eaten at breakfast or for supper – the list is endless. Strangely, they are a good source of vitamin D, which is essential for us when we lack sunshine yet they themselves grow without it.

The 4th Earl of Carnarvon noted in his dairies that he was restoring the mushroom house just before Lord Salisbury and Benjamin Disraeli came to stay in 1866. In fact, they needed regular repair as the intensity of the heated dung in which the mushrooms were grown rotted the wooded slats onto which it was compressed as a growing platform.

AUTUMN PROJECTS IN THE GARDEN

FROM SEPTEMBER TO NOVEMBER vegetable gardens tend to over-produce, so that you will need friends, either to eat with or to share the crop. Yellow-flowered courgettes (zucchini) become almost wantonly abundant but you may well have cabbages, cauliflowers, potatoes, chard, spinach, runner beans, pumpkins, parsnips, carrots, leeks, celeriac and Brussels sprouts. In previous generations a successful autumn harvest used to be the difference between life and death but it is far less dramatic for most of us now.

OCTOBER JOBS

· Plant daffodils.
· Overhaul any borders which you may wish to change.
· Spread muck over some of the vegetable beds.

NOVEMBER JOBS

These are the months where many of the jobs are really about protection: from the cold and from the winds. It is best to choose days which are neither rainy nor windy to clamber up ladders or plant out. In the words of Winnie the Pooh: 'No one can tell me, Nobody knows, Where the wind comes from, Where the wind goes.'

· Plant tulip bulbs in pots and borders, covering them with at least twice their depth of soil or compost. If you have problems with squirrels, cover the area with chicken wire that is staked down so that they cannot dig the bulbs up.
· Lift dahlia tubers after the first frost, clean them off and store in dry compost in a cool, frost-proof place.

- Clear faded sweet peas, morning glory, thunbergia and other annual climbers from their supports.
- Cut down old perennials that are looking tatty, then mulch the surrounding soil with garden compost.
- Look after garden wildlife as winter approaches by providing additional food and shelter.
- Prune apple and pear trees once all the leaves are fallen.
- Trim the top third of buddleias against wind damage.

COMPOSTING

In the past very little was ever wasted. The horse manure and straw were used for the mushroom house whilst compost heaps turned all the kitchen and garden waste into a dark crumbly compost used to improve the soil in the gardens. The compost heaps are still valuable today and not at all difficult to set up. Find a warm sheltered spot and remove all the weeds or brambles from the area. Either line the areas with slatted wood or just start to pile it up. The secret is to vary the materials – peelings, weeds, spent compost, cut-down stinging nettles, grass cuttings, tea leaves and bits of carboard are all good to add. Avoid anything cooked and anything non-vegetable. Water it in dry weather and turn it over from time to time and do cover with cardboard or old carpet, which keeps the heat in and encourages the microbes which will break down all the materials into a lovely crumbly compost.

NOSTALGIA

AUTUMN EVENINGS DIMINISH as the darkness occupies ever more of each day. Every outside job, from feeding animals to working in the garden, is pulled forward. The curling smoke from an autumn fire is a favourite scent, whether a bonfire behind the gardens or from a fireplace in the Saloon. It speaks of the essence of warmth and cooking.

On the whole, autumn is a nostalgic and contemplative time of year. Traditionally it is a time to say thank you, whether in harvest festivals or thanksgiving, to reap the rewards of the complex landscape around us and to admire the richness of the myriad small details of nature, of antiquity, of history and wildlife which start to be laid bare around us.

> Rustling through a wood or rather rushing, while the wind
> Halloos in the oak-top like thunder;
> The rustle of birds' wings startled from their nests or flying
> Unseen into the bushes
> John Clare, 'Pleasant Sounds'

By the end of autumn all the glinting, twirling leaves have danced away, tiny mammals are tucked up and we are ready to eat stews and hearty puddings, to sit by the fire with a cup of tea and tell stories of what happens when things go bump in the night. ◗

AUTUMN COOKING

THE SENSE OF CHANGE PERMEATING THE AUTUMNAL AIR PROPELS GEORDIE AND I to search the hedges for blackberries, inspect the apple and damson trees and to walk the fields looking for mushrooms. Autumn fruits are very abundant and yet there is a sense of urgency to judge the ripeness and not miss out. It is about cooking, preserving and storing. This time of year offers such a visual feast of colour and taste, and all these fresh seasonal foods are packed with the vitamins and minerals that help sustain us as the year progresses towards winter. Try beginning the day with homemade Bircher Muesli which, properly made, offers such a wealth of goodness.

Bircher Muesli

Maximilian Bircher-Benner was born in 1867 in Switzerland where he studied medicine. Following his own ill health, however, he experimented with the health effects that raw foods have on the body and from this he created muesli, a dish based on raw oats, fruits and nuts. Later, at his own Zürich sanatorium, his patients followed an ascetic schedule including physical training and gardening, eating muesli, mostly raw vegetables, cold showers and some sun.

His muesli recipe called for lots of fresh apple with a small amount of oats, lemon juice, nuts, cream and honey. He served it to his patients as a healthy appetiser before most meals.

INGREDIENTS

2 eating apples, coarsely grated
100g (3½oz) jumbo porridge oats
50g (2oz) mixed seeds
  (such as sunflower, pumpkin,
  sesame and linseed)
50g (2oz) mixed nuts
  (such as almonds, hazelnuts,
  pecans and walnuts),
  roughly chopped
½ tsp ground cinnamon
200g (7oz) live yoghurt
1 tbsp lemon juice
50g (2oz) sultanas or raisins

PREPARATION TIME 5 mins, plus overnight chilling **SERVES** 4

Put the grated apple in a bowl and add the oats, seeds, nuts and the cinnamon. Toss together well.

Stir in the yoghurt and 100ml (3½fl oz) cold water, cover and chill for several hours or overnight.

Before you tip some into your bowl, add the lemon juice and sultanas or raisins. Top with extra apple, nuts, berries or whatever takes your fancy.

Celery, Grape and Walnut Salad

This is really a Waldorf salad but it is a wonderful way of using up the little green grapes we grow here at the Castle which are sometimes just a bit too tart to eat on their own as fruit.

INGREDIENTS

2 celery sticks, sliced diagonally
2 apples, cored and sliced
  into wedges
200g (7oz) grapes, halved
100g (3½oz) walnut halves
100g (3½oz) of your preferred
  blue cheese
175g (6oz) rocket leaves
275g (9½oz) endive, roughly torn

For the dressing

150g (5oz) natural yoghurt
3 tbsp lemon juice
1½ tbsp Dijon mustard
Salt and freshly ground
  black pepper

PREPARATION TIME 15 mins   **SERVES** 6–8

First make the dressing: simply mix all the ingredients together and season to taste.

Toss all the salad ingredients with the half the dressing in a large bowl, and put the remainder in a jug for people to help themselves to.

Sorrel Soup

Sorrel leaves are generally large, bright-green and arrow-shaped with a smooth, crisp texture. It is slightly bitter with a lemony flavour and probably shouldn't be eaten in large quantities as it contains a high amount of oxalic acid. It is, however, absolutely delicious in a soup.

PREPARATION TIME 10 mins   **COOKING TIME** 30 mins   **SERVES** 4

INGREDIENTS

4 tbsp unsalted butter
75g (3oz) shallots, finely chopped
900g (2lb) sorrel, chopped
3 tbsp plain flour
1 litre (35fl oz) hot stock
2 egg yolks
75ml (3oz) double cream
Salt and freshly ground
   black pepper

Melt 3 tablespoons of butter in a heavy-based pan. Soften the shallots for two or three minutes until translucent.

Add the sorrel leaves to the shallots and stir well. Cover the pan and cook on a low heat for 10 minutes. Stir occasionally. Add the flour and cook for a further 3 minutes.

Add the hot stock to the sorrel, stirring constantly to remove any lumps. Bring to a simmer for 2–3 minutes. Remove from the heat.

Whisk together the egg yolks and cream in a heatproof bowl. Add a spoonful of the hot soup to the cream mixture and whisk. Repeat this three more times. This prevents the egg mix from curdling when it is added to the hot soup.

Pour the hot egg-cream-soup mixture into the soup, whisking continuously. Add the final tablespoon of butter and cook on a very low heat for a further 5 minutes. Do not allow to boil. Serve at once.

Oysters

Traditionally you are supposed to eat oysters and other native British seafood when there is an R in the month, which allows them to focus on reproducing in the summer.

As with mussels, avoid any that are open or have a strong smell – they should be tightly shut and smell like the sea. To open them, or shuck them as it is officially called, you need a proper oyster knife and a thick kitchen tea towel. The top of an oyster is flat and at the thick end is the hinge. Rest one hand behind the thick towel and with the other wiggle the knife in to open the hinge. Then ease the knife along the opening to find where it attaches half way along.

I love to eat them raw, with a little Tabasco and lemon, and I think they are one of life's great pleasures. However, they are also, for example, excellent baked with a little buttered thyme and garlic.

Chicken with Tarragon

One of my mother's and my most favourite friends was a very special lady called Mary Crowdy and, like us, she spent as much time as possible in Cornwall by the sea. She loved travel and racing, singing songs and had the best stories and limericks. Rather like my mother, she had a few favourite dishes and Chicken with Tarragon was one of them. I rather hope Mary and my mother are in heaven clutching a (Highclere Castle) gin and tonic and watching EastEnders *on TV together.*

Tarragon is one of the four 'fines herbes' of French cooking (the others being parsley, chervil and chives), and the distinctive aromatic is particularly good with chicken and fish dishes.

INGREDIENTS

2 tbsp vegetable oil
6 skinless chicken breasts
2 onions, chopped
2 garlic cloves, crushed
500ml (17fl oz) chicken stock
Small bunch of tarragon
Cornflour (optional)
250g (9oz) asparagus, trimmed
Ready-made rough puff pastry
  (or see page 214 if you would
  like to make your own)
Salt and freshly ground
  black pepper

PREPARATION TIME 10 mins   **COOKING TIME** 20 mins   **SERVES** 6

Preheat the oven to 180°C/350°F/Gas mark 4.

Heat the oil in a large non-stick frying pan. Season the chicken and gently fry with the onion and garlic until the chicken is lightly browned and the onions are softened but not burnt. You may need to do this in batches.

Pour over the stock, add some sprigs of tarragon and bring to a gentle simmer. Cook for about 10 minutes.

Now thicken the sauce if needed with a little cornflour that you have first dissolved in a little water to avoid lumps.

Chop the remaining tarragon and add to the chicken with the raw asparagus, then transfer the mixture into an oven-safe dish.

Unroll some pastry and cut to the size of your dish, then run a lattice cutter firmly across it. Place on top of the chicken filling and crimp the pastry around the edges of the dish.

Bake for 20 minutes or until the pastry is golden brown.

This is fabulous served with new potatoes and a crisp green salad with the crème fraîche on the side.

Lamb and Quince Tagine

INGREDIENTS

3 tbsp olive oil
1kg (2¼lb) shoulder of lamb, diced
2 onions, sliced
5cm (2 inch) piece fresh ginger,
    finely grated
3 garlic cloves, finely chopped
1 cinnamon stick
2 tsp ground cumin
1 tsp ground ginger
2 tsp ground coriander
2 tsp paprika
200g (7oz) chopped tomatoes (fresh
    or tinned)
2 tbsp harissa paste
Small pinch of saffron
2 tbsp honey
1 preserved lemon, finely diced
Zest and juice of 1 lemon
750ml (1¼ pints) lamb stock
400g (14oz) tin chickpeas,
    washed and drained
Sea salt and freshly ground
    black pepper

For the quinces

1kg (2¼lb) quinces, peeled, cored
    and quartered
40g (1½oz) butter
Zest and juice of 1 lemon
2 tbsp honey
2 tbsp caster sugar
Pinch of ground cinnamon

To serve

50g (2oz) sliced toasted almonds
Handful each of coriander (cilantro)
    and mint, chopped

Traditionally a tagine is the North African name of both the stew and the earthenware dish. It is a shallow cooking dish which has a tall conical hat or lid, in which is slowly cooked the spiced meat and vegetables. You could make a tagine with chicken, olives, onions and preserved lemons, using the same typical mix of spices below, but here we have chosen lamb and quinces.

Geordie nearly shares a birthday with one of my sisters and we all spent a birthday week in Morocco together, so this dish reminds me of walks in the foothills of the Atlas mountains and the famous colourful Marrakesh bazaars. It was a wonderful week.

PREPARATION TIME 1 hour   COOKING TIME 1 hour 30 mins
SERVES 6 generously

Heat 1 tablespoon of oil in a large casserole and brown the lamb in batches. Remove the lamb from the pan and set aside.

Add the rest of the oil and soften the onions until translucent.

Add the grated ginger and garlic and cook for 1 minute. Add the rest of the spices except the cinnamon stick and cook for a further minute.

Add the tomatoes, harissa paste, saffron, honey and cinnamon stick and simmer for 2-3 minutes.

Put the lamb in the casserole and add the preserved lemon, lemon zest, juice and stock. Season well, cover with a lid and simmer for 1 hour, stirring occasionally to make sure nothing catches.

Add the chickpeas and simmer for a further 30 minutes uncovered until the sauce is slightly reduced and the lamb is completely tender.

Meanwhile cook the quinces in a pan of boiling water for about 15 minutes until just tender. Drain well and put in a frying pan with the butter, lemon zest and juice, honey, sugar, cinnamon and some of the lamb cooking liquid. Gently cook until the sauce is sticky and the quinces completely tender. Turn them occasionally to make sure they don't burn.

Place the quinces over the top of the lamb and scatter over the almonds, coriander (cilantro) and mint. Serve hot with couscous.

Confit of Wild Duck

Wild duck is a dense, rich meat and marries well with juniper and
warm spices.

INGREDIENTS

6 duck legs
4 tbsp coarse salt
   (approx. 15g/½oz salt
   per kilo of duck leg)
1 cinnamon stick
3 star anise
2cm (¾ inch) ginger,
   peeled and chopped
8 juniper berries
6 black peppercorns
1 shallot, chopped
3 garlic cloves, bruised
2 bay leaves
Duck fat, to cover
Salt and freshly ground
   black pepper

PREPARATION TIME 20 mins   COOKING TIME 3 hours   SERVES 6

To make the confit duck ...

Place the duck legs into a deep tray and season with the salt and pepper,
add the cinnamon, star anise, ginger, juniper, peppercorns, shallot, garlic
and bay leaves to the dish.

Preheat the oven to 140°C/275°F/Gas mark 1.

Cover the duck legs with duck fat, wrap in baking paper and tin foil and
cook for 2½–3 hours or until the duck is very tender and you can remove
the thin bone by simply twisting.

When cooked, remove the duck legs from the hot fat (be very careful),
reserving the fat, and place on a roasting tray, draining off any excess fat.
Leave to cool.

The confit legs can be kept for up to four days in the fridge if fully
submerged in oil or the fat released in cooking.

To finish the dish ...

Heat some of the duck fat in a frying pan. Add the confit legs, skin-side
down, and fry for 2–3 minutes, or until the skin is crisp and the duck
meat is warmed through.

Plate up the duck legs with autumn vegetables, cooked as you prefer.
We used turned carrots, squash and turnips.

CHEF'S TIP

Confit duck legs can be made well in advance and kept for various uses.

If you're going to do this, as soon as they are cooked, put them in a sterilised
jar or airtight plastic container. Cover them with all the hot fat. Leave to cool
before sealing the jar or container.

In theory they will keep for several months in a jar, or several weeks in a
plastic container, stored in the fridge ... however, they are so delicious and
such a handy thing to have for a quick but luxurious lunch or supper, that they
are unlikely to hang around that long!

Beer-simmered Beef Pie

Everyone likes pies. This version includes a few vegetables as a proper
pie should but goes well served with a sliced green cabbage. It is delicious
and perhaps the note to self should be to remember the motto 'everything
in moderation'.

INGREDIENTS

6 tbsp olive oil
2 large onions, thinly sliced
4 carrots, sliced
3 celery stalks, sliced
½ garlic bulb, bashed
3 tbsp plain flour, for dusting
1kg (2¼lb) shin of beef, diced
570ml (20fl oz) ale or beer
300ml (10fl oz) beef stock
3-4 sprigs of rosemary
Rough puff pastry
   (see below, or use ready-made)
1 egg, beaten
Salt and freshly ground
   black pepper

PREPARATION TIME 25 mins   **COOKING TIME** 2 hours   **SERVES** 6

To make the filling ...

Preheat the oven to 160°C/325°F/Gas mark 3.

Heat 2 tablespoons of the oil in a large heavy-bottomed frying pan over a
medium heat. Add the onions, carrots, celery and garlic and soften gently
until they start to colour. Do not let them burn. Place them in a large
lidded casserole dish.

Put the flour in a shallow bowl and season with salt and pepper.
Coat each piece of beef in the flour and shake off any excess.

Turn up the heat in the pan used to prepare the vegetables, add the
remaining oil and brown the beef in batches. Add the beef to the
vegetables.

Add 2 or 3 tablespoons of the beer to the frying pan, scrape off any bits
from the bottom and pour everything into the casserole.

Pour the remaining ale and stock over the beef and tuck in the rosemary.

Cook for 2 hours or until the meat is really tender and the sauce has
thickened.

To assemble and bake the pie ...

Take your pastry out of the fridge and roll out to a thickness of about
½cm (¼ inch) to the shape of your pie dish.

Pour the filling into the dish, top with the pastry, brush with beaten egg,
season well, and bake in the oven for 20 minutes or until the crust is
golden brown. Serve immediately.

Rough Puff Pastry

INGREDIENTS

90g (3¼oz) cold butter
175g (6oz) plain flour
Pinch of salt
Splash of ice-cold water

PREPARATION TIME 10 mins, plus at least an hour chilling

Cut the butter into cubes and rub into the flour and salt with your fingers
to make a crumb.

Add a little cold water to form a dough (do not over work it).

Wrap in cling film and chill in the fridge for a good hour before use.

Wild Mushroom Lasagne

*The meatiness of mushrooms is an excellent alternative to meat,
but there is no need to pretend they are meat, they are a compelling
ingredient in their own right. My husband, like his mother and great-
grandparents, have always enjoyed cream, but I would recommend a good
walk before you sit down to lunch to enjoy this.*

INGREDIENTS

100g (3½oz) unsalted butter,
  plus 1 tbsp for the mushrooms,
  plus extra for greasing the dish
60g (2oz) plain flour
1·2 litres (40fl oz) full-fat milk
Pinch of freshly grated nutmeg
284ml (10fl oz) double cream
3 tbsp flat-leaf parsley,
  roughly chopped
75g (3oz) Parmesan, grated
1 tbsp olive oil
600g (1lb 5oz) mixed wild
  mushrooms, thickly sliced
1 garlic clove, crushed
50ml (2fl oz) dry white wine
25g (1oz) dried porcini mushrooms,
  soaked in 100ml (3½fl oz)
  vegetable stock
300g (10oz) fresh lasagne sheets
Salt and freshly ground
  black pepper

PREPARATION TIME 30 mins, plus chilling time
COOKING TIME 30 mins   **SERVES** 6–8

Preheat the oven to 200°C/400°F/Gas mark 6.

Melt the butter in a pan over low heat and add the flour. Stir for
1 minute, then, continuing to stir, slowly add the milk, a little at a time,
until smooth and thick.

Season with salt, pepper and nutmeg, stir in the double cream, parsley
and 30g (1oz) Parmesan. Remove the pan from the heat and allow to cool
to room temperature.

Heat 1 tablespoon of butter and the olive oil in a large, heavy-based
frying pan and sauté the mushrooms for 2 minutes.

Stir in the garlic and cook for a further minute. Season with salt and
pepper, pour in the wine, porcini and their soaking liquid and cook,
stirring continually, until the liquid has evaporated.

Stir this mixture into the flour/milk mixture.

To assemble the lasagne, butter a rectangular oven dish, approximately
25 × 15cm (10 × 6 inches), and cover the bottom with a layer of slightly
overlapping lasagne sheets. Top with a quarter of the mushroom sauce,
then continue layering the pasta and the sauce, finishing with a layer of
sauce. Scatter over the remaining Parmesan, cover with cling film and
chill for 30 minutes.

Remove the cling film and cook the lasagne for 30 minutes.

Shared Stuffed Pumpkin

Sharing a pumpkin, putting it in the middle of the table and digging out a helping, makes a fun family supper. This particular recipe is vegetarian and you could equally stuff another pumpkin with rice and mushrooms, macaroni cheese or a soup.

INGREDIENTS

Zest and juice of 1 lemon
1 large fennel bulb, thinly sliced
1 cooking apple, peeled cored and
   thinly sliced
1 medium-sized pumpkin,
   around 1kg (2½ lb)
4 tbsp olive oil
100g (3½oz) wild rice, rinsed
1 tbsp fennel seeds
½ tsp chilli flakes
2 garlic cloves, crushed
30g (1oz) pecans,
   toasted and roughly chopped
50g (2oz) parsley, roughly chopped
3 tbsp tahini
Sea salt and freshly ground
   black pepper
Pomegranate seeds, to serve

PREPARATION TIME 15 mins   **COOKING TIME** 1 hour   **SERVES** 4

Preheat the oven to 200°C/400°F/Gas mark 6.

Pour half the lemon juice over the fennel and apple to stop them discolouring.

Cut the top off the pumpkin and scoop out the seeds. Put the pumpkin on a baking tray, rub with 2 tablespoons of the oil inside and out, and season well. Roast for 45 minutes or until tender, with the 'lid' on the side.

Meanwhile, cook the wild rice according to the packet instructions. Drain.

Heat the remaining 2 tablespoons of oil in a frying pan. Fry the fennel seeds and chilli flakes, then stir in half the garlic and the fennel once the seeds begin to pop. Cook for 5 minutes until softened then mix with the apple, pecans and lemon zest. Remove from the heat and add to the rice.

Stir in the chopped parsley and season to taste.

Pack the mixture into the cooked pumpkin and return to the oven for 10–15 minutes until heated all the way through.

Make the dressing by whisking together the remaining lemon juice with the tahini, the rest of the garlic and a splash of water. Pour it over the stuffed pumpkin and scatter with pomegranate seeds.

Pumpkin Soup

At pumpkin season, every child or childlike grown-up eagerly sets to work
carving out pumpkin faces. But don't waste the scooped-out flesh as it
makes an excellent soup to later feed exhausted sculptors.

INGREDIENTS

2 tbsp olive oil
2 onions, finely chopped
1kg (2¼lb) pumpkin flesh,
    deseeded and chopped
    into chunks
700ml (25fl oz) stock,
    either vegetable or chicken
150ml (5fl oz) double cream
    or coconut milk

For the croutons

4 slices wholemeal seeded bread,
    crusts removed
2 tbsp olive oil
Handful of pumpkin seeds

PREPARATION TIME 20 mins   **COOKING TIME** 30 mins   **SERVES** 6

In a large saucepan gently heat the oil and soften the onions for
5 minutes.

Add the pumpkin and cook for another 8–10 minutes, stirring
occasionally until it starts to soften and turn golden.

Pour in the stock and season to taste. Bring to the boil and simmer for
about 10 minutes until the squash is very soft.

Take off the heat, add the cream and purée with a hand blender.
If you would like it extra smooth, you can pour it through a fine sieve
after blending.

To make the croutons: cut the bread into small squares. Heat the oil in
a frying pan, then fry the bread until it starts to crisp.

Add a handful of pumpkin seeds to the pan and cook for 1-2 minutes
until they are toasted.

Serve the soup scattered with the croutons and pumpkin seeds.

Fig *Tarte Tatin*

The carefully cut, sticky slices of fig tuck round a comforting blanket of buttery pastry which is all cooked until caramelised and entirely decadent.

The hazelnuts are optional as some guests may be allergic to nuts. If you do enjoy them they are very protective of your heart and are full of vitamins.

INGREDIENTS

50g (2oz) butter
50g (2oz) caster sugar
1 vanilla pod, split lengthways,
   seeds scraped out
6-7 figs
320g (11oz) ready-rolled puff pastry
1 egg, beaten
25g (1oz) hazelnuts,
   chopped and toasted

PREPARATION TIME 15 mins   **COOKING TIME** 25 mins   **SERVES** 4

Preheat the oven to 200°C/400°F/Gas mark 6.

In a heavy-based frying pan that will fit in the oven (and which is oven-safe) melt the butter and sugar over a medium heat, then add the vanilla pod and seeds. Wait for it to turn a golden caramel colour then remove the pan from the heat and take out the vanilla pod.

Halve the figs and place cut-side down in the pan so they cover the base snugly. Leave to cool and set in the caramel for 2 minutes.

Cut a circle out of the pastry that is 2cm (¾ inch) wider than the pan and place it over the figs, pressing the sides down so that the pastry is snug against the sides of the pan. Prick the pastry with a fork, brush with the beaten egg and bake for 20–25 minutes.

Cool for 5–10 minutes in the pan, then carefully turn the *tarte tatin* onto a plate. Scatter with the hazelnuts and serve warm.

Peach and Oat Crumble

INGREDIENTS

30g (1oz) cold butter, diced,
  plus extra for the peaches
150g (5oz) plain flour
100g (4oz) brown sugar
50g (2oz) oats
8 peaches, skin on, stoned
1 vanilla pod
Zest and juice of 1 lemon

PREPARATION TIME 20 mins   **COOKING TIME** 25 mins   **SERVES** 6

Preheat the oven to 200°C/400°F/Gas mark 6.

Rub the butter, flour and half the sugar together until you get a fine crumb. Try to keep the butter as cold as possible, and only use the tips of your fingers.

Now add the oats and mix.

Take the peaches, cut into quarters and gently cook in a pan in a little butter. Add the remaining sugar, vanilla pod and the lemon zest and juice. Taste and add more sugar if needed. Do not overcook – it should only take a couple of minutes.

Put the peaches in an ovenproof dish and top with crumble mix. Place in the oven and bake for 20 minutes or until golden brown.

Serve hot from the oven, giving everyone a large spoonful. Have some cream, custard or ice cream to hand if you like!

Baked Peaches

White peaches (and apricots, as above) grow against the back wall of the peach house in the Monks' Garden. There are few better moments than picking and eating the peaches. If there is a surfeit or if you are buying peaches that are not quite ripe or indeed too ripe, bake them. All they need is a little honey to caramelise as here, or you can try thyme or cinnamon with thick, soft brown sugar.

INGREDIENTS

12 ripe peaches
8 tsp clear honey
1 tsp vanilla extract

PREPARATION TIME 10 mins   **COOKING TIME** 15 mins   **SERVES** 6

Preheat the oven to 180°C/350°F/Gas mark 4.

Cut the peaches in half and remove the stones. Place them cut side up in an ovenproof dish, drizzle with the honey and add a drop of vanilla extract into each peach.

Bake for 10–15 minutes until soft but still holding their shape.

Serve with cream or crème fraîche.

Banana Bread

This is such an excellent use of bananas that are slightly past it.
However, please peel them and dispose of the skins most carefully so that
you do not slip on them.

INGREDIENTS

140g (5oz) unsalted butter,
  plus a little extra to grease
  the loaf tin
140g (5oz) caster sugar
2 large eggs, beaten
140g (5oz) self-raising flour
1 tsp baking powder
2 very ripe bananas, mashed

PREPARATION TIME 15 mins   **COOKING TIME** 50–55 mins   **MAKES** 1 loaf

Preheat the oven to 180°C/350°F/Gas mark 4.

Butter a 1kg (2¼lb) loaf tin and line with baking paper.

Put the butter and the sugar in a mixing bowl and cream together until
light and fluffy.

Slowly add the eggs a bit at a time along with a tablespoon of the flour.

Fold in the remaining flour, the baking powder and the bananas.

Pour the mixture into the tin and bake for about 50 minutes, or until
cooked through. Check the loaf at 5-minute intervals by testing it with
a skewer (it should be able to be inserted and removed cleanly).

Cool in the tin for 10 minutes before turning out onto a wire rack.

Blackberries

Blackberries grow in clusters along hedges and woodland edges, deepening in colour with the summer sun. They are ripe from late August and tend to be smaller than those grown commercially but are far sweeter. Pick well above knee height. Any surplus will freeze well. Don't wash the berries until just before use.

Blackberry Upside-Down Cake

INGREDIENTS

For the cake

350g (12oz) blackberries
150g (5oz) butter
200g (7oz) caster sugar
3 large eggs
150g (5oz) self-raising flour
30g (1oz) ground almonds

For the topping

50g (2oz) butter
115g (4oz) caster sugar

PREPARATION TIME 15 mins   **COOKING TIME** 50 mins   **SERVES** 4–6

Preheat the oven to 180°C/350°F/Gas mark 4.

First make the topping. Stir the butter and sugar in a pan over low heat until melted. Simmer for 3–4 minutes, stirring frequently. Pour into a greased 25cm (10 inch) diameter round cake tin and spread over the bottom. Arrange the berries in a single layer on top.

Beat the butter and sugar together until pale and creamy. Beat in the eggs one at a time.

Sift the flour into the batter and fold it in, then fold in the almonds.

Gently spoon the batter over the blackberries and bake for 50 minutes. If the cake starts to brown too much, put some foil over the top.

Allow to cool in the tin for 10 minutes before turning out. Cool for another 10 minutes before serving so that the fruit is not still piping hot.

Blackberry Clafoutis

INGREDIENTS

300g (10oz) blackberries
   (blueberries or even prunes
   are just as good)
Juice and zest of ½ lemon
1 tbsp granulated sugar
50g (2oz) plain flour, sifted
70g (3oz) caster sugar
25g (1oz) butter,
   plus extra for greasing
2 eggs, lightly beaten
275ml (9fl oz) full-fat milk
Pinch of salt

PREPARATION TIME 20 mins   **COOKING TIME** 30 mins, plus resting time
SERVES 6–8

Preheat the oven to 200°C/400°F/Gas mark 6. Grease a 24cm (9½ inch) diameter round cake tin. Shake the granulated sugar over the tin to coat it.

Gently melt the butter in a pan over a low heat. Remove from the heat and gently stir in the eggs and milk.

In a bowl, mix together the flour, caster sugar and salt. Slowly pour in the egg mixture, whisking continually so all combines with no lumps.

Place the berries, lemon zest and juice in a bowl and carefully press down with the back of a spoon, gently mixing and crushing without losing the structure of the berries. Spread over the bottom of the cake tin and pour the batter over. Gently shake the tin to remove any air and bake in the oven for 30 minutes, or until fully set and nicely browned.

Let it rest for 10 minutes. It will deflate but don't worry: it's not a soufflé.

Best served with plenty of double cream, at the end of summer, either outside or with the doors and windows open.

BLACKBERRY UPSIDE-DOWN CAKE →

Hedgerow Banquets

Hedgerows primarily offer feasts for birds but we can forage too. Instead of installing a wooden fence, plant an edible hedge and forage on fat hips from the dog rose (Rosa canain) which are packed with vitamin C. Likewise, Rosa rugosa can also be picked and bottled. Elderberry (Sambucus) grows well and is best placed at the end of a hedge for more flowers in spring and fruits in winter. Sloes have prickly thorns but are a good hideaway for birds ... and what is better on a cold day than homemade sloe gin.

Damson or Sloe Gin

INGREDIENTS

500g (1lb 2oz) damsons or sloes
250g (9oz) caster sugar, or up to
   50 per cent more if using sloes
1 litre (35fl oz) bottle gin

PREPARATION TIME 30 mins plus freezing and maturing time
MAKES 1½ litres (50fl oz)

Wash and pat dry the fruit, put into a freezer bag and freeze overnight. The next day bash the bags with a rolling pin a couple of times to split the skins, and divide the fruit equally between two sterilised 1 litre (35fl oz) Kilner jars.

Divide the sugar and gin between the jars, put the lids on and shake thoroughly. Sloes are very bitter so I usually use quite a bit more sugar with them.

Each day for a week, give the jars a good shake until all the sugar has dissolved, then put them in a cool, dark place and leave for 2–3 months.

After it has matured, strain the gin through a fine sieve and decant into sterilised bottles.

Rosehip Syrup

Memories of childhood flood back at even the thought of rosehip syrup. It was always such a pretty pinky-orange colour and irresistibly delicious, whether diluted with water to drink or trickled neat onto rice pudding or semolina.

Weight for weight, rosehips have over 20 times the vitamin C of oranges and their anti-inflammatory properties can help relieve symptoms of arthritis. During the Second World War, the Ministry of Food established a national week for the collection of rosehips in late September. Scouts, guides and other groups would head out to harvest the nation's hedgerows. Records from 1941 suggest that 200 tonnes of hips were collected, which turned into 600,000 bottles of commercially produced rosehip syrup.

INGREDIENTS

PREPARATION TIME 30 mins   COOKING TIME 15 mins

1kg (2¼lb) rosehips
1 litre (35fl oz) water
Caster sugar

Thoroughly wash the rosehips and roughly chop in a food processor. Transfer to a large saucepan and add the water. Bring to the boil, turn the heat down and simmer for around 15 minutes.

Firmly fix a double layer of muslin over a large bowl and pour the rosehip mixture onto it. Let all the liquid slowly drip through, gently squeezing out the last remaining drops. Rinse out the muslin and strain the liquid a second time.

Measure the rosehip juice and add 400g (14oz) sugar for every 500ml (17fl oz) juice.

Put the sugar and juice mixture into a saucepan and gently heat, stirring to dissolve the sugar. Bring to the boil for 2 or 3 minutes. Skim off any scum as necessary and bottle immediately in sterilised jars.

Keep for 3 months. Refrigerate once open.

Jams and Preserves

The general rule is to use roughly the same amount of fruit as sugar but if the fruit is particularly tart – as with damsons – you may need to use a little more. Use the special preserving sugar with added pectin as it makes it easier to set the jam. Equally, fruits that are particularly juicy need less water. If you don't have a cooking thermometer, put a saucer in the freezer so that you can test if the jam is set.

Mulberry or Blackcurrant Jam

Mulberry trees grow slowly and were fashionable in the seventeenth century; the fruit is delicious, sharp and intense and stains fingers as well as tablecloths. Best eaten quickly as they perish quickly – otherwise they make an excellent jam, cooked in the same way as the more commonly available blackberries.

INGREDIENTS

2kg (4½lb) mulberries or
  blackcurrants
600ml (1 pint) water
2·3kg (5lb) sugar

PREPARATION TIME 15 mins   **COOKING TIME** 20 mins

Tip the fruit into a heavy-based saucepan with about 100ml (3½fl oz) water. Bring to the boil and simmer for 5 minutes until the fruit has broken down to a chunky pulp. Leave to cool slightly.

If you don't like seeds and bits in your jam, sieve it and then put it back in the pan. If you are happy as it is, leave it there.

Add the remaining water and the sugar and return to the heat, stirring gently until the sugar dissolves.

Then turn up the heat and boil hard for about 10 minutes or until it reaches 105°C (220°F) (setting point) on a cooking thermometer. If you don't own a thermometer, test for setting point by spooning a little jam on to a saucer that has been in the freezer for a few minutes. After a couple of minutes gently poke the jam on the saucer – if the surface wrinkles, it's ready. If not, return to the boil for another couple of minutes and re-test.

Take off the heat. Skim off any froth and cool for 10–15 minutes. Stir gently to make sure all the fruit is distributed evenly (unless you sieved it) and pour into sterilised jars. Keeps for 6 months.

Cranberry Sauce

In this country we like this slightly sour-tasting, whereas for Thanksgiving in America they prefer it sweeter. Cranberries do grow wild and are farmed here but not on as large a scale as in the USA.

INGREDIENTS

1kg (2¼lb) caster sugar
Juice and zest of 2 oranges
100ml (3½fl oz) water
1kg (2¼lb) cranberries
Pinch each of ground cinnamon
   and five-spice powder

PREPARATION TIME 5 mins   COOKING TIME 10 mins

Tip the sugar, orange juice and water into a pan and bring to the boil.

Stir in the cranberries, orange zest and spices and simmer until tender but still holding their shape – between 5–10 minutes. Take off the heat.

The sauce will thicken as it cools. Store in an airtight jar in the fridge.

Medlar Jelly

Whilst medlars are the oddest-looking fruits, cooking them transforms them. Medlar jelly is fragrant and blush pink, tasting both sweet and spicy and complements cold meat, stews and gravy.

INGREDIENTS

1kg (2¼lb) medlars, chopped
600ml (1 pint) water
Sugar
2 tbsp freshly squeezed lemon juice

PREPARATION TIME 20 mins plus overnight resting   **COOKING TIME** 30 mins

Put the fruit in a pan with the water and simmer until soft. Strain through a muslin bag, retaining the juice.

Measure the juice and return it to the pan, adding 500g (1lb 2oz) sugar for each 600ml (1 pint) of juice.

Gently dissolve the sugar and add the lemon juice. Boil rapidly until setting point. Strain through a muslin cloth into a bowl.

This is often best left to strain overnight as it can be a slow process.

Seal into sterilised jars.

WINTER

WINTER IS A FORCE TO BE RECKONED WITH, A CHALLENGING TIME OF THE YEAR
and one that impacts minds, hearts and bodies. It's a cold and blustery season and both culture and farming traditions remind us of it, in what we eat and what we abstain from, in its feasts, celebrations and thanksgivings. Every one of us is brought together by invisible threads, a beguiling combination of rationality and emotion, of nature and nurture that, despite our increasing urbanisation, is still not totally divorced from the cycle of seasonal life.

OLD MAN WINTER

The blessings of fruitful fields and healthful skies. To these bounties, which are so constantly enjoyed that we are prone to forget the source from which they come, others have been added, which are of so extraordinary nature that they cannot fail ... to restore full enjoyment of peace, harmony, tranquillity and Union.

Abraham Lincoln (1809-65)

THE FIRST INTIMATIONS THAT AUTUMN IS WANING and darker times are coming is the arrival of Halloween in the diary, when the worlds of the quick and the dead merge. Originally part of the church's All Souls Day celebrations, it is a time when ghosts may wander the Earth. One way to avoid them is to dress in similar guises and thus be mistaken for spirits and be left alone.

Behind the Castle lies the remains of a seventeenth-century church, yet that is not the whole truth as it was built on the site of a much earlier Anglo-Saxon place of worship. At the back is a yew tree reputedly 1,000 years old and, moving gently towards it, between the remains of pillars along the grassed over aisle, it feels as if I am walking back into a sacred place. Lying thinly under my feet are ancient vaults and in the dwindling grey winter light, the gap between worlds seems just a few inches deep.

If the colour black is associated with death, and the dark green of yew trees with burial grounds, the orange tones brought out for Halloween remind us of the harvest and the end of summer. Today, Halloween is most commonly represented by the pumpkin, carved with

Sketch of the Old Church at Highclere now, pulled down. built by Sir Robt Sawyer

enthusiasm and displayed in and around everyone's homes. Less commonly known, fennel can also be hung over doorways to keep the devil at bay or used in cooking if you feel spiritually strong.

The date for All Souls Day remains 2 November and is when we remember the dead and make fruit cakes spiced with cinnamon to give to the poor in the parish. Following the old traditions, Martinmas day on 11 November was considered the last day to eat unsalted meat, thankfully long since abandoned as a food, then comes Stir-up Sunday when Christmas cakes are made, before we reach Thanksgiving, almost entirely an American celebration but creeping over here as well. It was President Abraham Lincoln who proclaimed Thanksgiving a national holiday in 1863.

From then on we are into winter proper, with short days and long nights when the land sleeps. The winter solstice, Christmas and the succeeding days to Epiphany give light and structure before we reach Plough Sunday, traditionally the start of the farming year despite being deep in the winter. St Hilary's Day on 13 January is reputedly the coldest day of the year and perhaps also the bleakest: Christmas is long gone but January, that longest of months, is less than half way done. Ironically, the derivation of this name is from the Latin *hilaris*, meaning hilarious or happy. The fact that some universities, schools and the courts of law still refer to this period as the Hilary term ensures its survival.

During this time of deep darkness in our latitude, ghouls and spirits, whether wistful, soliciting attention or just plain mischievous, stay with us in myth and literature. On the plus side we also have more helpful creatures such as elves to help us, so named from the Anglo-Saxon word *aelf* meaning 'genius' – always a good start.

Burns' Night celebrates the end of January with haggis and whiskey, just before the month which the Anglo-Saxon historian Bede called 'the Sol-Monath' – February – is ushered in. Often nicknamed the month of cakes as so many were offered to the gods on various dates, in today's world Valentine's Day gives a welcome pop of colour and light relief before the privations of Lent and the end of winter.

The ancient, austere landscape of Beacon Hill, barely changed for centuries

Cooking at Highclere still very much takes its inspiration from the seasons and the antiquity and heritage of our surroundings. These days we have more machinery and technology in our lives but it is still the same fields growing similar crops, the same orchards and gardens growing many of the same types of fruits. Likewise, the vegetables, herbs and animals in the pasture lands are interchangeable with those grazing here 1,000 years ago.

THE BRITISH LOP-EARED PIG

WALK DOWN THE HILL, AWAY FROM THE CASTLE and just past the walled garden and there are various cottages with wooded areas behind them, overgrown with brambles and scrub. The track drops down further towards a park field grazed by sheep and before you reach a 'Brownian' planting of cedars and oaks. Originally part of the *ferme ornée* in past centuries, this area had become a preferred ground in which sheep, as is their wont, would tangle themselves up disastrously and would be hard to find and rescue.

Leaning on a bent old metal gate, looking down the slope, Simon the Farm Manager and I thought that perhaps the answer would be to acquire and rear some pigs. We each left in some excitement to research breeds and thoughts.

Engrossed in the pig-breeding enterprises of earlier Carnarvons, I was still reading when Simon rang and said he thought we should buy some British Lops. Simon has proper knowledge of pigs and innovative enthusiasm. Within a week two 'gilts' (young female pigs) arrived from Trevaskis Farm in Cornwall. I was imagining little cuddly piglets such as in the film *Babe*, but these two were quite large already. They took to their new life well but, to start with, seemed to make little or no impression on the mess and intertwined scrub. A few short weeks later it was a very different story – they had completely transformed the area and the soil looked as if it had been professionally rotavated.

We named our two gilts Thelma and Louise. British Lop-eared pigs are an old endangered breed, friendly and good at living outside. At one point there were only 100 breeding sows left in the world so they are still very much on the at-risk list. There have, of course, been pigs at Highclere before. The 5th Earl had an award-winning herd of old Berkshires. His father was also a pig breeder, as was his grandmother Henrietta, the 3rd Countess of Carnarvon. My father-in-law was a hands-on farmer after the end of the Second World War and established a pig herd around some farm buildings on the downland above Highclere.

Welcome therefore to the boar Ernie who was borrowed from Trevaskis for a month in order to look forward to some more piglets in the spring. The breeding period of pigs is very short: three months, three weeks and three days from when Ernie mated with them, the exact timing of which we are not quite sure of, so the precision is somewhat lost.

Our pig endeavours have now expanded to a boar of our own, Arthur, named after King Arthur of Tintagel. Thelma and Louise have been joined by three more gilts, Lady Mary, Lady Edith and Lady Sibyl, although the latter now lives with another farmer, Adam Henson, and appears on the BBC's *Countryfile*. With Lady Violet and Lady Cora we have now increased the number of breeding sows to the limit of what we can just about manage.

Despite our different shapes and lifestyles, humans and pigs do share some fundamental characteristics. As I walk towards them, I always call out to say hello and chat to them. British Lops love a scratch and can differentiate who is coming towards them. They can store information and distinguish scents and are remarkably clean-smelling. They rootle round and plough up the fields and are not always very easy to move around and direct. When they last came into season, Thelma and Louise were two fenced fields away from the boar but, notwithstanding, just headed through all impediments to present themselves to him leaving a trail of broken fences. They are inquisitive, brave and have been excellent animals to integrate into our farming cycle.

The ancient settlement of Beacon Hill lies in the middle of the Highclere lands, and Stonehenge, one of the great wonders of the world, is just 30 miles west of us. The latter has been much explored and reassessed, each time sharing more of its secrets from very small clues which we are ever better at interpreting with modern technology. Two miles north-east of Stonehenge in the direction of Highclere lies Durrington, the largest Neolithic settlement find so far with perhaps 1,000 houses.

Unsurprisingly, thousands of animal bones have been found at these sites, of which some 90 per cent were from pigs, the remainder from cattle. Many of the pigs were probably killed for midwinter food and, as in today's world, there would have been feasting and celebration during the winter nights.

In fact, our ancestors lived at Beacon Hill and Stonehenge and other similar settlements for far longer than we have lived here in the time frame recorded by words, language and art.

ROOM WITH A VIEW

EAST ANGLIA

IT WAS THE THIRD EARL OF CARNARVON who, in 1842, commissioned Sir Charles Barry to create the inspirational Italianate gothic castle (or 'palace' as it was initially described) that everyone sees and knows today. Sadly, he died very young, in 1849, before he could even stay in it. His widow, Henrietta, continued with the great project but left some of the detail of the internal refurbishments to her son, the 4th Earl of Carnarvon.

Like his father, the 4th Earl was an assiduous historian, fascinated not only with the classical heritage of Greece and Rome but also that of the Anglo-Saxon world and earlier history. Later in life he would become President of the Antiquities Society, but his interest was obvious when he carefully named seven of the 35 family and guest bedrooms in the 'new' Highclere Castle in tribute. There were seven Anglo-Saxon kingdoms, hence the names for the seven bedrooms: Wessex, Mercia, Northumberland, Sussex, Kent, Essex and East Anglia.

East Anglia bedroom is a large, sunny corner room facing east and south. It has a bathroom which was converted from a small sitting room over 100 years ago and an adjoining dressing room. The aspect is outstanding, leading the eye towards both the tree-studded Siddown Hill and to the ancient escarpment of Beacon Hill. The 5th Earl (who discovered the tomb of Tutankhamun) apparently held seances in here and it seems appropriate that you can almost see his grave on the summit of Beacon Hill, where he was laid to rest in 1923:

The summit of Beacon Hill is crowned with a very fine British entrenchment. Several barrows at the foot of the hill were opened some years ago, and found to contain burnt bones, spear and arrow heads of bronze, and some small ornaments of thin gold, which had obviously been used as a covering to a nucleus long since decayed. The elevated barrows had contained the bones of warriors; the smaller ones, which were only slightly elevated above the surrounding ground, contained smaller bones (apparently those of females or young people), which were unaccompanied by implements of war.

The original name for Beacon Hill was *Weald Setl* – literally the settlement of the chieftain, the one possessed of the wealth. The remains of that community, farming and fort walls which can be seen today point to what must have been at that time a large engineering project, one undertaken with order and planning and the co-ordination and co-operation of most of the community. Ramparts and ditches mark where the earth was removed to create defences some 20 feet high which augmented the natural contours of the hill. A timber revetment was most likely created to hold back the earth and create a vertical face to protect from potential attackers (reverted rampart). The outer bank ditch beyond the rampart is later and it is likely that the site evolved over many generations. From the bottom of the ditch, the rampart might have been 30 or 40 feet high. Other forts from this time have several ramparts but here there is only one. This might be because the others had fewer natural topographical advantages than Beacon Hill or were sited on busier trade routes and therefore had a greater risk of attack. These sites were constructed for defence: intruders armed with flint arrowheads or bows of seasoned ash were as lethal in 2500BC as the later famous longbows of England were at the Battle of Agincourt in 1415. (The earliest bow found in England dates from around 2690BC.)

The enclosure within the contours amounts to around nine acres and it is still possible to discern the circular remains of stone huts both on their own and grouped together. There are also elongated hut remains which might have been communal areas for eating and are distributed throughout, although avoiding the highest points which would be less sheltered from winter winds. The circular huts are Bronze Age and if Iron Age immigration increased settlers' numbers, it did not alter all their traditions. Times of year and season were marked by gatherings, to fast or feast together and remember those who had passed on. Faint symbolic stone lines link down the hill from the living towards the dead.

Their survival and life were centred around farming and food, what they could eat, how it could be grown and hunted, how it could be stored and the rituals that developed around these imperatives. It must have been a busy community, full of bustle and activity.

It all changed with the arrival of the Romans, not only with their military might and stronger armaments but with their more sophisticated farm implements and heavier ploughs, which could turn the soil and allow more areas to be farmed. As the Roman Empire faded, around 350AD, there are the first indications that this area began to be called the lands of 'clere', the first link to Highclere. Gradually new raiding parties arrived, led by Anglo-Saxons, new smaller kingdoms and fiefdoms developed, and around 740AD King Cuthred of Wessex established the independence of his Kingdom and issued a number of Charters.

There are five Anglo-Saxon Charters which relate to the lands of 'clere', and in one the boundaries of Highclere are for the first time to our knowledge defined in words that describe ways and trees and natural markers. The map is drawn along the *Hunig Weg* (presumably an old way with a good source of wild honeybees or where hives were traditionally kept) via large stones, along a brook, to a coferan tree (*feran* means to travel, so perhaps the traveller's tree, the rowan), to a broad oak and so on.

East Anglia is a room with a view through time as well as distance.

IMAGINATION AND WINTER

ALMOST UNIVERSALLY in countries where the seasons are marked, winter lives deeps in our minds, stories and literature. 'Winter is coming', the ominous refrain from the hit TV series *Game of Thrones* could equally be a refrain from a Shakespeare play or from one of Tolkien's epic fantasy tales. Likewise, the White Witch casts C.S. Lewis's Narnia into a hundred years' winter with no Christmas, no feasts and no celebrations: the ultimate punishment. In the cold and the gloom, our imaginations run riot, fear is easy to stir up, death stalks the land and melancholy and isolation are constantly threatened companions.

Families and communities have lived at Highclere for thousands of years, although little primary data has survived from those early days. Divisions of time are a retrospective invention but the division between day and night, warm and cold are never changing.

Shakespeare's King Lear says: 'I have a journey, sir, shortly to go. You can stand outside one experience only by stepping inside another', and so we can imagine the commonplace tragedy of this small family living here at Highclere in 1500BC ...

THE SILHOUETTE OF THE LITTLE GROUP sitting huddled on some large logs was ageless. Around them in the gloaming wintry evening, were eight or nine rounded barrows, made up from earth and timber, grouped at the foot of the huge hill of the chieftain. Silently reflecting on those they had laid to rest in the arched home of the dead that stood just before them at the foot of the windswept hill, the logs gave them some convenient protection from the chill of the grass. They had yet to close the small wooden door to the barrow, separating the other world from theirs and, above them, the enormity of sky was studded with pinpricks of bright light which pierced the cold night in the darkness of the year. It was not yet the solstice and the shortening days marked the daily rhythms of their life.

The elderly woman stood up, signalling the two half-grown boys to follow her. It would be better to return to their home and the safety of the stockaded village before the deepest hours of night. She reached for their hands and then patted them gently on their backs as they went with her, heads bowed in loss for the mother and brother who had left them. Walking across the open ground, they found the path leading them back. It was good land: the chalk ensured it was well drained, there were flints for axes and the higher ridgeways in day time offered long views unobscured by vegetation. Their homestead was in the shelter of the trees, below the great hill, on the side of the rising sun.

In contrast to their thoughts, the night was never silent, from the mysterious rustle of stiff grasses to the circling breathy owls and swooping bats. The dark solid outline of a large dog padded reassuringly by the boys as they carefully skirted the dewpond, made in the chalk depression with puddled clay. They had helped their father lay some hedging around it to keep out the animals, lest they went through it with their hooves.

They all knew the path and before long could see the shape of the two large oak trees which marked the entrance to the homestead. Hazel had been cut into similar lengths and bent into shape to create fences to hold in the large sows who would soon give birth again. Scratchy hedges were newly planted around to offer further support. The sheep were nearby and a large dog stood up and pricked its ears as they approached. The dogs were on guard for wolves but this had been a year of plenty and they had other resources just now. One of the boys whispered something to the animal who settled back down.

They bent down to enter into their home, a circular construction with a welcome fire in the middle of the one room. Wattle and daub had long been used to make the walls which were substantial enough to withstand the winter weather. Their grandmother checked the great stewpot over the fire and went to the pot in the corner, dipping in small beakers and offering each boy in turn some ale flavoured with juniper gathered from the hill. Quietly she settled down and began to sing the old songs of their forbears, lamenting the passing of the sun which spent ever less time in the sky, hiding itself in darkness behind the dense hills of the high downland.

They knew these old songs and stories of their ancestors who had made the journey of fable across the low-lying, marshy land, Doggerland, between what would, in the future, become Denmark and England. Their ancestors were following the herds of animals, horses and deer across the continent as the Ice Age receded. This was good pasture with clean water and a diverse topography where it was possible to hunt and find food on the woodland edge. As the climate warmed, the land gradually flooded and became a great cold sea which neither man nor horse could now cross.

The boys stared into the fire, acutely missing those who were gone. In any home there was nothing stronger than a mother's love – her laughter and hugs, her cooking of course and the sewing of skins for their shoes. Tomorrow they would run with their father and the men outside, learning to hide, to track, to move with silence to bring down the buck or the wild pigs, but not yet.

Generations continued to live where once that family had. Their settlements could expand because farming was productive and the valley behind the tumuli provided good sheltered grazing for animals. Crops were planted, barley, rye, wheat, and later on grains of wheat and barley would be found beneath the remains of timber posts. The wild woods were pushed further back. They grew flax and hemp, beans and turnips at this time of year. It was a time when men and women tried to make nature work for them: deer were hunted, birds netted and cattle were herded and carefully taken from pasture to pasture.

The dead were buried near the living, a custom that lived long into later medieval times where the chapels were at the heart of the community and the graveyards and cemeteries near-by. It was ever thus: the attempt to propitiate the gods as well as remember our forbears and look after them in death.

As the light faded, the shadows acted as an echo of those who walked here in a different time, many lives and generations before their life.

Millennia later, in 1781, a man and his family came to live near the same place, and found the ten or twelve round hills or barrows and wondered who was buried inside. They found the curled-up skeletons of the woman and younger person and pondered who they were.

A letter found in the archives here, from Lord Carnarvon to his son, records:

> ... in one we found the unburnt skeleton of a child about 8 or 9 years old in a small barrow, his knees bent up to his chin; the bones laying together but without adhesion, the ligatures all perished, it fell to pieces on being moved, the jaw contained teeth and the second teeth under them ready to supply the first as they should have shed; nothing was found besides in the Barrow. In a Hattish barrow of the bell shape, we found in a hole in the foil of the old down, heaped over with Earth we found half-burnt bones and charcoal, with a Brass spear head; two gold fibulae very much like a Birmingham button rising in the center to a point. The gold very thin it has probably been fixed to wood; in another we found a hole which had the bottom covered with a piece of wood about 2 inch thick, it seemed to have been lined with cloth, as we found many bitts of cloath very visible by the webb and something which was like a composition which might have been Glew or cement. We found also a brass spear head and 2 bone tops of arrows very pointed with a hole where they might have been fixed to the wood; In another was found a disjointed skeleton the bones a large size, half the jaw containing all the teeth very large, bone arrow tops; in another Bones half burnt skull and other parts not burnt and a broken urn.

Still treeless, Weald Setl or Beacon Hill commands the landscape around it, rising steeply 900 feet above the open fields. Our knowledge of how the people from this time lived is derived primarily from the observation and excavation of their rituals at death, as no writing has survived from this era in Europe. The settlement was abandoned before or during the Roman invasion and new villa homes were made at the foot of the hill. Remains of life from walls, coins, dress brooches, shoe nails exist to remind us of our ancestors. The same fields as then are still used to grow grain and pasture sheep, deer remain abundant and hares and rabbits have become part of the animal landscape.

WINTER TREES

ROBERT HERBERT'S FORMAL EIGHTEENTH-CENTURY GARDENS had long since disappeared by the twenty-first century. A closely planted soft-wood tangle of trees from the 1960s wantonly obscured the earlier landscape but hidden amongst the newcomers were eight smooth, soaring beech trees which clearly marked the beginning of an earlier avenue. Taking those as our inspiration, we have cleared and re-interpreted Robert's 'Great Wilderness' in a new way and renamed it the Wood of Goodwill. Over the last fifteen years it has developed and grown and even in winter has a recognisable shape, re-formed with meandering paths to echo earlier footsteps through glades of native trees.

The name 'Wood of Goodwill' came about during a walk with my number six sister and, in fact, a tulip tree marks her wedding here at Highclere. Other friends have given viburnums, forsythia and malus trees. A weeping birch tree is planted in honour of Nora Sutcliffe who worked here for 42 years, whilst other trees mark the passage of past team members from Albert Saxton, Clerk of Works, to Stan Ansty, a bricklayer.

One way or another most projects seem to begin in mud and winter and, with the music of the four seasons in my head, I thought the garden plan could be drawn up so that each season would be highlighted in a different area, with the eighteenth-century beech avenue creating the backbone.

We knew from the start that we wished to concentrate on British native trees. Arguably there are only 30 of them. In fact, the beech might be a bit of a usurper as it may only have been brought to Britain with Stone Age settlers which is not regarded as native! It was the botanists of the eighteenth and nineteenth centuries who introduced the extraordinary variety of exotic trees which flourish here in this climate now and offer us the infinite variety of species to which we are used.

Many of the native trees were already to be found in the Wood of Goodwill but they needed resuscitating from hibernation: juniper, crab apple, lime, oak, birch, box, rowan, maple, holly, hazel, yew,

hornbeam and poplar were all here but we have planted others that were missing. Then, in homage to my husband's predecessors, we added in a few exotic trees as well, such as the tulip tree, Japanese cherry trees, acers for autumn colour, elms, walnut trees and shrubs such as winter viburnums, forsythias plus a few hydrangeas too.

Some of our native trees such as Black Poplar have become rather rare and hard to find. Popular in medieval times, its trunk can reach 100 feet tall and 6 feet thick and it has both female and male species. Nearby is a 'Quaking' Aspen (*Populus tremula*), already twice the height of its neighbour and so named because the leaves shimmer and tremble in the lightest of breezes and turn a rich golden yellow in autumn.

JUNIPER

A MASSED DARK EVERGREEN JUNIPER HEDGE provides wind protection between the Wood of Goodwill and the more tender Secret Garden. Again, a British native, it grows in the fosse of Beacon Hill as it has for millennia. Steeped in folklore, its thorny needles would catch witches and protect villagers from malevolent beings. Once prolific, it has declined despite its berries, which are the most essential ingredient in gin. The aroma and taste of juniper is – or at least should be – the signature note in any gin. The name juniper in French is *genièvre* or in Dutch *jenever*, which was shortened to produce the English name of the spirit: gin. Its value was appreciated long before gin was invented though: the Egyptians and Romans consumed it like pepper but, outside gin production, today it is mostly used dried to add flavour to game dishes.

Gin production uses fresh berries and we have gradually been planting more as we really need around 30 plants to allow them to successfully self-seed and survive. Juniper has very precise germination requirements but, once it is seeded, will cope with most soil and planting situations. It is diecious – i.e. individual plants are either male or female – and it blooms with small yellow flowers, followed by the 'berries', which are actually fleshy cones, that start life green but ripen to a deep blue-black.

BIRCH AND HOLLY

BIRCH HAS A RELATIVELY SHORT LIFE but produces seeds with ease, freely dispersing their light fruits in the wind. The wood is still used for maypoles and fires whilst the white-barked trees bring good luck in summer. For the Irish, a child placed in a birch cradle was protected from malicious spirits. The poet Samuel Taylor Coleridge described them as the '... most beautiful of forest trees, the Lady of the Woods', grateful for the brilliance of the bark in winter months. Freya, one of our pale Labradors, is simply delighted to sit and pose by them as in Norse mythology they were sacred to the goddess Freya, wife of Odin. In contrast to both dog and bark, we have underplanted with dark hydrangeas and weigela.

Like the birch, holly is a survivor from the last Ice Age. The Latin name *Ilex* means 'evergreen oak', perhaps by reason of the fact they often grow together. Browsed by many mammals and animals it tends to survive and merely come back with more prickly leaves. The 2nd Earl of Carnarvon developed not only the spring-flowering *Azalea altaclerensis* but also *Ilex × altaclerensis* – hollies. They make up a group of hybrid hollies that are more robust than the common holly (*Ilex aquifolium*) and bear larger leaves and berries. It is very easy to take hollies for granted but they are impressive in their own way as they provide garden structure and colour, from the brightly coloured winter berries to their year-round foliage.

Again, they are diecious (either male or female), thus ideally you need a pair. The most obvious choices are the female varieties which produce berries, unlike the male, but the latter make plants of great beauty and their puffs of pollen carry a sweet scent, so don't entirely reject the male. One of the brightest of all the hollies available is *Ilex × altaclerensis* 'Lawsoniana' (above right) which has unusual, almost spineless leaves, with bold, irregular central splashes of bright yellow and green. It bears generous bunches of brown-red berries throughout the winter months, which are much loved by garden birds. Amusingly the names do not reflect the sex of the holly. 'Golden King', another Highclere holly, is in fact female.

Other hollies grown at Highclere include *Ilex × altaclerensis* 'Belgica Aurea', which produces leaves that are dark green with a yellow edge, and then fast-growing, hardy *Ilex × altaclerensis* 'Hodginsii', which has big green and lime-green leaves, purple stems and honey-scented flowers and is a reliable male partner.

As one of Britain's most common native trees, holly wood has been used by furniture makers for centuries. Prized for its whiteness, it is popular in decorative marquetry and inlay work and often acts as a beautiful contrast to walnut or other woods, and, of course, no Christmas is complete without wreaths of holly with bright green leaves and berries.

WORKING FOR THE WOODS

THE WOOD OF GOODWILL IS A LARGE AREA and from muddy beginnings it has begun to give much delight, not just to us but to the myriad wildlife and the old chalk downland wildflowers which have re-colonised it, from bee orchids to wild thyme, all currently hibernating but proliferating more each year. It is not all neat and tidy but then it is not supposed to be and it is all the richer for that. Old fallen trees have been sliced through to become tables, the walnut walk provides winter sustenance for squirrels who always beat us to it, shrubs bearing berries support the birds, coppiced hazel trees proliferate, whilst the trunks of long-gone trees still standing are a haven for insects and beetles against which rose and honeysuckle will scramble up in summer.

The starting point for us fifteen years ago was the avenue and tree moving but we were far from being the first at Highclere to undertake such great tree projects. Capability Brown and the 1st Earl of Carnarvon had moved huge trees 250 years ago to create instant results and some of the vistas across parkland which we still enjoy today. Diaries from the 1st Earl record the process:

> The best way of planting large beech trees of any size is, to cut in the lateral branches, not close to the body, in the beginning of February; and, in the autumn following (or even in the same spring), to cut round the roots, and fill the earth in; letting it stand till the succeeding autumn, or longer, by which time the tree will have made young branches and young roots, and be in vigour, and fit, upon removal, to push immediate roots. It should be taken up without cutting the roots much more, and put into a hole with the earth in mud, filled in and well staked. The young roots will immediately strike, and the young branches shoot. Planting in earth made thick nod is an excellent way. The tree should be planted level with the ground; it suffers, if sunk below the level of the ground. The top or leading branch of a beech, indeed of any tree, should not be cut off.

We were less ambitious with the size of the trees we moved but also undertook the work in winter. Fortunately, we have graduated to the help of a tractor with horsepower to move them rather than horses and cart. We reduced the head height of the selected beech on the estate by one-third, digging it out using a tree spade. Meanwhile, in the new location, a larger hole than was needed was dug using a digger before positioning in the tree, backfilling and firming everything down. It all went very well until springtime when we realised one of the beech was in fact a copper beech, but that is life – imperfect – and we left it there. In this way we established the first part of the avenue and later planted the second stage of the original avenue leading to the mound on which sat Robert Herbert's Octagon. Further oak and beech were gradually also transplanted to begin to recreate the wooded glades of earlier delight.

ANCIENT OAKS

SO OFTEN ASSOCIATED WITH HOLLY is the oak tree, *Quercus ilex*. In England, they are part of our architecture when cut and used as timber; the British navy would not have become a global force without its ships of oak and no woodland is complete without them. Their seeds – acorns – are distributed by the wind, they can re-grow from fallen oaks as well as survive coppicing. Even today, the timber is used as supports in our homes, for furniture, for floorboards and to smoke salmon.

With their deeply ribbed bark and etched leaves they will grow in groups but are perhaps at their most spectacular as pioneer trees, standing alone, gloriously expansive and beautiful as the seasons turn and outstandingly venerable in winter. The old oaks in the park here have survived because the land has not been ploughed but instead used to graze sheep. As a result, we are lucky to have some that are full of an ancient grandeur which is hard to surpass. The oldest tend to be those

trees standing alone as they have no competition during times of hardship and retrenchment. Neither are the oldest oak trees necessarily the tallest, as oaks tend to pull back from the top most branches in times of adversity and, as they hollow out, they then transfer minerals to the roots. At such an age they become supportive habitats of myriad other species and their age brings lichens and diversity. Some of these trees have lived and grown here for over 500 years, outliving generations of humans.

'CAPABILITY' BROWN

TWO HUNDRED AND FIFTY YEARS AGO during the winter days of 1770, a mud-spattered coach swept into the courtyard of Highclere, horses steaming. Harassed and tired, a stout, well-dressed man descended, looking forward to a warm fire and bed. His name was Lancelot 'Capability' Brown, and the then heir to Highclere, having met him through his father-in-law, wanted the celebrated landscape architect and gardener to transform his house and park in the new fashion. At the height of his renown and experience, Brown was a successful and canny businessman. His schemes were often on a huge scale, his modus operandi being to construct apparently boundless worlds, fading into the horizon, with curving woods all linked by circular carriage drives sometimes miles from the main house. He was certainly not inexpensive.

The farm buildings and old medieval courtyards and cemetery were to be deconstructed, although the remains of the walls can still be seen in the sunk fence or 'ha-ha' which led the eye smoothly out over the uninterrupted vistas. The ha-ha was a favourite ruse of his as it allowed his designs to appear seamless by confusing the eye into believing that various pieces of parkland, though managed and stocked quite differently, were as one.

Having made his site visit to understand the topography of Highclere, Brown later sent down his colleague, John Spyers, to carry out full surveys of the house and grounds, on the basis of which three plans were submitted to Col. Henry Herbert, Robert Herbert's nephew. One was a general plan for the alteration of the grounds and gardens (£40); the second a plan for the intended water (£10); and the last 'many plans for the alteration of the house and office — a great deal of trouble to me' (£25). Spyers' expenses amounted to £52 10s whilst he charged £127 for his own journeys (see below). Further payments made by Colonel Henry Herbert (later the 1st Earl of Carnarvon) to Brown's bank account at Drummonds amount to £400, well over £200,000 in today's money. This marked one of the biggest changes ever seen at Highclere as the views and parkland were enormously expanded from the formal structure of earlier garden styles to the carefully constructed Arcadia which is still in place today.

Brown's vision was as much an intellectual and philosophic impulse as a practical one of landscape gardening and was very much in tune with the philosophy of the time. Horace Walpole MP, the son of Britain's first Prime Minister, Sir Robert Walpole, was regarded as an arbiter of taste, of antiquarian knowledge, of letters and art. His life spanned the intellectual and Arcadian impulses of the eighteenth century and in 1770 he wrote an *Essay on Gardening*:

> We have discovered the point of perfection. We have given the true model of gardening to the world ... original by its elegant simplicity ... proud of no other art than that of softening Nature's harshness and copying her graceful touch.

Brown's signature feature was water and, in particular, moving it around to create diversity and interest. Most of his plans contained it and so naturally one of the features he designed for Highclere was a never-ending curved lake. The place chosen for this was Dunsmere, part of the old medieval landscape. The existing water (*mere*) was expanded to provide a larger habitat for water-loving creatures of all varieties and the outline was snaked around to form a single body of water, as if a river flowed through the landscape and ran on indefinitely. Above it would be a Rotunda to lead the eye as part of the arrival story on horseback or carriage. In fact, many of the finest views and perspectives at Highclere today are still best observed from horseback: cars are too low to the ground and you cannot smell the trees or be still for the wildlife if you are sitting beside a rumbling engine.

This effortless coherence that is taken so much for granted today, the fact that it simply appears that the whole landscape was ever thus, was predicted in Brown's obituary: 'where he is the happiest man he will be least remembered, so closely did he copy nature, his works will be mistaken'. His nickname of 'Capability' is thought to have come from his describing landscapes as having 'great capabilities'.

Highclere's Arcadia is an outstanding combination of Brown's structure and planting and the natural topography. Come and stand on the south lawns, outside the Castle, looking south: there are two lines of sight, one to the south-east and Beacon Hill and the other to the south-west and Grotto Copse. Paler-leaved beeches and limes dominate the line of sight towards the eastern valley, whilst specimen cedars are grouped to the west to show the trees and their lengthening shadow to the best advantage in the setting sun.

Standing on the other side of the house facing north, the level pasture leads the eye towards Sidehill, a valley sculpted on either side which is almost perfectly orientated north–south. Its slopes provide a foil for the dark cedars of Lebanon with a few eye-catching oaks and beeches at the far end of the valley whilst further clumps of trees border it far to the north and render the borders indistinct.

Colonel Henry Herbert was full of enthusiasm, and with sufficient plans to start work on the park, his new house could wait. Brown's overarching theme was to remove all the internal boundaries from within the outlined park, whether walls, hedges or avenues, and Brown's map showed that two belts of trees to the north of the house were to be removed, and new approaches created.

Capability Brown often used the language of grammar to help his clients visualise his plans and imagine the future:

> 'Now there,' said he, pointing his finger, 'I make a comma, and there,' pointing to another spot, 'where a more decided turn is proper, I make a colon; at another part, where an interruption is desirable to break the view, a parenthesis; now a full stop, and then I begin another subject'.

Dismissed by his Victorian successors and out of tune with the wildness promoted by the romantic movement, his parks have nevertheless withstood the test of time, and in their scale provided the permanent old pasture, woodlands and space for nature that are valued so much today.

THE MEDIEVAL DEER PARK

OF COURSE, MUCH OF THE SPACE that Brown was working within was technically the remains of a medieval deer park, identified as such on maps over 700 years earlier. Meat was expensive and hunting and forestry rights were jealously guarded privileges of the nobility, with fearsome punishments for those who broke the law. The Bishop of Winchester owned Highclere throughout the medieval era and such game was highly valued for food: Bishop John Stratford of Winchester took 'rabbits, partridge and fesanon for the diet of the King at Merewalle' circa 1330, whilst Bishop William Edyington took 30 fallow deer

by the gift of the King in around 1350. Later, in Victorian times, a Highclere herd of deer was held in a new paddock but today we just have a field named Deer Park for reference and deer are entirely wild throughout the estate.

In winter it is much easier to see fallow or roe deer shyly fading into the edge of the woodlands along Siddown Hill or silhouetted in the open spaces. Fallow deer were first brought to Britain from the western Mediterranean during the Roman period whilst roe deer are a true native of the British Isles. Just as light fades from the world in nature, during winter their coats fade to a dull grey colour, a very different colour from the bright rusty red coats of summer.

Above the deer, pheasant croak and call as they flap up to roost in the trees with the approach of evening. Pheasants have not been resident quite as long as the deer but again live along the woodland edge. The burnished feathers of male birds are a traditional symbol of our countryside whilst the female birds are a more indistinguishable stony colour which may attract less predator attention as they are left entirely alone each spring to bring up the chicks.

Along the shoulder of Beacon Hill are small coveys of grey partridge. As the remaining day fades you can sometimes hear the chirpy click calls of these now less-familiar birds. They run with quick steps before lifting off low in a fan of wings and calls, diving across the tufted pasture at great speed. Arriving after the last Ice Age they were prevalent until the herbicides of the early 1950s. These eliminated many of the weeds growing in the crops which were habitat for the insects that were the main food source for these birds. Combined with increased predation during the nesting times the population has decreased by 80 per cent since then. Now that we are becoming more aware of the impact on the environment of human actions, each year there are a few more birds as we try to help them by providing them with uncultivated areas and less tended hedges. In contrast, French red-legged partridge have thrived perhaps as they can raise two clutches of eggs simultaneously.

WINTER IN THE GARDEN

LIVING INSIDE WELL-LIT CENTRALLY-HEATED HOUSES it is easy to forget the turning points of the year and the dance of the seasons. If spring was marked by the vernal equinox on 21 March, autumn is marked by the 21 September equinox. By late November the garden and trees are aware that winter is approaching, when the world will pause and change direction. Likewise, in November, there are still fingers of sunshine and some daylight by which to get some work done in the garden, but by December the ground is starting to get cold and hard. It is a time to read seed catalogues, clear out the greenhouse and plan for the spring.

WINTER JOBS
· Send off for seed catalogues and start planning what to grow next year. Dare to dream.
· Take stock of the previous year, the successes and failures, and plan accordingly. Work out what might need to be moved.
· Some planting can be done in December – fruit bushes spring to mind - as long as the ground isn't waterlogged or frozen.
· Harvest the last of the carrots and parsnips.
· Winter is the harvest time for kale, Brussels sprouts, celery, cabbages and winter spinach.
· Now that they are dormant, winter-prune apple trees.
· Divide snowdrops as soon as they have flowered.
· Start growing winter salad and other seedlings in the greenhouse.
· Plant bare-root hedging, roses, trees and shrubs, before the weather turns really cold and the ground freezes.
· In February you can sow *in situ* garlic cloves, Jerusalem artichokes, parsnips and shallots.

PLANTING GARLIC
· Always buy 'seed' garlic to grow, rather than use bulbs from a supermarket, to minimise the risk of disease. Supermarket varieties are often bred for warmer climes than the UK.
· Aim to plant between November and February when the ground is available and not too wet or too frosted– hard to dig.
· Where possible, choose a sunny spot with well-drained soil.
· Break the bulb into individual cloves and push into the soil – use a trowel to avoid damaging them – so the tip is just covered.
· Space cloves 15cm apart in rows 30cm apart, so it will be easy to hoe off weeds.

PLANTING TREES
· Choose a dry, cool day for planting. If the soil's sticky enough to cling to your boots, it's too wet for planting.
· Dig a hole that's at least twice as wide but also deeper than the roots of your tree and fork over the base and sides to loosen the soil and allow roots to spread easily.
· Generous watering is vital and when we planted our beech avenue in the Wood of Goodwill one of the biggest challenges was keeping all the newly installed trees hydrated. Transplanted trees are often short of water as their roots take hold in the new environment.

BARE-ROOTS AND POTS

Bare-root shrubs, trees and hedges are the least-expensive method of planting and produce strong plants. They can be planted between November and March and, if you take the time to do it properly, they will do their best to live and thrive. The scale of Highclere is sometimes overwhelming, with the sheer number of plants required to fill a space, so where possible I buy bare-root plants.

It's a good idea to soak the roots in a bucket of water when the plant or tree arrives before you plant. You can also add some root-grow powder at this point. Dig the hole to be much bigger than the root ball of the plant. Fork over the bottom of the hole, and then add some compost so the roots can easily begin to grow downwards. Before placing the plant in the hole, tease out the root ball to loosen it, especially if the plant is pot bound. Most plants prefer the firmed soil to be filled back just above the root ball. Once in the soil their roots will be warmed and strengthened and put out new growth in the springtime.

Aside from new planting, Highclere's Head Gardener and his team use the winter months to work through the gardens and the Wood of Goodwill. By pruning back the cornus (dog wood), the vibrant colour of the stems is retained. It is also a good time to trim back the wisteria, clematis and the buddleia. Compost is dug into the Secret Garden and White Border and paths are repaired.

PLANTS FOR INDOORS

Glass houses of all types and for all purposes were hugely popular during Victorian times. Deeply fashionable, they were also invaluable in bringing variation to the dining table during the winter months. From pineapple houses, to melon houses, orangeries, vineries, peach houses, carnation houses and camellia houses, every south-facing garden wall at Highclere was embellished with greenhouses, whilst facing north behind the orangery was a fernery. Whilst many of these have sadly now disappeared, the eighteenth century orangery still stands with a Victorian fernery behind offering dappled shade to help preserve the rich green of the fronds.

Many of these buildings were in a parlous state when we first took over here but we have gradually been repairing them and putting them to use once again. Behind the buildings are both cold frames and vegetable beds, fenced and protected from rabbits. Again, whilst many of these have disappeared over the years, others have found new roles. The orangery provides flowers year-round for the Castle and oranges and lemons which are sent to the gin distillery. The carnation house now grows indoor plants, again for use inside the Castle, and the vinery, newly repaired, traditional table grapes. A further more modern greenhouse grows tomatoes of all colours and types as well as peppers.

The Victorian author Charles Kingsley, who stayed at Highclere, was one of those who publicly recognised the Victorian passion for ferns as a phenomenon. There was a name for it – *pteridomania* (fern fever) – and Highclere did not escape. The fernery was likely built around 1860 and was a symbol of wealth and position. Beyond fashion, every home benefits from the cheerfulness and the air-cleansing effects of a series of houseplants throughout the year. In winter cyclamen, amaryllis and indoor hyacinths

are followed by tête-à-tête narcissi and early orchids which, in turn, are replaced by pelargoniums and geraniums in summer.

Orchids inspired a similar obsession to ferneries, despite the difficulties in growing them. It is essential to replicate the correct growing conditions that each different one requires. In the home, they need bright light and therefore flourish by south- or east-facing windows, and it is very important not to over water them. Wait until they nearly dry out before doing so and make sure you have suitable compost.

A Winter Picnic

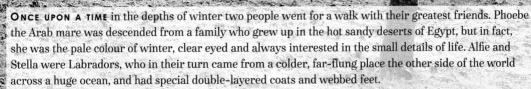

ONCE UPON A TIME in the depths of winter two people went for a walk with their greatest friends. Phoebe the Arab mare was descended from a family who grew up in the hot sandy deserts of Egypt, but in fact, she was the pale colour of winter, clear eyed and always interested in the small details of life. Alfie and Stella were Labradors, who in their turn came from a colder, far-flung place the other side of the world across a huge ocean, and had special double-layered coats and webbed feet.

The sun was rising but it was so pale that only a little light without any warmth filtered through the trees. The two people were tucked into thick coats, their heads down against the cold air, and the fallen leaves formed tapestries laced with frost underfoot. Phoebe was delicately stepping alongside them between the bare smooth winter trees. She chose to go with them as she enjoyed their friendship and she listened as they talked and walked ...

... Alfie and Stella padded nearby, sensing the peace of the morning and aware that a repast of some sort might be forthcoming. It was so cold that flakes drifted and touched them all like feathers. The collection of chairs and tables that came into view looked promising and everyone in turn took much interest in what might be there to enjoy. Phoebe, wary of the smell of woodsmoke, stood upwind from the eddying haze, although the two people seemed to like it.

They began to discuss what they might like to eat, from soup to thick homemade bread. Phoebe was patient but wondered what the oranges tasted like, although she was offered crisped kale instead whilst Alfie and Stella believed it was their duty to try the bread and cheese. The two people kept asking each other where they should start but Phoebe could see it was all together in one place so that was the wrong question. She decided to try everything and it tasted as good on the ground as on the table. Likewise, Alfie and Stella knew that space and time did not matter, only their tummies.

The two people seemed happy to be there. They ate and chatted and said it was just like a fairy tale, *A Winter's Tale*, perhaps – 'A sad tale is best for winter, I have one of sprite and goblins' – whilst the animals watched and waited, knowing the walk was not yet over.

Sourdough Bread

Bread has been a staple part of our diets for thousands of years. Once you have made a loaf, smelled it baking and enjoyed the texture you may well repeat the experience.

The principle is pretty much the same for all loaves: create a mixture, knead it to activate it, return it to the bowl to let it rise and mark it with a cross to let the devil out – a nice superstition but it does also help it rise! However, in many ways making sourdough bread is much more a labour of love. The absolute key to success is patience over a number of days. It can take between one and five days for the starter to begin fermenting, depending on the temperature and environment. Persevere for up to six days but if you still don't see any signs of life, or it starts to smell nasty, throw it away and start again.

If you plan to make sourdough every 2–3 days, keep your starter at room temperature and 'feed' it every couple of days. If less often, keep the starter in the fridge, feed it once a week, then leave it at room temperature for 24 hours before using it. Always try to use your starter when it is 'hungry' (i.e. if it has not been fed for 24 hours) and always leave about 200ml (7fl oz) of it in your jar for the next loaf.

INGREDIENTS

For the starter

700g (1lb 10oz) strong white flour

For the loaf

500g (1lb 2oz) strong white flour,
  plus extra for dusting
1 tsp fine salt
1 tbsp clear honey
300g (10oz) sourdough starter
Flavourless oil, for greasing

PREPARATION TIME 1 hour, plus 8 days for the starter and 3 hours rising
BAKING TIME 40 mins   **MAKES** 1 loaf

For the starter ...

In a large bowl, mix together 100g (3½oz) of the flour with 125ml (4fl oz) slightly warm water. Whisk together until smooth and lump-free.

Transfer the mixture into a large jar (a 1-litre/35fl oz Kilner jar is perfect). Leave the lid ajar for 1 hour or so in a warm place, then seal and set aside for 24 hrs.

For the next 6 days, you will need to 'feed' the starter. Each day, tip away half of the original mixture, add an extra 100g (3½oz) flour and 125ml (4fl oz) slightly warm water and stir well. It is best if you do this at the same time each day.

After 3–4 days you should start to see bubbles appearing on the surface and it will smell yeasty and a little acidic. This shows it is working.

On day 7, the starter should be quite bubbly and smell sweeter and is now ready to be used in baking.

For the bread ...

Tip the flour, 225ml (7½fl oz) warm water, salt, honey and the starter into a bowl and stir with a wooden spoon until combined. You can use a mixer with a dough hook for this. Add some extra flour if it is too sticky or a little warm water if it is too dry.

Tip onto a lightly floured surface and knead for 10 minutes until soft and elastic. You should be able to stretch it without it tearing.

Place the dough in a large, well-oiled bowl and cover. Leave in a warm place to rise for 3 hours. Don't worry if it doesn't seem to grow very much – sourdough takes much longer to rise than conventional bread dough.

Line a bowl with a clean tea towel and flour it thoroughly. Tip the dough back onto your work surface and knead briefly to knock out any air bubbles. Shape the dough into a smooth ball and dust it with flour. Place the dough in the bowl, cover loosely and leave at room temperature until roughly doubled in size.

The time it takes for your bread to rise will vary depending on the strength of your starter and the temperature in the room, anywhere from 4–8 hours. You can also prove your bread overnight in the fridge. Remove it in the morning and let it continue rising for another hour or two at room temperature.

Place a large baking tray in the oven, and heat to 230°C/450°F/Gas mark 8. Fill a small roasting tin with a little water and place this in the bottom of the oven to create steam.

After 5–10 minutes, remove the baking tray from the oven, sprinkle with flour, then carefully tip the risen dough onto the tray. Slash the top a few times with a sharp knife, then bake for 35–40 minutes until golden brown. It will sound hollow when tapped on the bottom.

Leave to cool on a wire rack for 20 minutes before serving.

Toum

Toum is a Lebanese garlic sauce that is a slow and steady emulsion process of garlic and oil. It is not merely utter heaven but very supportive of your health. Raw garlic is known for its antibacterial properties in association with lungs and breathing. I make a batch of this most weeks during the winter months.

Traditionally a pestle and mortar and a lot of patience was used to break down the garlic with the salt but these days it is infinitely quicker to use a hand blender or food processor.

INGREDIENTS

½ bulb of fresh garlic
   (about 6 cloves) with any little
   green hearts cut out
Pinch of good sea salt
Juice of ½ lemon
200ml (7fl oz) sunflower or
   rapeseed oil (not olive oil as it
   is too strong a flavour and will
   overpower the garlic)

PREPARATION TIME 20 mins   **MAKES** 1 jar

Put the garlic and salt in a bowl and pulse in short bursts until finely minced, occasionally scraping down the sides of the bowl so all the garlic is caught.

Add 1 teaspoon of lemon juice and continue processing until a paste begins to form. Then add a second teaspoon of lemon juice and process until completely smooth and slightly fluffy.

Keep the blender running and slowly drizzle in the oil in a very thin stream, 1 tablespoon at a time, followed by a little lemon juice. Repeat with another tablespoon of oil and the remaining lemon juice. Continue the process, alternating the oil with a smidge of water, until all the oil has been incorporated. Transfer the toum to a jar and store in the fridge for up to 1 month.

Toum can be used as a dip and a sauce. I love to dip fresh sourdough into it, drizzle it over roasted vegetables, use as a condiment for cold or even hot roast meat, and it is particularly delicious with grilled chicken. I find it utterly addictive!

Carrot and Ginger Soup

*We grow carrots in large pots or tubs as well as in the ground.
The Labradors, however, are also partial to them, which leads to utter
chaos if they have tipped up any of the tubs and nicked the carrots.
An exasperated Geordie immediately starts saying 'far too many dogs'.
I'm not exactly sure how we do have this many ... They often nip into the
horses' stables and find a spare carrot supply as a mid-morning treat,
only to be chased out by an exasperated Maggie.*

PREPARATION TIME 15 mins **COOKING TIME** 25–30 mins **SERVES** 4

INGREDIENTS

1 tbsp rapeseed oil
1 large onion, chopped
2 tbsp coarsely grated ginger
2 garlic cloves, sliced
½ tsp ground nutmeg
850ml (30fl oz) vegetable stock
500g (1lb 2oz) carrots, sliced
400g (14oz) tin cannellini beans
  (no need to drain)

Heat the oil in a large pan, add the onion, ginger and garlic, and soften
gently for 5 minutes. Stir in the nutmeg and cook for 1 minute more.

Pour in the stock, add the carrots, beans and their liquid, then cover and
simmer for 20–25 minutes until the carrots are tender.

Scoop a third of the mixture into a bowl and blitz the remainder until
smooth. Return everything to the pan and heat until bubbling.

CHEF'S TIP

If you would like, serve topped with roasted sliced almonds and a sprinkle of
nutmeg to make it even better.

Flapjacks

PREPARATION TIME 10 mins **COOKING TIME** 15 mins **SERVES** 6–8

INGREDIENTS
350g (12oz) butter
250g (9oz) golden syrup
250g (9oz) demerara sugar
550g (1¼lb) jumbo rolled oats
Pinch of salt

Preheat the oven to 180°C/350°F/Gas mark 4.

Melt the butter and syrup together in a pan. Add all the remaining
ingredients and mix well.

Press firmly into a greased and lined 25 × 35 cm (10 × 14 inch)
baking tin.

Bake for 10–15 minutes.

Leave to cool slightly before turning out, and cut into portions once cool.

THE SIX SISTERS

BEYOND THE WINTER PICNIC TABLE lies a short avenue. Each of my five sisters and I have planted a pair of walnut trees there which are growing over time into a light and spacious pathway linking the Wood through a rose arbour to the Pinetum and Wild Garden. It is something of a frost pocket and we have had to keep replacing trees until at last they all seem to have grown beyond it.

The common walnut (*Juglans regia*) and the black walnut and its allies are prized for their timber, which is hard, dense, tight-grained and polishes to a very smooth finish. The colour of the wood ranges from creamy white in the sapwood to a dark chocolate in the heartwood. The nuts produced each autumn are a good source of both food and of essential oils and are valued in traditional medicine.

It is a competition with the squirrels as to who picks all the walnuts and, due to localism on their part, they seem to be by far the most successful. They undoubtedly feed well from the chestnut trees, too, which offer alternative winter sustenance. Charles Dickens featured chestnuts in his novels, red hot and dipped in salt, whilst blowing on your fingers. It has always been a good land for hazels; fast-growing and tolerant, their stems are much used in fencing and, whilst the hazelnuts are also loved by squirrels and dormice, they are so prolific that occasionally there are some left over for us.

The hazelnuts and walnuts can be whizzed up to make nut butter, which contains a wonderful mix of nutrients including fibre, protein, B vitamins, phosphorous, zinc, vitamin E and oleic acid or omega-3. It is delicious spread on crunchy vegetables ... but highly calorific, which may be good for dormice and squirrels but slightly trickier for us.

WINTER WALKING

Roads go on
While we forget, and are
Forgotten like a star
That shoots and is gone.
Edward Thomas, 'Roads', 1916

WALKING HELPS US THINK, whether we are doing it from necessity or for exercise. It is a fundamental part of being a human, of understanding that we are on a journey: *'mens sana in corpore sano'*.

In winter, the bare trees reveal the framework of an older landscape and the old Iron Age fort is clearly visible above the Wood of Goodwill. Our forbears have left us a multitude of tracks and markers, whether pathways, trees or exposed stones, as a form of communal heritage, like ghosts of the past placed there to guide us. Local history is held together by the stories of those who have walked along the old driveways and depressed paths that run through these chalk escarpments and, in the faded light of winter, they can often take on a slightly eerie aspect.

On either side of the trackways above the Castle are the visible remains of the old field systems. They may have changed shape slightly from when they were first hacked out of the woodland and scrub by Stone Age settlers, but later fields were, for the most part, just fitted around the old ones. The field enclosures on the lower-lying land with its better soil are now hedged but the value of these chalk headlands is that they still are as they always were. To help preserve them, they are used as permanent pasture, lightly grazed by sheep with few fences which allows wildlife to be unconstrained and unconfined.

If the land and soil is still and sleeping, it is the quietest, toughest time of year in the fields and woods, the edible hedgerows vital for the birds and some extra hay or turnips much welcomed by

the sheep. Every light-filled part of the day is devoted to ensuring ice is broken for horses and ponies, for the chickens, the sheep and pigs who with their weight are able to take a more robust view towards sorting out icebreaking. The soil, open to the sky, absorbs the pure rainfall whilst microorganisms convert tilled-under fodder into usable nutrients for the next crop of plants. Ben the keeper and Simon on the farm go out to scatter bird seed and all of us watch as the natural world draws down through quieter months, before the sap will rise again.

CROCUSES, SNOWDROPS

CROCUSES FLOWER FROM AUTUMN RIGHT THROUGH TO SPRING, depending on variety, particularly lighting up the winter ground with all shades of violet and white as well as unexpected saffron colours. Like other bulbs, they are poisonous if ingested, although too often much enjoyed by mice and voles!

They will happily multiply and come back year after year, bringing more blooms with them each time. Crocuses like well-drained soil in a partial to full sun location. Plant crocus bulbs (corms) in informal groups, just 8cm (3 inches) deep and 5–8cm (2-3 inches) apart.

Unfortunately, as with so many bulbs here at Highclere, the most common crocuses, various hybrids of *Crocus vernus*, are particularly delicious to squirrels (and mice) and whilst the gardening team have numerous strategies to discourage them, it remains true that the best of these is simply to plant crocuses that squirrels don't like. There are such varieties and they are quite attractive. The purple and white species and hybrids of *Crocus tommasinianus* bloom from late winter to early spring. They look lovely and taste terrible so that the squirrels don't like them, and early foraging bees appreciate their nectar as well.

Legend relates that Eve was in the Garden of Eden and about to give up hope that winter would ever end. An angel appeared and transformed a snowflake into a snowdrop as a promise that spring would indeed appear again. Likewise Candlemas, which is celebrated on 2 February, marks 40 days after Christmas and the end of the festive season, though I suspect fewer people than in the past will remember either the date or what it signifies. Traditionally, candles would be lit to symbolise the hope of spring as it was a day to mark leaving the darkness of winter behind before entering a lighter month. Metaphorically, it also symbolises a holy illumination of the spirit of truth, which would be most useful.

The word 'candle' comes from the Latin word *candere* (to shine) and candles generally radiate thoughts of romance, security, warmth and the comfort of light, just as, similarly, out in gardens and churchyards snowdrops, those resolute little white bells of flowers, are associated with the coming of spring. They are nature's counterpart to the candles lighting up homes.

In a whirling and rather discordant time, these small flowers both bring a smile and offer focus. Nor are they alone as they break through the earth. Hellebores, also known as Lenten roses, flower from late winter until spring and are both frost-resistant and evergreen. They can vary in colour from snow white to yellows, pinks and lime greens, and will slowly spread by surface-rooting rhizomes. Some of the flowers look up at you, others are shyer and droop down. They are an early source of nectar for bees and for that reason alone are good to include where you can. Winter viburnums, an evergreen shrub, add shape and form to the border in the garden as well as in woodland and can perfume a winter walk.

Behind the statue of Charlemagne by the Monks' Garden are a mass of large architectural shrubs – *Mahonia japonica*. Much of the year they are just a backdrop, large and bushy with bright-green prickly leaves, but at this time of year they have fragrant lemon-yellow flowers which are produced in pendulous racemes. On a still day you catch the scent on the air and walk in circles until you find the source. On a different scale, delicately wound round fences, the small cream bells of winter clematis ignore all weather warnings whilst bright yellow winter jasmine adds a pop of colour to a wall. It is strange how so many of these early spring flowers, harbingers of light and warmth, are either white or yellow, light and sunshine.

Around these glad tidings, the main effort in the garden at this time of year is the practical work of preparing for spring and summer: digging, mulching, pruning, planting and moving and, just as Paul and his team work in the garden, so the Castle team are working with me to plan and prepare for our tours and events for the next eighteen months. Just like a snowdrop, a symbol of positivity, we all need something to look forward to as the day length increases.

HEAVENS ABOVE

AT THE END OF EVERY EVENING, whatever the weather, a melée of enthusiastic dogs and I head out for a final walk. Without the compelling need of the dogs, I am sure I would stay inside and some evenings, when I walk out into dense swirling rains and blustery winds, my sortie is brief.

On most evenings, however, I look up at the skies with awe and amazement, glad I have stepped out. To quote Vincent van Gogh: 'For my part I know nothing with any certainty, but the sight of the stars makes me dream.' Each evening walk marks a more peaceful time away from noisy human activity and a rarely found space to pause and stand and stare.

The night sky is an extraordinary, immense, eternal, curving sphere, lit by thousands of stars, both the same and everchanging. From different vantage points we all see the same half circle; our ancestors saw it and we hope that our descendants too will look up and wonder in years to come. The stars and planets move through their cycles depending on the seasons of the year and where we are standing. Over this year, I have watched the hero Arcturus move around the sky, Jupiter and Saturn were brilliant and sitting just above the Castle to the south as I walked across the field, whilst Mars, clearly visible at many times, is as fascinating today as the legendary figure after which it was named.

Since the earliest stories and myths, our behaviour both good and bad has been translated into patterns in the stars: the Bear, Cassiopeia, Perseus, the zodiac signs, Orion and so on. Archaeologists found the earliest-known depiction linked to the constellation of Orion in a prehistoric carving in a cave in the Ach valley in south-west Germany and dated it as more than 30,000 years old. In ancient Egypt the stars of Orion were thought to represent the god Sah, whilst his consort Sopdet was the goddess of the star Sirius. Homer's *Iliad* charts the story of Orion the hunter and the star Sirius, which is mentioned as his dog. Today this collection of stars remains attributed to Orion the hunter, wearing his belt with the faint suggestion of an arrow. He was brave but also flawed.

Bravery and heroism, happy endings and failings, they are all represented:
Silently, one by one, in the infinite meadows of heaven,
Blossomed the lovely stars, the forget-me-nots of the angels.
Henry Wadsworth Longfellow, 'Evangeline: A Tale of Acadie', 1847

◇

SHORT DAYS AND LONG EVENINGS AND NIGHTS LEND THEMSELVES TO HEARTY STEWS and slow cooking: dishes that reflect the plethora of game and winter vegetables available at this time of year. The winter months are about returning from invigorating walks, well wrapped up in soft scarves and thick coats against the pale icy sunshine and frost-painted hedges, to pies, warming curries and marmalade pudding, dripping with orange glaze. Nature and the weather have a different energy, one which calls for dishes to help us survive and celebrate these months.

WINTER
COOKING

The Easiest Pancake Recipe

This is where the USA and the UK can be divided by a common language. USA pancakes are fluffier; whereas here we prefer the thin British pancakes perfect for tossing on Shrove Tuesday. They have just three main ingredients and may bubble but do not rise. They are more similar to French crêpes and can also be the basis of a delicious dessert – Crêpes Suzette. The latter just requires you to cook some pancakes, folded into quarters, in a syrup of orange juice, sugar and Grand Marnier. It begins, however, with the basic pancake recipe.

INGREDIENTS

100g (3½oz) plain flour
2 eggs
300ml (10fl oz)
    semi-skimmed milk
1 tbsp sunflower or vegetable oil,
    plus extra for frying
Pinch of salt

PREPARATION TIME 5 mins   **COOKING TIME** 10 mins   **SERVES** 4–6

Put the flour and a pinch of salt into a large mixing bowl. Make a well in the centre and crack the eggs into the middle. Pour in about 50ml (2fl oz) of the milk and the oil and start whisking, gradually incorporating the flour into the eggs, milk and oil. Once all the flour is incorporated, beat until you have a smooth, thick paste. If it is too stiff to beat, add a little more milk.

Add a good splash of the remaining milk and whisk to loosen the batter. Continue whisking whilst gradually pouring in the rest. Continue pouring and whisking until you have a batter that is the consistency of slightly thick single cream.

Heat the pan over a moderate heat and wipe it with oiled kitchen paper. Ladle some batter into the pan, tilting it to spread the mixture into a thin and even layer. Quickly pour any excess batter back into the mixing bowl.

Cook, undisturbed, for about 30 seconds or until the pancake is a light golden colour on the bottom.

To turn the pancake, slide a palette knife under it and quickly flip it over. Cook for another 30 seconds before turning out onto a warm plate.

Continue with the rest of the batter, occasionally wiping the pan with the oiled kitchen paper as necessary.

Serve with lemon wedges or golden syrup.

CHEF'S TIP

For *Crêpes Suzette*, make an orange sauce by combining the juice of two oranges, the zest of one, 175g (6oz) butter and about 75g (3oz) caster sugar in a saucepan, heating and simmering until wonderfully syrupy. Lay folded, pre-cooked pancakes in the warm sauce, add Cointreau or Grand Marnier, light it with great care, and *flambé*.

Parsnip and Apple Soup

Geordie loves parsnips, whether roasted or in a soup, and they partner very well with apples. I love walnuts and a few, toasted, give a delicious crunch to the soup.

INGREDIENTS

50g (2oz) butter
2 tbsp olive oil
1 large white onion,
    peeled and chopped
4 medium parsnips,
    peeled and sliced
2 apples, peeled,
    cored and chopped
1 tsp curry powder (optional)
1 litre (35fl oz) stock
A few sprigs of thyme
200g (7oz) crème fraîche
Salt and freshly ground
    black pepper
Toasted walnuts and/or apple slices,
    to garnish (optional)

PREPARATION TIME 15 mins   **COOKING TIME** 30–40 mins   **SERVES** 4

Heat the butter and oil in a large pan and soften the onions and parsnips over a medium heat for around 15 minutes until soft.

Add the apples and curry powder (if using) to the pan, and cook for 2–3 minutes.

Add the stock and thyme, season with salt and pepper, and simmer over a low heat for 30 minutes or until the vegetables are tender

Remove from the heat and blitz with a hand blender until smooth. Stir in three-quarters of the crème fraîche.

Spoon the soup into bowls and top each with some of the remaining crème fraîche, garnishing if you like with a little sliced apple or gently toasted walnuts.

Celery

Celery leaves were found in the tomb of Tutankhamun, so its excellent health properties have been known for a long time. Although made up mainly of water, it has antioxidant properties and contains selinene, limonene, kaempferol, p-coumaric acid, vitamin K, folate, vitamins A, B2, B6, C and potassium. The Romans thought it helped gout, insomnia, arthritis and, of course, the libido, and fenland celery became a much sought-after delicacy in the Victorian kitchen. Celebrated as a vegetable in French cuisine for over 400 years, it more often tends to adorn a Bloody Mary cocktail here. It does, however, make a truly delicious soup, whilst braised celery is a lovely accompaniment to meat and fish dishes.

Roasted Celery and Fennel Soup

INGREDIENTS

1 head celery, chopped into chunks
1 bulb fennel
1 garlic clove, chopped
2 tbsp olive oil
750ml (1¼ pints) chicken stock
2 large potatoes, peeled and diced
2 tbsp chopped parsley
Salt and freshly ground
   black pepper
Cream, to serve

PREPARATION TIME 16 mins   **COOKING TIME** 45 mins   **SERVES** 4

Preheat the oven to 180°C/350°F/Gas mark 4.

Put the celery, fennel and garlic into a large roasting tin, drizzle with oil and season with salt and pepper. Toss it all together so the vegetables are nicely coated. Cover loosely with foil to prevent browning and Roast for about 45 minutes or until the vegetables are soft.

Meanwhile, heat the chicken stock in a saucepan. Add the chopped potato, and cook for 20 minutes until the potato is entirely soft. Add 1 tablespoon of the parsley.

Add the vegetable mixture to the stock, blitz until smooth and season to taste. Serve in bowls sprinkled with the remaining parsley and with a swirl of cream.

Braised Celery

INGREDIENTS

2 heads celery
1 tbsp chopped mixed herbs
150ml (5fl oz) white wine
250ml (8fl oz) double cream
2 garlic cloves, crushed
25g (1oz) butter
Salt and freshly ground
   black pepper

PREPARATION TIME 5 mins   **COOKING TIME** 1 hour   **SERVES** 6–8

Preheat the oven to 180°C/350°F/Gas mark 4.

Wash and peel the celery stems and lay them in rank in a rectangular dish. Scatter with the herbs.

Combine the wine, cream and crushed garlic in a jug. Season with salt and lots of freshly ground black pepper. Pour the wine mixture over the celery and dot the butter on top.

Cover with foil and bake in the oven for 45 minutes. The celery will now be soft. Take the foil off and continue to bake for a further 15 minutes.

BRAISED CELERY →

Honeyed Winter Salad

Honey makes most things better in life, spread on toast, drizzled over porridge and even in a salad.

A day without a friend is like a pot without a single drop of honey left inside.

'I don't feel very much like Pooh today,' said Pooh.

'There, there,' said Piglet. 'I'll bring you tea and honey until you do.'

A.A. Milne, Winnie-the-Pooh, 1926

INGREDIENTS

1 butternut squash,
   cut into thin wedges
2 red onions, halved and cut
   into wedges
4 parsnips, cut into wedges
3 tbsp olive oil
1-2 tbsp clear honey
1 small ciabatta, roughly torn into
   pieces
1 tbsp sunflower seeds
225g (8oz) spinach
2 tbsp white wine vinegar
1 tsp Dijon mustard
Salt and freshly ground
   black pepper

PREPARATION TIME 15 mins   **COOKING TIME** 30 mins   **SERVES** 4

Preheat the oven to 220°C/425°F/Gas mark 7.

Put the vegetables into a large roasting tin, drizzle with half the oil and season to taste. Roast for 25 minutes, turning once in a while until softened and the butternut squash has just started to brown at the edges. Drizzle with the honey. Scatter the torn ciabatta and sunflower seeds over the top and return to the oven for a further 5 minutes or until toasted.

Put the spinach into a large bowl and tip in the vegetables and ciabatta.

Whisk the vinegar, mustard and remaining oil together, season to taste and toss into the salad until the spinach wilts slightly.

Serve immediately.

Smoked Haddock Mornay with Spinach

*This is one of our mother's favourite recipes and I can still see her
cooking it for supper with our father. She far preferred it if I were to
cook it, however, so she could enjoy a delicious gin and tonic and good
conversation with Geordie.*

INGREDIENTS

300ml (10fl oz) full-fat milk
1 small onion, peeled,
   cut lengthways into 6 wedges
1 bay leaf
2 strips lemon peel
450g (1lb) smoked haddock fillet
   (or any other decent white fish
   with skin)
40g (1½oz) butter
25g (1oz) plain flour
2 tbsp white wine
50g (2oz) Gruyère, finely grated
½ tsp English mustard
3 tbsp double cream
500g (1lb 2oz) spinach
Salt and freshly ground
   black pepper

For the gratin topping

25g (1oz) fresh white breadcrumbs
15g (½oz) Gruyère, finely grated
½ tsp chopped parsley

PREPARATION TIME 25 mins   **COOKING TIME** 20 mins   **SERVES** 4

Pour the milk into a large, deep frying pan and add the onion, bay leaf
and lemon peel. Place the fish skin-side down in the pan and bring to
a gentle simmer over a medium heat. Cook for 5–6 minutes, basting
the fish occasionally, until it is just starting to flake. Leave to stand for
5 minutes.

Drain the fish, reserving the milk.

Melt the butter in a large non-stick saucepan and stir in the flour to form
a *roux* (chef's term for a cooked butter and flour mix). Slowly add the
reserved warm milk, stirring constantly. Bring the sauce to a simmer and
continue to stir until it is smooth and thick. Stir in the wine, Gruyère,
mustard and cream. Cook over a low heat for a further 2–3 minutes,
stirring all the time. Season to taste.

Flake the fish into chunky pieces and discard the skin, onion, bay leaf and
lemon peel. Add the fish to the cheese mixture and heat very gently for
2 minutes to warm it through.

Cook the spinach in a pan of salted boiling water for 1 minute.
Drain thoroughly. If making the gratin topping, keep warm.

For the gratin topping, preheat the grill to hot and mix the breadcrumbs,
Gruyère and parsley together. Pour the fish mixture into a shallow
ovenproof dish and sprinkle over the gratin mixture. Place under the grill
for 3–5 minutes until it is nicely browned and the filling is bubbling.

Serve on a bed of spinach.

Winter Vegetable Curry

*My niece Marina has become vegetarian and always complains
that her mother, Sarah, my number two sister, does not cook. This is not
exactly the truth as Sarah does in fact cook boiled eggs. Therefore, I have
included a lovely vegetarian curry for both of them to cook together.*

INGREDIENTS

1 tbsp vegetable oil
1 tsp mustard seeds
5 fresh curry leaves (if you can't
    get these, try kaffir lime leaves
    instead)
2 medium onions, finely chopped
2cm (¾ inch) fresh ginger,
    finely chopped
1 red chilli
½ tsp turmeric
1 tsp fennel seeds
1 tsp fenugreek seeds
400ml (14fl oz) coconut milk
250g (9oz) mixed diced turnip and
    swede (rutabaga)
3 tbsp vegetable stock
1 small cauliflower, broken into
    florets and chargrilled
Handful of fresh coriander (cilantro)
    (optional)

PREPARATION TIME 25 mins **COOKING TIME** 35 mins **SERVES** 4

Heat the vegetable oil in a frying pan and add the mustard seeds and
curry leaves. Cook gently until the mustard seeds start to pop but be
careful not to burn them. Add the onion and ginger and soften for
3–4 minutes.

Add the rest of the spices and fry for 1 minute.

Add the coconut milk, turnip and swede (rutabaga) and a splash of
vegetable stock.

Season, cover with a lid and simmer for 20 minutes, adding more
vegetable stock as necessary.

Stir in the cauliflower and cook for a further 10 minutes (we cooked
the cauliflower separately in boiling water, dried and chargrilled it for
presentation).

Scatter with the coriander (cilantro), if using, and serve.

Fabulous with Fragrant Rice (see below), naan bread, poppadums and
mango chutney (of course!).

Fragrant Rice

INGREDIENTS

1 tsp cumin seeds
3 or 4 cardamom pods
1 tsp cloves
400ml (14fl oz) vegetable stock
    or water
1 cinnamon stick
1 small onion, unpeeled
    but cut in half
250g (9oz) basmati rice
25g (1oz) butter (optional)

PREPARATION TIME 10 mins **COOKING TIME** 20 mins **SERVES** 4

Heat a heavy-bottomed saucepan and toast the cumin seeds, cardamom
pods and cloves over a medium heat until the aromas of the spices are
released.

Add the stock or water, the cinnamon stick and the onion, then bring to
the boil, turn down the heat and simmer for 15–20 minutes.

Meanwhile, put the rice in a sieve and rinse under cold running water to
remove a little of the starch. Transfer to a saucepan.

When your stock is ready, strain it into the rice. Turn on the heat under
the rice and bring rapidly to the boil. As soon as it boils, cover and turn it
down to the lowest possible heat.

Cook for about 10–12 minutes until the rice is cooked. Fluff up with a
fork before serving, incorporating the butter, if using, for extra flavour.

Baked Three-Cheese Soufflé

Mrs Mackie was the cook for the 6th Earl and Countess of Carnarvon in 1932. Timing was all and, in order to encourage the footmen to hurry along the corridors to the Dining Room with her pièce de résistance, she would chase them.

Twice-baked soufflés are a fantastic idea as you can make them in advance, taking away any worries about them not rising at the critical moment. Perfect for a casual lunch served with a crisp salad. I do love cheese.

INGREDIENTS

For the soufflés

40g (1½oz) butter,
  plus extra for greasing
1 small onion, peeled and cut into
  wedges
275ml (9fl oz) full-fat milk, plus
  extra for topping up if needed
1 bay leaf
40g (1½oz) plain flour
40g (1½oz) mature Cheddar,
  coarsely grated
40g (1½oz) Gruyère, coarsely grated
40g (1½oz) mild goat's cheese
1 tsp English mustard
  (or 2 tsp Dijon mustard)
Freshly grated nutmeg, to taste
1 heaped tbsp chopped chives,
  plus extra for garnish
3 free-range eggs, separated
Salt and freshly ground
  black pepper

For the second baking

50g (2oz) Gruyère or mature
  Cheddar, finely grated
6 tbsp double cream

PREPARATION TIME less than 30 mins   **COOKING TIME** 40 mins   **SERVES** 6

Preheat the oven to 200°C/400°F/Gas mark 6.

Generously butter six 150ml (5fl oz) ovenproof ramekins and line each with a disc of baking paper. Place on a baking tray.

Put the onion in a saucepan with the milk and bay leaf and simmer for 5 minutes to infuse the flavours. Remove from the heat and set aside for a couple of minutes.

Melt the butter and stir in the flour, mixing well. Cook for a minute, stirring continually as it cooks and begins to bubble. Remove from the heat.

Strain the milk and gradually stir it into the flour and butter paste. Then return to the heat and cook for 2 minutes, stirring constantly, until it is smooth and thick. You will need around 250ml (8fl oz) of infused milk.

Add the cheeses, mustard and a grating of nutmeg and continue to cook for a further 1–2 minutes until the cheese melts.

Stir in the chives and season to taste. The seasoning should be reasonably strong at this point as the egg whites still have to be added. Transfer to a heatproof bowl and leave to stand for 5 minutes.

Beat in the egg yolks one at a time until thoroughly mixed.

Whisk the egg whites until stiff peaks are formed and fold a couple of tablespoons into the cheese mixture with a metal spoon. (This loosens the mixture and makes it easier to fold in the rest.) Then gently fold in the remaining egg whites to preserve as much volume as possible.

Spoon the soufflé mixture into the ramekins until it almost reaches the top. Bake in the centre of the oven for 15-20 minutes until very well risen and golden brown on top. (Do not open the oven door for the first 10 minutes of cooking.) Once cooked, remove the tray from the oven and leave the soufflés to cool in their ramekins.

Once the soufflés are cold, line a baking tray with baking parchment and slide a knife around the edge of each ramekin. Carefully turn the soufflés out onto your hand. Remove the baking paper disc from the base and place upside down on the baking tray. At this point they can be covered with cling film and left in the fridge for up to 24 hours before baking again.

When you wish to finish them for service...

Preheat the oven to 200°C/400°F/Gas mark 6.

Sprinkle each soufflé with the grated Gruyère or Cheddar, spoon a tablespoon of double cream over each one and bake for 10 minutes until they are hot and the cheese topping has melted. Serve immediately, sprinkled with more chives.

Baked Gnocchi with Spinach

INGREDIENTS

1kg (2¼lb) good potatoes
  (King Edward or Desirée)
2 garlic cloves, peeled
3 eggs, beaten
300g (10oz) plain flour
600ml (1 pint) béchamel sauce
  (see recipe below)
400g (14oz) spinach
Salt and freshly ground
  black pepper

Baked gnocchi are simply classic Italian potato dumplings, which make for a hearty meal no matter how you serve them. Recipes vary from region to region but this is the one we have always used.

PREPARATION TIME 10 mins   **COOKING TIME** 30 mins   **SERVES** 4

Preheat the oven to 190°C/375°F/Gas mark 5.

Place the unpeeled potatoes in a pan of cold water with the peeled garlic and bring to the boil. Cook until just soft.

Whilst the potato is still hot, remove the skin and mash with the cooked garlic for a lovely flavour.

Place the warm potato on a worktop, make a well in the middle and start to add the beaten eggs.

Mix in the flour, salt and pepper so that it forms a light dough that's easy to shape and does not stick.

Roll out the mixture, divide into three and roll into sausage shapes about a thumb's thickness. Cut into little barrels. Use extra flour if needed.

Bring a large pan of salted water to the boil and poach the gnocchi for about 2 minutes, a few at a time.

When cooked, remove from the water and chill in cold water.

Warm the béchamel sauce over a medium heat and drop in the spinach and gnocchi. Gently mix together and pour into an ovenproof dish. Bake for 15 minutes.

CHEF'S TIP:

Add a cheese of your choice to the sauce or dried chilli flakes (for an extra kick). You can also try a sprinkle of chopped herbs — chives, parsley or sage work so well.

Béchamel Sauce

INGREDIENTS

1 small onion, peeled and studded
  with 4 cloves
1 litre (35fl oz) milk
100g (3½oz) unsalted butter
100g (3½oz) plain flour

PREPARATION TIME 10 mins   **COOKING TIME** 30 mins   **MAKES** 600ml (1 pint)

Place the studded onion in the milk and bring to a simmer over a low heat. Take off the heat and set aside.

In another pan gently melt the butter.

Add the flour to the melted butter and mix over a low heat without colouring. Cook for 4 minutes.

Slowly add the warmed milk to the roux and keep stirring until a smooth sauce is formed.

Remove the onion and discard. Strain the sauce if necessary.

CHEF'S TIP

For extra flavour leave the studded onion in the sauce and simmer over a low heat for a while before removing.

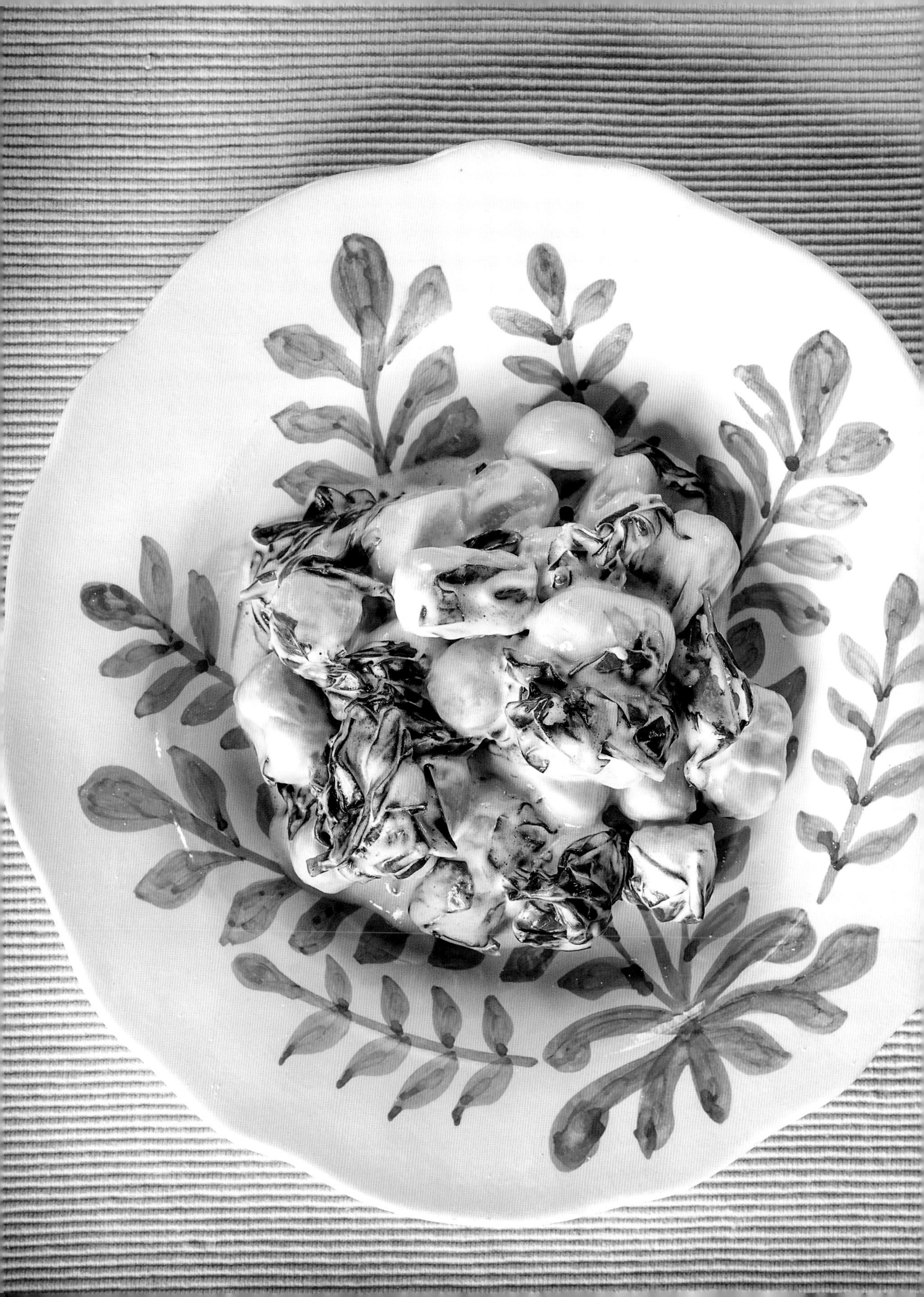

Pork Belly with Fennel

Fennel hung over doorways helps keep the devil at bay and used to be stuffed into keyholes on Halloween when the worlds of the quick and the dead merge. Fennel is crunchy and strongly aniseed when eaten raw, but when roasted or braised, its flavour becomes softer and simply aromatic. Full of vitamins including manganese and other health-giving compounds, it is delicious and offers support to your diet during the winter.

INGREDIENTS

3 garlic cloves
2 tsp fennel seeds
1 tsp coarse black pepper
3 lemons (zest of 3, juice of 2)
2 tsp chopped rosemary
2 tbsp olive oil
1·2kg (2½lb) piece pork belly
1 bulb fennel
400ml (14fl oz) dry white wine
Sea salt and freshly ground
   black pepper

PREPARATION TIME 20 mins   **COOKING TIME** 3 hours   **SERVES** 4

Preheat the oven to 190°C/375°F/Gas mark 5.

Place the garlic, 1 teaspoon of sea salt and fennel seeds into a mortar and pound them together to form a paste. Mix in the pepper, lemon zest and juice, rosemary and oil.

Score the skin of the pork at 5mm (¼ inch) intervals, just deep enough to cut through the skin and no further, and place 1 teaspoon of the seasoning mixture into each slit. Rub the scored skin with the rest of the mixture and the remaining lemon, cut in half. Sprinkle with more sea salt and place on a rack in a roasting tray. Cook in the oven for 1 hour.

Meanwhile, remove the fronds from the fennel and set them aside. Cut the bulb into slices 4mm (¼ inch) thick, season and place on a baking tray. After the belly has cooked for 1 hour, pour its rendered fat over the fennel, then cook separately for 1 hour more. If the crackling is already well browned, cover it with foil to prevent scorching.

Once the fennel is browned and the meat tender, transfer the pork to sit on top of the fennel. Pour any remaining fat out of the pork roasting tray, pour in the wine, then heat the tray on the hob and scrape up all the juices in the pan. Pour these over the pork and fennel, then turn the oven temperature down to 150°C/300°F/Gas mark 2 and cook for a further hour until very tender.

Remove the crackling and serve in thick slices.

CHEF'S TIP

This dish is fabulous with beetroot (beets); we have used baby beetroot – red, candy and golden – but large diced ones are just as good. You can simply peel and boil them and serve with lots of seasoning.

For the most strikingly colourful result, cook different colours in separate pans.

Roasted Pork Cutlet and Tinned Prunes

Pork and prunes are a classic combination for good reason, and prunes whether tinned or dried are an excellent source of fibre. High in potassium and key vitamins, choose the amount you serve with pork and enjoy them. This recipe is for one – it's always handy to have a quick tasty supper dish in your repertoire for when you're left alone on a winter evening.

INGREDIENTS

1 sprig of thyme, leaves picked
1 sprig of rosemary
1 garlic clove, crushed
200g (7oz) pork cutlet on the bone
290g (10oz) tin of prunes
100g (3½oz) chilled butter, cubed,
  plus extra for cooking
1 tbsp olive oil
1 shallot per person,
  sliced into thin wedges
1 apple, cored and cut into wedges
50ml (2fl oz) chicken stock
Salt and freshly ground
  black pepper

PREPARATION TIME 20 mins   **COOKING TIME** 20 mins   **SERVES** 1

Preheat the oven to 190°C/375°F/Gas mark 5.

Crush the thyme, rosemary and garlic roughly together in a mortar and pestle and rub on the cutlet. Leave for a good hour (best left overnight).

Open the tin of prunes and strain out and reserve the juice. Destone the prunes and put to one side for later.

In a hot pan, add a small knob of butter and splash of oil, then the cutlet (take care as this may spit). Add the shallot and gently brown.

After 2 or 3 minutes turn over the pork and shallot. Add the apple and cook for 2 more minutes.

Turn everything out on to an oven tray and roast for no more than 5 minutes. This is not long, so don't forget about it and let your pork go dry!

Return the frying pan to the heat and deglaze with the chicken stock, scraping up any tasty, brown caramelised bits from the bottom. Reduce by half, then add the prune juice and as many prunes as you like.

When the sauce is hot, remove from the heat and add the butter, a piece at a time, stirring all the time until all the butter has melted into the sauce. Chefs call this *monter au beurre*, and it adds great shine, flavour and richness.

Now plate and enjoy – great with sautéed green beans or just a salad.

Game from the Highclere Estate

Our ancestors would have depended on game to survive wintertime, cooking over a fire, grilling, roasting or smoking the various meats. Still today it is about using seasonal ingredients to add flavour to the heat. The woodlands and fields are as much a larder in which to 'forage' for game, as for berries and nuts, bringing what is wild into the kitchen.

Game is an incredibly healthy source of food, leaner than farmed meats, given the natural diets and life. Often locally sourced, the carbon footprint of game tends to be relatively small, with very few miles from field or wood to table.

Roast Pheasant with Smoked Bacon

Game such as pheasant is one of the healthiest meats available, lean and very low in fat and cholesterol. It also tends to be high in iron as well as other beneficial minerals. My son claimed not to like it particularly but I always used to tell him it was chicken, because it has a similar taste but a little bit stronger.

INGREDIENTS

1 oven-ready pheasant
1 tbsp oil
2 slices dry-cured bacon
   for covering the breast,
   plus 80g (3oz), diced
1 small onion, sliced
2 carrots, roughly chopped
1 leek, roughly chopped
Sprig of rosemary
1 garlic clove, crushed
100ml (3½fl oz) red wine
100ml (3½fl oz) vegetable,
   chicken or game stock
Small handful of sage leaves,
   chopped
2 bay leaves
Salt and freshly ground
   black pepper

PREPARATION TIME 20 mins   **COOKING TIME** 1 hour   **SERVES** 2

Preheat the oven to 180°C/350°F/Gas mark 4.

Brown and seal the pheasant in a hot oiled pan, season and place in an ovenproof dish. Wrap the slices of bacon over the top.

Put the bacon trimmings, onion, carrots, leek, rosemary and garlic in a pan and sauté for 2–4 minutes.

Pour in the wine and stock and add the sage and bay leaves. Simmer for 2 minutes, then add to the pheasant.

Cover the dish and bake in the oven for about 1 hour.

When the meat is tender, remove and let it rest. Strain the liquid into a saucepan, boil until it has reduced by half, then serve.

Tagliatelle with Venison Ragu

A genuine ragu is often made with different meats, and every Italian family has the best recipe in the world. Compared to other sauces a ragu has red wine and tomatoes and is quite thick, which is why the pulled venison works so well. The discussion and enjoyment of such recipes, the time devoted to cooking and eating is the greatest of talents and a reason to sit and eat in Italy.

INGREDIENTS

For the ragu

1kg (2¼lb) venison
6 tbsp olive oil
200g (7oz) pancetta or
   streaky bacon
1 carrot, finely chopped
1 celery stalk, finely chopped
1 medium onion, finely chopped
3 tbsp tomato puree
1 × 400g (14oz) tin of tomatoes
   or passata
1 bouquet garni (or tie together
   2 bay leaves, a sprig of rosemary
   and some thyme)
4 garlic cloves, chopped
1 tsp mixed spice
500ml (17fl oz) red wine
500ml (17fl oz) beef stock
Salt and freshly ground
   black pepper
Grated Parmesan, to serve

For the pasta

500g (1lb 2oz) fresh tagliatelle
50g (2oz) butter

PREPARATION TIME 40 mins   **COOKING TIME** 4 hours   **SERVES** 6

To make the ragu ...

Season the venison with salt and pepper, place in a roasting tin and drizzle with half the olive oil. Roast for 2 hours until browned on the outside and cooked. Reserve the pan juices and leave to cool.

Using a heavy casserole dish with a lid, cook the pancetta or bacon in the remaining oil for 5-6 minutes.

Tip in the vegetables, the tomato puree, the tomatoes or passata, the bouquet garni, the garlic and the mixed spice and cook over a low heat for 20 minutes until the vegetables have softened but not coloured.

Pull the roast venison apart with two forks and add to the vegetable mix. Cook on a high heat for 10 minutes until the meat starts to brown. Add the roasting juices, wine and stock.

Bring to a simmer, cover and cook for around 90 minutes in the oven, stirring occasionally. If it is still too liquid, cook for a little longer.

Season to taste.

To cook the pasta and serve ...

Cook the pasta in boiling water for two or three minutes.

Drain, reserving a small amount of the cooking liquid and add the pasta to the meat ragu. Add the butter and gently coat the pasta with the sauce. Use the cooking liquid to loosen the sauce if necessary.

Top with Parmesan and serve.

For a more complete meal, this is delicious served with asparagus spears and a couple of roasted baby carrots stirred through the ragu.

Local Pot Roast Venison with Dumplings

Venison is a delicious lean meat and, given it has little fat running through it, it is important not to let it dry out. The deep mellow richness of the stew is entirely irresistible, and who does not love dumplings? The slower you cook it the better, and remember to rest it before you serve.

Venison partners well with mushrooms and berries but the strong flavour of the meat also works brilliantly with bitter ingredients like red wine, as here, or dark chocolate and chilli.

INGREDIENTS

1·2kg (2½lb) venison haunch, diced, with any sinews removed
100g (3½oz) butter
2 tbsp olive oil, plus extra for browning
2 large parsnips, peeled and chopped into large chunks
4 large carrots, peeled and chopped into large chunks
½ swede (rutabaga), peeled and chopped into large chunks
2 onions, chopped
300g (10oz) potatoes, peeled and quartered
4 garlic cloves
Large sprig of rosemary
Juice of 1 lemon
3 fresh bay leaves
100ml (3½fl oz) port
300ml (10fl oz) stock
2 tbsp redcurrant or cranberry jelly (as you prefer)
Salt and freshly ground black pepper

For the dumplings

50g (2oz) suet
100g (3½oz) self-raising flour
Pinch of salt
Cold water

PREPARATION TIME 30 mins **COOKING TIME** 90 mins **SERVES** 6

Preheat the oven to 220°C/425°F/Gas mark 7.

Brown the venison in a pan in batches with a good knob of butter and a little oil.

Place all the vegetables except the potatoes with the garlic in a roasting dish and drizzle with olive oil, salt and pepper. Place the rosemary over the vegetables.

Rub the browned meat with the lemon juice, sprinkle with salt and pepper and place on top of the vegetables. Tuck in the bay leaves.

Cover with port, stock and your jelly preference and place in the oven for 1 hour. Top up with extra liquid if necessary.

For the dumplings, mix together the suet, flour, salt and enough water to make a dough consistency (credit for this foolproof recipe goes to the Atora suet box). Divide into 6 balls.

When the stew has 20–30 minutes left to cook, add the potatoes and place the dumplings on top.

Remove from the oven and serve from the dish.

CHEF'S TIP

Add chopped sage or picked thyme leaves to the dumpling mixture for a better flavour.

Game Pie

Game pie is one of the oldest noted dishes and is often made with the meat entirely encased in a pastry. In fact this process of raising the sides of a rectangular pie to form a pastry box was described in old cookery books as 'raising the coffin'. It was a way of preserving and carrying food. The extraordinary diversity of game became almost competitive and was the subject of elaborate still-life paintings.

Moving on to slightly happier thoughts, however, a lattice pastry top as here is delicious and a slightly lighter version which just references the cooking heritage.

INGREDIENTS

2 tbsp sunflower oil
675g (1½lb) mixed game meat such
   as pheasant and partridge or
   pigeon
225g (8oz) venison steak, cut into
   2.5cm (1 inch) cubes
2 red onions, peeled and sliced
1 garlic clove, peeled and crushed
120g (4oz) smoked streaky bacon,
   de-rinded and chopped
120g (4oz) wild chanterelle and
   oyster chestnut mushrooms,
   cleaned
30g (1oz) plain flour
1 bay leaf
Zest and juice of 1 orange
1 tbsp redcurrant jelly
300ml (10 fl oz) chicken stock
300ml (10 fl oz) red wine
Ready-made puff pastry
   (or see page 214
   to make your own)
Sprigs of thyme
1 egg, beaten
Salt and freshly ground
   black pepper

PREPARATION TIME 40 mins   **COOKING TIME** 2 hours   **SERVES** 6

Heat a tablespoon of the oil and fry the game and venison in batches until well browned. Put on one side.

Heat the rest of the oil and soften the onions for 5 minutes. Add the garlic, bacon and mushrooms and cook for 2–3 minutes.

Stir in the flour and cook for 2 minutes. Season well and stir in the bay leaf, orange zest and juice, redcurrant jelly, stock and wine.

Bring to the boil, add the meat and simmer gently for 40–50 minutes until the meat is tender. Leave to cool.

Preheat the oven to 200°C/400°F/Gas mark 6.

Put the meat mixture in a pie dish.

Roll out the pastry to a thickness of about ½cm (¼ inch), cut into strips and plait together to make a lattice topping. Or just roll out the pastry to make a simple lid and cover the dish, then decorate with the pastry trimmings and cut a steam hole in the centre.

Garnish with picked thyme and season well with black pepper and sea salt. Glaze with beaten egg.

Bake for 20 minutes and then reduce the heat to 180°C/350°F/ Gas mark 4 and continue to bake for 30 minutes or so until the pastry is golden and risen and the filling is piping hot.

Highclere Lemon Cake

Whilst this cake uses neither gluten nor dairy, that is not the reason to make it – bake this because it is simply gooey and you cannot resist trying a slice, and perhaps another ...

INGREDIENTS

175g (6oz) vegetable shortening
  or vegan butter
175g (6oz) caster sugar,
  plus an extra 100g (3½oz)
Zest and juice of 2 lemons
3 medium eggs
100g (3½oz) gluten-free
  self-raising flour
75g (3oz) ground almonds

For the icing

120g (4oz) icing sugar
Zest and juice of 1 lemon

PREPARATION TIME 20–30 mins   **COOKING TIME** 40–45 mins   **SERVES** 8

Preheat the oven to 180°C/350°F/Gas mark 4.

Line a 900g (2lb) loaf tin with baking paper.

Beat together the vegan butter and 175g (6oz) caster sugar, add half the lemon zest and beat until pale and fluffy.

Add the eggs one at a time and beat thoroughly before adding the next.

Sift the flour into the bowl and fold it into the mixture. Fold in the ground almonds.

Spoon the mixture into the prepared tin and bake for 40–45 minutes until golden and a skewer inserted into the centre of the cake comes out clean.

To make the drizzle, mix together the juice of 2 lemons, the remaining zest and the 100g (3½oz) caster sugar.

Remove the cake from the oven and poke holes over the top with a skewer whilst it is still hot. Gradually pour over the drizzle. Keep pouring as it takes time for it to soak into the cake.

Wait until the cake is cool before removing it from the tin.

If you would like to ice the cake ...

Mix together the icing sugar and lemon juice to a drizzling consistency.

Once the cake is completely cold, drizzle the icing over the top of the cake and sprinkle over the lemon zest.

Lord Carnarvon's Marmalade and Ginger Pudding

*There can be few more traditional puddings than Marmalade, and,
considering lunch menus for friends during the winter, this pudding
simply makes Geordie happy. He has it with custard and cream. I think
Paddington Bear would also like this pudding, but he might need extra
marmalade.*

INGREDIENTS

110g (4oz) salted butter,
  plus extra for greasing
175g (6oz) thick-cut marmalade,
  plus extra for Paddington!
150g (5oz) self-raising flour
2 tsp ground ginger
1 tsp ground cinnamon
¼ tsp ground cloves
¼ tsp grated nutmeg
1 tsp baking powder
Pinch of salt
110g (4oz) light muscovado sugar
2 large eggs
1 tsp freshly grated ginger
3 tbsp fresh orange juice

PREPARATION TIME 30 mins   **COOKING TIME** 35 mins   **SERVES** 8

Preheat the oven to 180°C/350°F/Gas mark 4.

Grease a 1·8kg (4lb) pudding bowl with butter and load the marmalade
into the bottom (easier when using slightly warm marmalade). Set aside.

Sift the flour, spices, baking powder and a pinch of salt into a bowl.

In another bowl beat the butter until pale and fluffy then add the sugar
and beat for a further 5 minutes until paler. Beat in the eggs one at
a time, adding in 1 tablespoon of the flour with the second egg.

Beat in the grated ginger and gently fold in the remaining flour mixture
with a metal spoon, followed by the orange juice. Pour this batter on top
of the marmalade in your pudding bowl.

Bake for 30–35 minutes until a skewer inserted into the centre of the
pudding comes out clean. Leave to cool in the bowl for 10 minutes then
carefully turn out onto a warmed serving dish.

Serve with custard or cream (and a dish full of the extra marmalade).

EPILOGUE

Therefore, am I still
A lover of the meadows and the woods
And mountains; and of all that we behold
From this green earth; of all the mighty world...
The anchor of my purest thoughts, the nurse
The guide, the guardian of my heart, and soul
Of all my moral being

William Wordsworth, 'Lines Composed a Few Miles above Tintern Abbey', 1798

THE LANDSCAPE AT HIGHCLERE is the result of the inspiration of successive generations who have lived here. It is shaped by personality and vision, observing and celebrating the 'art of Garden-Making' in England. Gardens offer both recreation and solitude, as well as a built-in acceptance of the cycle of life, but here the heart of our success is the topographical setting in which Highclere stands: its position in the extraordinary landscape that surrounds it. The house has developed through cycles of scale and importance and the gardens and wider estate both extend and reflect this life.

From the beginning it has been a farm, and that still lies at its heart. Extending to some 5,000 acres, the evidence of the human hand has been visible in the chalk landscape for over a millennium: the ancient paths and trackways a continuing reminder of a communal history. In an uncertain world, such Arcadia is both a nostalgic memory and consoling in its perpetuity.

Looking forwards, as custodians of this landscape, our task is to preserve, renew and reinvigorate. Once lost, ancient woodlands, grass uplands and field boundaries cannot immediately be recreated. Such landscapes provide us with all our basic needs of food and shelter and embrace both the living and those who once lived here.

The contribution of nature to human life cannot be over-emphasised. We are intrinsically bound to the world in which we live and have shaped it like no other being. It is therefore imperative that we look forwards, to nurture and conserve, to farm with care and responsibility, and to enjoy the simple pleasures of growing, cooking and eating together. Whether it is ancient trackways for walking, history to explore, the colourful patchwork of fields, hedges, woods, downland and hill-country, the deeply anchored sense of place offers tranquillity and happiness.

May the road rise up to meet you.
May the wind be always at your back.
May the sun shine warm upon your face;
the rains fall soft upon your fields
and until we meet again,
May God hold you in the palm of His hand.

Traditional Irish blessing

ACKNOWLEDGEMENTS

AS EVER I OWE A HUGE THANK YOU TO THE HIGHCLERE TEAM. The past eighteen months have been such a challenging journey, emotionally, mentally and physically (as well as, of course, economically) for everyone wherever they live. On top of which I have immersed myself in the research and intensity of writing this book. It has focused my thoughts on nature and time.

Thank you to all for the team effort: to Adam Hillier, from his extremely early morning photo shoots in the depth of winter to the beautiful roses in the rose arbour; to Paul Winch-Furness for tempting photographs of the food and dishes, all of which were prepared by the Highclere team led by Head Chef Paul Brooke-Taylor, who also helped compile the recipes and offer more precision. Luís and the banqueting team are always cheerful and help provide the setting for the enjoyment of every meal as well as creating gorgeous cocktails. Meanwhile, John Gundill would kindly hike upstairs bringing sustenance, to find me at my desk – still – and regale me with the latest challenges of Highclere.

Sally Popplewell worked tirelessly, editing both text and recipes with thought and flair. My husband Geordie contributed some beautiful photographs, edited and commented, spotting errors and missing ingredients. My son Edward remained calm, positive, helpful and encouraging. Hannah Gutteridge helped style the food and photography, directing all with her forthright approach. Paul Barker, our Head Gardener, has helped us plant trees, shrubs and innumerable bulbs which produce amazing flowers for us all to enjoy at Highclere. Simon Andrews and the farm team work all hours to grow crops for all of us to eat and leave space for nature. Paula Jones, PA to Geordie and I, continually reminds me what is still to be done. And Reuben Privett kept reading and re-reading, spotting tiny details we all had somehow missed.

Finally, a tremendous thank you to Trevor Dolby and Tim Barnes for setting the book out with precision and exquisiteness, and Zennor and team at Penguin Random House for believing in the book.

INDEX

Page references in *italics* indicate images
Recipes are listed in **bold**

319

First published by Century in 2021

www.penguin.co.uk

A CIP catalogue record for this book is available from the British Library.

ISBN 978 1 5291 3558 9

Edited by Trevor Dolby

Designed by Tim Barnes, herechickychicky.com

Printed and bound in Italy by L.E.G.O. S.p.A.

The authorised representative in the EEA is Penguin Random House Ireland, Morrison Chambers, 32 Nassau Street, Dublin D02 YH68.

Penguin Random House is committed to a sustainable future for our business, our readers and our planet.

This book is made from Forest Stewardship Council® certified paper.

3 5 7 9 10 8 6 4

Century
20 Vauxhall Bridge Road
London SW1V 2SA

Century is part of the Penguin Random House group of companies whose addresses can be found at global.penguinrandomhouse.com.

Penguin
Random House
UK

Photographs by Adam Hillier, Paul Winch-Furness, Lord Carnarvon, Edward Herbert, Emma Chandler, Chaz Oldham, Lady Carnarvon, and from the Highclere Castle Archives

except: p43 (bottom) by RhubarbFarmer (Creative Commons Attribution-Share Alike 3.0 Unported); p251 (left) by David Whelan (Creative Commons CC0 1.0 Universal Public Domain Dedication); p251 (right) by Country, Farm and Garden Photo Library, cfgphoto.com; p254 (bottom right) by MacDurk (Creative Commons Attribution-Share Alike 4.0 International license).